At Bay

Cultures Converging Through Southwest Washington

Jay Miller, ed

© 2018

At Bay
Cultures Converging Through Southwest Washington

At Bay

Introduction

Washington State has wet west and dry east sides because of the high Cascade Mountain range, broached by the Columbia River. Along the shore, Coast Salishan languages are spoken, with across the mountains, along the Columbia and its tributaries, Interior Salishans are to the north and Sahaptin are to the south. Unique to the state and the world, along the northwest corner of the Olympic Peninsula are the Chimakuans (Quileute, Hoh, Chimakum), ancient residents pushed aside by Nootkan Makahs at the very tip to watch for whales and Straits Salish Klallams along the north shore across from their close kin on Vancouver Island.

In the southwest corner between the mouth of the Columbia and the Pacific shore are Tsamosan Salish, former called Olympic Coast Salish, comprised of Upper and Lower Chehalis, Quinault, and Lower Cowlitz. Upper Cowlitz are Sahaptin-speaking Taytnapams who crossed the Cascades with their horse herds. Along the Skookumchuck River and Willapa Hills are the Swaal, Pacific Athabaskan speakers, and adjoining them along the Columbia are the numerous Chinooks, whose network contributed to the spread of a trading jargon known as Chinuk WaWa.

Chehalis

The Chehalis River bends and twists along its ⊃-shaped route. At its headwaters, first flowing north, it loops eastward toward Centralia at Claquato, and then shifts west by north from Oakville to enter Grays Harbor at Aberdeen. Upriver, Klaber and Boisfort are on the South Fork, while the main course includes Ceres, Rainbow Falls, Dryad, and Pe Ell. The Newaukum River joins at Chehalis City and the Skookumchuck River enters the main river at Centralia, as does Hanaford Creek. Scatter Creek borders the prairie at Grand Mound, a hill where part of a Star stayed on earth and the Upriver and Downriver dialects diverged (Appendices A, B).

"The original territory of the Upper Chehalis was along the Chehalis River and its tributaries from just east of Elma to just north of Pe Ell. They fished in the rivers and creeks of the area, hunted in the woods and mountains, and gathered plants throughout the region. A particularly important feature of this area was and is the large number of prairies, large and small, that were kept burned off and free of forest. These prairies provided valuable grounds for berries and such important roots as camas and bracken fern. Prairie often features prominently in the folktales of the Upper Chehalis" (Kinkade 2008: 350).

The Upper Chehalis River, in particular, was the interface between four language stocks. Sahaptians known as Taynapams, or Upper Cowlitz, neighbored Salishan-speaking Upper Chehalis and Lower Cowlitz, along with Athapaskan-speaking Willapas (Swaal), sometimes known as Mountain or Upland Cowlitz. Indeed, despite speaking languages of very different stocks, all of these Cowlitz, according to Dr. Verne Ray, their expert witness, identified them as a single tribe among themselves and to others. The Willapas lived in the hills drained by the river of the same name. The Cowlitz River headwaters were on the slopes of Mount Rainier, near others flowing into eastern Washington. Ancestors of Sahaptians now on the Yakama Reservation walked along these waterways, upriver and across to trade and intermarry among Salishans, establishing bilingual Taytnapam-Cowlitz Salishan villages on the Lewis and Upper Cowlitz Rivers.

The headwaters of the Chehalis River approach those of the Willapa River, which drains into Willapa Bay after passing through Raymond and South Bend. On the north side of Willapa Bay at Toke Point, the Shoalwater Reservation was established for the Lower Chehalis, Chinook, and Willapas who refused to move to the Confederate Chehalis Reservation near Oakville or upcoast to the Quinault Reservation at Taholah. On the south shore at Bay Center, Franz Boas (1894 and 1901) collected texts from Charles Cultee, one of the last fluent speakers of two Chinook dialects, as well as Chehalis.

Upper Chehalis [q̓ʷay̓ayiɫq] lived along the Chehalis River from around modern Chehalis to a little west of Oakville, including Oakville and Rochester prairies, large parts of Mima and Grand Mound prairies, and many smaller ones (Adamson 1934: ix).

Upper Chehalis was once spoken from Elma upstream almost to Rainbow Falls. Silas Heck identified 5 bands: Mud Bay and Black River (called here the Bays), Teninos, Chehalis town (called here Ilawiqs), Pe Ell - Boistfort (Boisforts), and Oakvilles (Kinkade 1991a: v).

Among these 5 bands were 3 Chehalis dialects: Satsop, Oakville (ch series, Bays and Oakvilles), and Tenino (k series, Teninos, Boisforts, Ilawiqs). Satsop, while speaking Upper Chehalis, interacted more with the Lower Chehalis. In this rearranged collection, Tenino Chehalis was spoken by Marion Davis, Mary and Peter Heck, Robbie Choke; Oakville Chehalis by Dan and Jonas Secena, Pike Ben, Joe and Maggie Pete. For unknown reasons, Silas Heck spoke the Oakville dialect while the rest of his family used Tenino (Kinkade 1991a: vii). By 1927, the Satsop language had replaced the older form of Upper Chehalis among the younger generation {md 58 ThA}.

Mary Heck testified to both number of houses and location for Upper Chehalis villages, specifying those at (with number of six-fire houses in parenthesis) Elma (4), Klukwulum (4), unnamed (7), Cedarville (3), Oakville (2), Grand Mound (7), Centralia (10), Chehalis City (3), Edna [Adna] (4), and Pe Ell (6). She ended by stating, "And she likes to lay before you every word that Governor Stevens spoke at the council they had. Do you want to know?" But the lawyer responded, "Tell her no; it is not material in this case" (Duwamish and others 1933: 534-5, 341).

Thelma Adamson's notes mention specific place names and foods. For example, the land from Rochester to Tenino, where Scatter Creek flows, had a distinct designation as Q!waxtn [K1689]. Among the Lower Chehalis, Westport was literally called "sand" [čaxe?s K329, cf 57] and was an aggregate of Lower Chehalis more than a distinct tribe. Wynoochee lived across from Porter Creek, where they hunted elk. They dug wild carrots at Malone [downriver from Oakville].

Chehalis rarely married east of the Cascades. Spencer, a Yakama chief, married the daughter of *Yawnish* but had no children before they separated. She then married Chehalis Jack. Alice (Mrs Dan) Secena, a shaman from Ellensburg, married into Chehalis and told her life's story to Melville Jacobs (1934).

Chehalis later went to Monticello, called mansela [mansla, modern Longview], to work for the French during harvest time.

An Upper Chehalis town was located at Cedarville (a fish trap, 4 large houses, smaller ones), where Santos was the last person to live. Satsop came to spend the winter there {ph 240 ThA}.[1] In turn, Upper Chehalis stayed with Satsop at their town at that river mouth.

Upper Chehalis lived between Rochester and Ceres. The Willapa were below [west, beyond] Ceres {ph 69}. An important town was located on the open prairie near [modern] Centralia.

Only the Teninos [ɬməšluws K906] had an account of their own origins, traced to the marriage of a royal daughter and a Wolf. Mary Heck's husband, Sam Smith, Mrs. Marion Davis, and the Sanders "belong" there. [Sanders ~ Sandersons were also southern Lushootseeds.] Teninos were like soldiers, mean fighters and good hunters. Each of them could eat a quarter of a deer. To insult them, people called them "dogs," meaning less than wolves.

Trails to Olympia went from Tenino to Tumwater, or along the Black River through Waddle Creek {ph 241 ThA}. Suckers were dried at a lake on the Tenino trail. Women gathered moss and sank it into the lake on Black River to catch [entangle] small fish, but people could only canoe as far as Little Rock, where they portaged upriver.

Grand Mound, where part of a Star stayed on earth, had a spring half way up the side. The Star was too big to live on the earth so it left only a small bit behind. Just to the east are many small mounds that once were porpoises [q^{w}siyu' K1612] before the Flood.

Brush Creek divided Grand Mound Prairie and was known for its winter abundance of red salmon. It was dry in the summer.

At Lequito [Claquato], Moon was born, according to the epic. Before the Flood separated everyone into animals and humans, birds were the boss of all the people. Moon changed all that.

At Black Creek, across from Lequito, a man killed his wife and ran off with his five daughters into the mountains. Later, Taytnapam hunters saw smoke, found them, and thought they had gone wild. But someone convinced this family to settle among the Taytnapams [ƛ'alamux^w K941], where the girls married {ph 69 ThA}.

At nearby Lincoln Creek, Chehalis and others dug camas. Hunters followed it up into the Blue Mountains for elk. [Chehalis call the Blue Mountains what the map shows as the Black Hills, and there is also a Blue Mountain in the area to the south.]

Upper Chehalis and Black River [sacəl'ɬ 'made lake' A17] languages were close, but the people were different. Black River town was at Gate City, where Maggie Pete's father came from. Many of these people were fair, with black eyes and brown hair.

A monster bird lived near the Black River bridge, perhaps a condor, but people were afraid of it because it was able to bite off heads {sh 151, md 164 ThA}.

Upper Chehalis and Newaukum spoke the exact same language, and most Upper Chehalis summered there for hunting and berrying [also wild carrots, camas]. Newaukum was named for the crayfish there [nawaq^{w}m literally means "big prairie" A62, its South Fork name is the one that refers to crawfish [nəx^{w}c'al'x̱ A66]. A village there was jointly occupied by Chehalis and Cowlitz].

---

[1] Codes for source people and places of Thelma Adamson & Dale Kinkade are on page 25.

Two first cousins ran away and married. They had three children, one of whom was Mary Heck's father, when Mary Iley's great grandfather found them among the Upper Chehalis and welcomed them back to Newaukum {mi 1}. Thereafter, the Ileys and this family called each other cousins.

Some Upper Chehalis summered at Dryad and Ceres, but hunted at Willapa. Good camas prairies were located near Robbie Choke's and Pierson's.

The people at Klaber spoke another language, more like Cowlitz. Boisfort people were Cowlitz, marrying among Upper Chehalis and Lower Cowlitz. Fred Wesley and Julia Pete belonged there.

Chehalis went to Cowlitz to borrow canoes to go to Vancouver and Portland to trade. They dried eels at Willamette Falls in Oregon City. French and other traders wanted beaver hides from them. Later they went there on horseback.

Cowlitz

Cowlitz were rich, with many horses and packed storehouses. Each kind of stored food had a separate house, such as for dry camas, dried berries, dried fish, dried venison, or for hide blankets {ly 120 ThA}. They had five good salmon creeks with prized trap locations. They owned many shells, horns, beaver pelts, deer hides, baskets, songs, and names {ly 121 ThA}. Charles Roblin (1919), a special BIA inspector, in his census of landless tribes of Washington, referred to Cowlitz as the regional blue-bloods (Wilson 2001, also Kiona 1953, Suttles 1990, Wilson 1999).

The Cowltiz community included speakers of three distinct languages, as well as fluency in those of their neighbors (Ray 1966, 1974, VRC). Lower Cowlitz spoke an inland Tsamosan Salishan language, Upper Cowlitz Taytnapam spoke Yakama Sahaptin, and Upland Cowlitz spoke two dialects of Pacific Coast Athapaskan (described below) = Willapa and Swaal.

Taytnapam were Sahaptin-speaking Upper Cowlitz, including those at Mossy Rock (the *Wanukwt*), at Nesika, and at Silver and Tilton Creeks (Adamson 1934: x). Other Upper Cowlitz were on the Lewis River near Mt Rainier.

The Tsamosan Coast Salishan Lower Cowlitz lived along that river from Toledo to Castle Rock, roaming as far south as Kelso. Subgroups included the Toutle River Cowlitz (si:'q'w), those at Newaukum River, and those near Pe Ell and Boisfort.

Lower Cowlitz lived on the prairie half a mile above present Toledo, where they had a trail through Mossy Rock to Klicktat across the Cascade Mountains {md 32 ThA}. They had a big village [stop'omux^u A153], down the hill from the Catholic mission, that had plank houses 30 feet long.

Cowlitz were "prairie oriented": "In a geographical region noted for its unbroken forestation (western Washington) the lands of the Cowlitz were the exception. Their territory was dotted with open prairies, all small and widely scattered, but numerous. Without them Cowlitz economy would have been impossible" (Ray 1966: A-12).

Cowlitz comprised 4 bands, Lower (Salishan), Upper (Tay napam Sahaptian), Willapa (Diné Athapaskan), and Lewis River Taidnapam Sahaptian. Movement of Plateau (Yakama) people into the coast was facilitated by four nearby passes within a twenty-miles stretch of the Cascade Mountains. These passes were, north to south, Carlton (at 4100 feet high), Cowlitz Pass

(5191 feet) 5 miles further south, White Pass (4500 feet) 9 miles south, and Tieton Pass (4800 feet) 19 miles to the south of Carlton (Smith 2006). Motivating much of this historic movement was a concern with horse pasture, giving Cowlitz an equestrian focus.

Cowlitz leaders were multilingual, though migration, hostilities, and epidemics so reduced the number of speakers of Swaal~Willapa~Kwalioqua that Cowlitz Salish speech predominated among the survivors. Washington Athapascan word lists were collected by Gibbs in the 1850s and by Franz Boas and his students until a century ago (circa 1910).

Cowlitz were also at Jackson Prairie. Marion Davis's father was raised on the Jackson farm and took their family name. Peter Tom, half Wanukwt and half Newaukum, brother to Mrs. Jack and Frank Tom, lived there above the main store road. Frank Tom lived in the Willapa Hills. The population at Jackson died during an epidemic when many sweated and then swam in the cold river.

Lower Cowlitz went to Castle Rock for the fishing, and to Kelso. A big town was at the mouth of the Cowlitz River with many four-fire winter houses, each 40 feet long. Where they camped for camas or berries, they used cattail mat tents.

Upper Cowlitz went to Bay Center by getting to Boisfort, canoeing down the Chehalis river to Westport and then going on {ly 129 ThA}. Canoes, later horses, took them to Nisqually, Mud Bay, Puyallup, and, rarely, Skokomish [Hood Canal]. Cowlitz got clams at Olympia and Mud Bay, or traded for them from those at Tumwater. The trail was in woods from Chehalis to Centralia, then in prairie to Tenino and beyond.

Upper Cowlitz materials were supplied by Mary Iley, her sister Sophie Smith, James Cheholts, Lucy Youckton, Mrs. Northover [only in 1926], and Minnie Case. The sisters Mary, Sophie, and Lucy belonged to the bilingual Newaukum Cowlitz who intermarried with Taytnapam. The father of Mary and Lucy was Lower Cowlitz, their mother was Taytnapam and Yakama. Mary was married to a Taytnapam. James was born on the Toutle River, as were his mother and father. Mrs. Northover was born near Toledo. Minnie Case belonged to the Boisfort group (Adamson 1934: xi). They spoke Sahaptin among themselves and the Wanukwt, but used Chehalis with others. Lucy Youckton lived at Oakville and suggested the names of others, who were scattered because the Cowlitz had neither a reservation nor a land base (Adamson 1934: x).

Lucy Youckton's father, a great hunter, was Lower Cowlitz, her father's mother was from Tenino, her father's father was Cowlitz, and her mother's mother was Taytnapam. She was born on *lakamasili* [Lacamas Illahee, "camas land" in Chinuk jargon] Creek, a little more than half a mile from Cowlitz Prairie, where many camas and cattails grew. She had a Lower Cowlitz uncle, named *wvk'm-nos Kal*, who was a great old man "to tell her everything. When get to be a woman, be kind to people." He had about 4 wives at the same time and 2 or 3 houses, with round, hanging doors. Each house was located near a food source like a salmon stream or berry patch {ly 117, 122 ThA}. Joe Peter and his wife Agnes were mentioned because he was Mrs. Youckton's sister's boy {ly 118 }.

Mary Iley, about 70, lived at Nesika on the Upper Cowlitz River, but visited widely {ph 250}. ThA finally met her in 1926 at Wapato on the Yakama Reservation staying with her sister, Sophie. Minnie also lived at Wapato. Mrs. Johnnie Johnson, a sister of James Cheholts, lived among the Yakama but refused to give any tales. In 1927, Mary was with her son at Morton, where Melville Jacobs worked with the entire family collecting Sahaptin texts. Their brother James was then at Rochester.

Modern Cowlitz efforts toward federal recognition began with a 1915 meeting above George Bertrand's general store at Olequa, called by Dan Plomondon. Cowlitz found ready employment at Olequa at local hop yards. Because of its more central location, Cowlitz met at Chehalis City on 6 June 1912, and again on 17 September 1915.

While local native peoples continued to share space and labor with local settlers, the land they reserved as CTCR were guaranteed by Secretary of the Interior JP Usher near Oakville in 1864 (Ott 2008b). Cowlitz had only family homesteads until they became federally recognized by the US government as the Cowlitz Indian Tribe in 2002.

Swaal

ThA found no fluent speakers for the upland Athapaskans (called by her Willapas or Tinneh [Diné]), who lived as far as Dryad, intermarrying with the Pe Ells [A86]. They used a trail between the Willapa and Chehalis rivers to go and dig clams at Tokeland, now paved as State Route 6 between Chehalis and South Bend. Old Youckton belonged at Willapa, where people went to hunt elk. Perry Youckton (about 70 in 1927, half Willapa and half Tokeland) was married to Mary Heck's aunt, who was Black River and Chehalis. Tokeland was home to Lizzie Johnson's mother's father. Her husband was part French and named Pierre Charles. The town Pe Ell was named for him, being the native pronunciation of his name with a shift from R to L.

These Athapaskans were called upstreamers or inlanders in Chehalis [čucia K473]. They spoke Salish with Chehalis and Athapaskan with the Pe Ells {ph 35 ThA}. They were known by their Chinookan names of Kwalhioqwa in Washington and Klatskanie in Oregon, though the place is spelled Clatskanie. Early researchers, such as Horatio Hale, George Gibbs, James Teit, and Franz Boas documented these communities when they were in steep decline. Dale Kinkade reported the tribal name as Swaal (rather than Su'wal) and Swaal is the preferred name used herein.

Franz Boas thought Kwalhiokwa derived from Penutian Chinook meaning "at a lonely place in the woods". Horatio Hale "estimated them at about 100, said that they built no permanent habitations, but wandered in the woods, subsisting on game, berries, and roots, and were bolder, hardier, and more savage than the river and coast tribes" (Hodge 1906 I: 746).

The Oregon branch originated from the Skookumchuck, and probably moved south along the Cowlitz corridor.

> According to a tradition recorded by [George] Gibbs, [Edward] Curtis, and [James] Teit, the Clatskanie once lived on the Skookumchuck River but migrated across the Columbia where the hunting was better (Kraus 1990: 530).

The names Kwalhioqua and Klatskanie (Tlatskanai) are Penutian Chinook words, the first a village name "lonely place in the woods" and the second meaning "those of the place of little oaks", or "little-oak-ers". Like other Athapaskans, they probably referred to themselves by some version of the term diné, tinneh, or din-nay, "people, humans".

> "Tlatksanai. An Athapascan tribe that formerly owned the prairies bordering Chehalis r., Wash., at the mouth of Skookumchuck r., but, on the failure of game, left the country, crossed the Columbia, and occupied the mountains on Clatskanie r.,

Columbia co., Oreg. [Anson Dart, Oregon territorial Superintendent of Indian Affairs, in 1852 said] This tribe was, at the first settlement of the Hudson's Bay Company in Oregon, so warlike and formidable that the company's men dared not pass their possessions along the river in less numbers than 60 armed men, and then often at considerable loss of life and always at great hazard. The Indians were in the habit of extracting tribute from all the neighboring tribes who passed in the river, and disputed the right of any persons to pass them except upon these conditions" (Hodge 1910 II: 763).

Population estimates have been as high as several hundred, testifying to the good hunting in their new home.

Lastly, as general background, the Athapaskan diaspora was precipitated by the CE 803 White River eruption on the current Alaska-Yukon border, and featured small contracting stemmed points, rectangular houses, and possibly microblades. Earlier eruptions there in CE 50 and 450 may have also played a role. Over four hundred years later, Pacific Coast Athapaskans further relied on a stored salmon-acorn economy (Matson and Magne 2007: 151).

Pacific Coast Athapaskans split from the Canadian branch, after it split from the Alaskan homeland. Like others of the diaspora, they retained their own language while learning to speak those around them and borrowing features of economy and technology. They continued a concern with death taboos, and with girl's puberty, but shifted the focus to the menstruant herself rather than her potentially dangerous impact on the community. Unlike the matri-emphasis of other Athapaskans, Pacific Coast communities were more patrilineal and patrilocal, with settled towns and territories. Land hunting remained important, though some coastal tribes regarded sea lions as "ocean deer" (Perry 1991: 40-49).

Multilingualism was typical, especially among noble families. Indeed, Cowlitz collectively spoke five languages: Salish Lower Cowlitz, Taynapam Upper Cowlitz, Chinook, Swaal, WaWa, with French from Metis fur trade inlaws and English added later.

Five is the pattern number throughout this region, as well as up the Columbia River. Thus, Chehalis trace five ages of their world, as told by Peter Heck, George Sanders, "blind" Dan & Jonas Secena, Marion Davis, Mary Eley, James Cheholts, Jack Williams, and others.

The Five Ages of Chehalis World

1) The world already exists, inhabited by bird-like spirits with great powers, potentials, and wealth. They have a shiny hoop to play games with until the four Coyote sons of Fox and the bowlegged Grandson of Dog, decide to steal it. The oldest Coyote boy watches; grabs the hoop; is chased after, and relays it to his next younger brother just before the oldest is caught and killed. The hoop continues in relay until finally Dog's Grandson gets it. Swan uses his own doctoring power to cure grandson's hip, and turns his own white feathers into a heavy fog that enables the boy to escape with the hoop and return to Dog, whose win over Fox results in the rainbow. Some spirits get lost in this fog and take on the forms of present-day animals, plants, and places.

2) Flood destroys everything after inlaws wrongly keep insisting that a bird (Junco or Thrush) wash his discolored face, thereby treating everyone alike. The son in law had been using dust baths, so changing to water upset expected conditions. Some animal spirits escape in canoes from the flood, and take turns trying to bring up soil from the ocean bottom. Muskrat succeeds; creates a mountain nearby (Capitol Peak); and the world is remade by earth spreading out from it.

3) Two sleepy girls talk of marrying Star husbands and are taken into the sky by an old man Star (white color) and a younger one (with red color). The grumbling wife of the old man becomes pregnant, escapes from the sky, and, at Claquato gives birth to Starchild, a boy destined to be Moon who is tended by his blind grandmother until stolen by two lonely women (Age # 4) carrying him off in relays. The distraught mother wrings a twin son from a diaper left behind. That twisted brother and the mother suffer greatly until Bluejay gets Starchild to return. Reunited, he straightens out his twisted brother, and joins with him in remaking the world of today. The twins avenge their family; burn up the old ways; and establish chiefly blood lines before becoming Moon and Sun in the sky. Starchild's own children become fish and trees.

4) X^{w}ane/ Changer/ Transformer/ Coyote/ Misp^h - originally a set of five brothers - travel through the land, mostly along rivers. They destroy cannibal women, provide regular foods, set rules for living right, and change things into their present forms and conditions - in preparation for the eventual world of today's humans. From salmon innards, X^{w}ane creates two girls, who flee from his amorous comments and, running in relays, steal Starchild from his blind grandmother (Age # 3). Beings wanting to hurt Changer are turned into deer, beaver, and other helpful creatures.

5) Human beings arrive in this prepared world by canoeing upriver. Each village and tribe receives special abilities as it settles along a namesake river branch with it own special foods and resources. Species of plants and animals become as they are now: Freshwater Clams were spirits whose canoes capsized, Spring Salmon and Silver Lamprey take shape from flesh and oil removed from Steelhead, and so forth. A visiting Star leaves behind a piece that becomes Grand Mound.

Background

Placing Chehalis epics in their proper chronological order is like working a jigsaw puzzle, one that was put together over centuries and now has to be put back together with some parts missing. The Chehalis River Valley is so complex and important because it became the outlet for the mile-high glacier that covered all of Puget Sound ten thousand years ago. The widened Chehalis became the "Salish Funnel" through which the ancestors of Tillamook and other Coast Salish languages got to the coast, thousands of years after it had also been the most northern coastal entry into North America.

As introduction to the regional range of people, studies, memories, and references involved in this genesis, we will review each epoch in terms of its supporting oral and written testimonies. The starting point for the big pieces of this puzzle is the Abstracts at the back of

NORTHWEST Pacific Coast

Penutian Stock
 Chinookan
  Kiksht Wishram Wasco
  Chinook
  Klatsop
  Kathlamet
  Clackamas
 Oregon Penutian
  Takelma
  Kalapuyan
  Yamhill
  Tualatin
  Santiam
  Yonkalla

Chinuk WaWa

Na Dine
 Swaal
 Umpqua
 Chetco
 Tututni
 Tolowa
 Hupa
 Nicola

Salishan Family
 Nuxalk
 Central
  Comox
  Pentlatch
  Sechelt
  Squamish
  Halkomelem
  Cowichan
  Musqueam
  Chilliwack
 Straits
  Lummi
  Songish Lkungen
  Sooke
  Klallam
 Nooksak
 Lushootseed Puget
 Twana
 Tsamosan
  Quinault
  Upper Chehalis
  Lower Chehalis
  Cowlitz
 Tillamook

Chimakuan Family
 Chimakum
 Quileute

Wakashan Family
 Nootkan
  Makah
  Nitinat
  Nuuchahnuth

Isolate
Ktunaxa Kootenay

NORTHWEST Plateau

Penutian Stock
 Sahaptian Family
  Klamath Modoc
  Cayuse
  Molala
  Shaptian
  Nez Perce
  Sahaptin
   Klickitat
   Kittitas
   Tenino
   Umatilla
   Walla Walla
   Wanapum
   Yakama Palus
    Taytnapam

Interior Salish Family
 North
   Secwepemc Shuswap
   Nlaka'pamux Thompson
   Stl'atl'imc Lillooet
 South
  Coeur d'Alene
  Selish Flathead Kalispel Spokan
  Lakes Colvile Sanpoil Nespelem >
    Okanagan Methow
  Snkyuse Columbia Wenatchee Entiat >
    Chelan Methow

Thelma Adamson's <u>Folk-tales of the Coast Salish</u>, where many stories in her collection are summarized and compared with similar ones throughout the region. On page 379 are, first, code letters for 8 tribes, then a list of 8 other collections of folklore in print or in manuscript, such as [Boas MS, Jacobs MS]. Each separate entry begins with the title and selection of other variant versions, the pages where versions appear in Thelma in a column along the margin of the page, and then a tight summary of the story along with [alternative incidents] set off in square brackets.

In addition, there is the book <u>Honne</u> by George Sanders and Katherine Van Winkle Palmer, as well as stories collected in 1927 in the Chehalis language by Franz Boas, many from Secenas (Goertz 2018). Boiled down ethnographic notes by Thelma Adamson from 1927 contain important clues, especially on page 41 under Origins mentioning the contest for the hoop at the beginning of the world. In addition, there is much scholarly work on particular themes or events that help with understanding. The new collection <u>Salish Myths and Legends</u>, <u>One People's Stories</u>, by M Terry Thompson and Steven Egesdal adds a lot. But knowing such contexts is rare, elite, chiefly, privileged knowledge.

1)   Hoop #1 / abstract is on page 390, but the context comes from a wider understanding of the world beginning at a time when land was scarce and spirits were more like birds. Animals became more important when they captured the hoop, with the spirit power of Swan especially significant since its downy feathers created the fog that helped animals win. Swan helped shift power from birds to animals, beginning the settling process since some spirits got lost in the fog and stayed where they were to become sacred places or persons. In one version, the birds are rich and the animals are poor until they get the hoop, rephrasing this shift of power in terms of possessions, which can also reflect power and success in the Euro-American or White world.

According to Mary Eyley, telling in Taytnapam Sahaptin Cowlitz a story she heard from her father in Salish Cowlitz, each of Coyote's sons gained his guardian spirit while fasting on a prairie. By age, name, and prairie, these sons are #1 pa'tawaswai @ sa'lk prairie, #2 pa'x̣ła @ kuku'łm (Jackson Prairie), #3   pa'swiyatkas @ nawa'qum (Newaukum), #4   pa'tcikwn @ q'qa'ya, and #5 patawaswa'ipatawaswai @ wax̣a'lat. During the fatal relay race each son presumably positioned himself on his own prairie to advance the hoop until Grandson ran with it onto Cowlitz Prairie (na'wq) and Animals won. Coyote dies in grief over his lost sons, old and young winners go toward sunrise, rain stops, and Grandfather holds up the hoop, which shows everywhere as rainbow.

Mary called the grandfather Dog both Naha´ntci and t'əpit'ə´pi. His grandson quested at lapa´ləm, a creek near Newaukum, which explains his Swan power. He is mostly likely the Cascade Golden-Mantled Ground Squirrel (*Spermophilus saturatus*), which lives only in the mountains of BC and Washington state, a range distinct from the more common species across the West. Though acting much like a chipmunk, it lacks their white facial stripes and instead has the orange-red head and nape for which they are named. It favors open areas in wooded terrain, such as prairies, and has July litters of 2-8 young. Omnivorous, it now begs from hikers and campers. During the fall it can add 50% to its weight in preparation for winter hibernation (Bowers, Bowers, and Kaufman 2004: 72-73). Because its habitat overlaps that of humans, and its weight gain can make its movements awkward, it is the most likely to be Dog's Grandson of the first epoch.

Nora Bowers, Nick Bowers, and Kenn Kaufman 2004 *Mammals of North America*. NY: Houghton Mifflin Co.

Melville Jacobs   1934   Northwest Sahaptin Texts.   NY: Columbia University Contributions to Anthropology XIX Part I ~ English: 168-169.

2)   Flood #2 / abstract is on page 413. There are lots, and lots of Flood stories, but the song in this epic is particularly important because it still brings on the rain. Certain families still have the right to sing it and they usually say the son-in-law bird is a Junco, though Thrush is also mentioned. Help here comes from Laurel Sercombe's 2001 UW PhD dissertation "And Then It Rained: Power and Song in Western Washington Coast Salish Myth Narratives". Bird's still have great power after epoch #1 so when Junco washes his face, exposing white places, these attract the dense white clouds that bring the rain that causes the flood.

The simplest geologic model for Capitol Peak is the Crescent [Metchosin Igneous Complex in Canada] deformation as a dome-like uplift from a continental margin rift extrusion with little or no overall displacement relative to North America (Suczek, Babcock, and Engebretson 1994: 1H-6).

Suczek, Christopher A.; Babcock, R. Scott; Engebretson, David C. Tectonostratigraphy of The Crescent Terrane and Related Rocks, Olympic Peninsula, Washington. Swanson, D.A. & Haugerud, R.A., Editors, Geologic Field Trips in the Pacific Northwest: University Of Washington Department Of Geological Sciences, vol. 1: 1H 1 - 1H 11 1994.

3)   Star Husbands #3 / abstracts are on page 379 and 418. This epic is a well known and widely distributed over North America, though in the NW it explains the origins of chiefly families, who come from the Stars. Vi Hilbert (Skagit elder and US National Treasure) and Jay Miller discuss it in "Lushootseed Animal People". Only the Chehalis explain that the two women who kidnapped baby Moon, who is born at Claquato, and marry him were created from salmon innards by a Changer.

4)   Changers #4 / abstracts are on page 379 and 384. Honne (1925) is good for this because it presents Changer as interconnected stories, weaving them together as they would have been drawn out to be told night after night during the winter inside the old cedar plank long houses. These Changer~Transformers have many names, varying by river, by tribe, and by language, but all try to set the world right because, in the title of a famous collection by Mel Jacobs, "The People Are Coming Soon". Many bad and dangerous beings were fixed and placed during this epoch, marking the land and water in ways that still vital for humans.

5)   Humans #5 / has no abstract, but a representative story is on page 241, its abstract on page 420. This is the epoch when what can be called "history" begins, and houses, towns, rivers, and regions take on their distinctive characteristics in terms of the staple foods they eat, the clothes they wear, and the customs they follow. Representative stories are in Salish Myths and Legends. A good example is Dog Husband who marries a girl, bringing the importance of Animals into the world now in the control of Humans. Also, lamprey eels are as important as salmon, as shown on the Lucky Eagle hotel lobby's back panel.

Jay Miller
1989 An Overview of Northwest Coast Mythology. Northwest Anthropological Research Notes 23 (2): 125-141.

1998 Chehalis Area Traditions: A Summary of Thelma Adamson's 1927 Ethnographic Notes. <u>Northwest Anthropological Research Notes (NARN)</u> 33 (1): 1-72 Spring 1999.
 Tsimshian Ethno-Ethnohistory: A "real" Indigenous Chronology. <u>Ethnohistory</u> 45 (4): 657-674.
 Jay Miller and with Vi taq^{w}shəblu Hilbert
1996 Lushootseed Animal People: Mediation and Transformation from Myth to History: 138-156. <u>Monsters, Tricksters, And Sacred Cows. Animal Tales and American Identities</u>. A James Arnold, ed. New World Studies. Charlottesville: University of Virginia Press.
 Vi taq^{w}sheblu Hilbert
1985 <u>Haboo</u>, Native American Stories From Puget Sound. University of Washington Press.
 Melville Jacobs
<u>Northwest Sahaptin Texts</u>. NY: Columbia University Contributions to Anthropology XIX Part I ~ English 1934: 168-169.
 <u>The People Are Coming Soon</u>. <u>Analysis of Clackamas Chinook Myths</u>. University of Washington Press 1960.

Ten Features

Among cultural convergences are characteristics of the Northwest Coast, as noted by Jon Daehnke (2017: 30), quoting Leland Donald and Kenneth Ames:

(1) marine ~ riverine orientation that directly shapes subsistence practices, ideology, and cultural outlook

2) highly evolved and sophisticated technology adapted for exploiting marine ~ riverine resources

(3) highly developed woodworking technology for the creation of plankhouses, canoes, artworks, watertight storage boxes, and basketry

(4) some of the densest human populations in Indigenous North America, in many areas even higher than densities found in agricultural societies;

(5) an emphasis on wealth and property, both tangible and intangible (such as the ownership of art forms, songs, and dances), with control of wealth and labor central component of social success

(6) tripartite system of social stratification, including a nobility, free commoners, and slaves

(7) true slavery, including owners controlling life or death of a slave

(8) no form of intercommunity political organization, with the village typically being the largest political unit

(9) no formal political offices

(10) large, coresidential households ~ big houses as the basic unit for economic production, food processing, storage, social life, and ceremonials, with two families sharing each hearth.

Indeed, there is a political system, but unlike mainstream America, it is embedded within kinship and class networks, enforced by applications of spiritual powers, especially by shamans in holy alliance with chiefs. It is also dependent on position of a town or village along a river waterway, with those nearer the mouth having more clout over those upriver, especially during salmon runs. Quileute tell of The Two Fishermen (Andrade 1931: 152-155) when an upriver town, acting through a shaman, destroyed a lower one after it cut off their salmon runs.

53. The Two Fishermen
Arthur Howeatle to Leo Frachtenberg

Well, the two had fish-traps one below the other quite far apart. The (man) below would not let the fish pass. So the one up the river hated him. But he (the latter) was not minded. The shaman began to study what to do, [translating Quileute line 5 >] because the one up the river was a great shaman. So he tried to make a salmon. Now, he went to the woods. He began to get what he intended to use. He began to gather snakes, lizards, frogs, toads, water-dogs. He got them. Then he made salmon by means of his magic power. The stripes of the salmon were made out of snakes. He made the roe [10] out of lizards, the liver out of frogs, the eyes out of toads, the heart out of water-dogs. Then he ended by making the fat out of shark oil. When he finished it he instructed it saying: "Do not let them catch you the first time. Only when those five brothers come after you, then allow yourself to be caught by the last one." [15] Then he threw it into the water.

The fish started down the stream. It came to the trap. It went along side of it. Only the males remained in the village. Their married women had gone to the prairie to dig roots. The salmon closed its eyes several times. Then one (man) saw it. "It has closed its eyes," he said. Then he himself [20] went into the water, but he missed it. Then he returned. He did not catch it. Not long afterward it closed '(its eyes). Then again one approached it. Then he pulled his net. He did not succeed. He went toward his home. Then again it closed its eyes. Then one approached it. He did not succeed. He just caught it by the tail and lost it. He only saw how big the fish was. Then he [25] went toward his home. He did not catch it. One of them did not go home: he went toward the water. That one touched it with the edge of his net, but lost it. He did not catch it (and) went back away from the water. Then it was the eldest brother's turn. He went toward the water. At once he saw the fish coming. It was big. Right away he went in (into the water), pulled up (the net) and finally caught it.

[30] At once he was going to roast it. Presently he cut up the fish, he soon had it ready and spread it over the fire. The fish was very fat. Soon it was cooked.

Then a youngster left the shore to give the news to those who were digging roots. Then he arrived. "A salmon was caught," he said, "by father." Said the boy, [35] "The fish that was caught is [155] big." Then the ones who were digging roots were glad, because they were going to eat when they would return home. The boy remained there. He did not start home.

What they had caught was cooked. Then they began to divide it. They gave a piece to each when it was cooked. Then they began to eat. They finished eating. Then, "I am getting sleepy," said one. "My lips have become greasy," he said, "what we ate [40] was too fat." So they lay down. They covered their faces with blankets. There they remained without budging again. Those who had eaten died.

Then not very late in the evening those who had been digging roots were on their way home. There was no smoke at the place from which they had started (their house). They entered the house. "Why are you sleeping ?" (one woman) said. "Get up, Sir, make a fire," said [45] one of them. The one addressed did not budge. Then she approached him; shook him. "Why are you sleeping? Come on, make a fire," she said. He did not budge. She pulled off the blanket. Then it was unbelievable. He was dead. Half soaked in blood. Thereupon she screamed. Then each one examined her own (and) it was unbelievable. They were dead. Soon they found out that it had been done by the salmon that they had caught. [50] So no one ate it. They cast away the fish and burned it.

The ones who had become widows went away to their parents. They did not touch their husbands. The next day they came back to where they used to live. They did not touch them. They left them right there. They just burned the house where they had lived. No one (tried) to avenge them, because the whole household [55] knew that it had been done by the one who hated them, and lived up the river. They did not touch the fish-trap. They left it right there. Now the only ones having fish-traps are those who live up the river. That was the reason for killing those who used to live down the river

Still and all, inlaw exchanges, trade, and barter served to level or paste over these differences during normal times.

Tribes speaking a language isolate are properly introduced by a recounting of their origin saga to provide a sense of being and belonging at their special place. Then we consider housing since it best represents this unique relationship to a particular environment. Forests mean trees for house posts and planks, marshes supply cattails for mat covering, arid conditions lead to the use of adobe or stone, and frequent movements encourage the use of skin tents. Moreover, houses mirrored the contours of the world. Not surprisingly, people who live in round houses regarded the universe as round, while those who live in square homes spoke of a world with four corners.

The dimension of time – of successive movements matching those of the sun, seasons, succeeding generations, and outside forces – is considered in terms of a day, a year, a life, and local history. In doing so, the symbolic importance of often doing things by fours is also recognized. Lastly, we consider how and what we know about this particular culture and its people from a variety of sources.

The coming together of space, time, people, and spirits into some kind of perfection is expressed by rituals. These provide a sense of identity and belonging to those in the same tribal congregation. More than any other feature, native memberships were defined by participation in rituals, formerly aboriginal and now a mixture of native, Christian, and truly ecumenical.

For example, Shiuchi Nagata, an anthropologist from Japan, tells the wonderful story of being at Moenkopi, an Arizona Hopi town on Third Mesa, during World Peace Day. He had the delicate task of remaining neutral while a Chinese Buddhist monk, through his Japanese translator, both of whom had been invited by the local Eskimo Bahai missionary, made a speech that simultaneously lauded Bahai beliefs and denounced the duly elected governments of the United States and the Hopi Tribe.

Creation

Kwati ~ k'ʷati changed things long ago so that they became as they are now. There are many versions of how he did this. According to one, he made humans from parts of the salmon, natives from the brown portion of livers, Europeans from light colored glands, and Africans from the veins. In another, he went all over improving things by slaying monsters and settling tribes in specific places. Then he instructed them in proper behavior.

In his travels, he met the humanoid prototypes of various animal species, with diverse results. Once, he encountered a man sharpening a knife. Kwati asked who he was and what he was doing. The man said, "I am Beaver and I am getting ready to kill the one they call Kwati because he is going all over messing things up." Kwati asked to look at the knife. He then implanted it as a tail on this being, changing him into the forerunner of all the beavers who were to come. He went on to other adventures.

At the Hoh River, he met people walking on their hands and carrying baskets between their legs. He turned them right-side up and told them to live by fishing. At the mouth of the Quillayute River, he changed Man and Woman Wolves into the ancestors of the Quileute. He instructed them that a poor man should have one wife, and a rich man four to eight wives. At

Ozette, he turned Dogs into people, who occupied a village there that became a famous archaeological site.[2]

During all this, the world remained in twilight or darkness. Kwati intended to change this, so he turned into a small boy to trick the people who kept sunlight. He visited them and went in a canoe to gather mussels. Also in the canoe was the box holding Sun and Moon. When the people went off to pick, he stole the canoe and box. He continued on, "liberating resources," until all the world was satisfactory; then he went up into the sky to live forever.

World

Immortals populating the known world included dwarfs, stars, Raven, Kwati, ghosts, and various monsters, including a kidnapper with kelp for hair. Thunderbird snatched whales out of the ocean and ate them at its home on the Blue Glacier of Mount Olympus on the so-called Olympic peninsula. The Universe itself was alive and addressed in prayers.

As the cedar tree provided materials for all Quileute necessities, from wood for tools and houses to roots for baskets, so the various salmon species, through the bounty of annual runs, provided the staple food.

Housing

Quileute lived in rectangular longhouses, framed in by using massive logs. Set on these four upright supports, were lateral beams and a single-slope or shed roof. The entire outside was covered with split cedar planks lashed to poles set at intervals. Side wall planks were set horizontally, while the end ones were vertical, allowing space for a door. Roof planks were troughed to carry off rainwater.

Inside, the floor was bare earth, excavated down a yard or so, with a row of fires along the center line. Interspersed along the sides were planks set into the ground for use as backrests. Paired families shared the same fire, living across from each other on bunks along the side walls. A large house, sixty feet long and forty feet wide, could hold six families and three fires. Most houses were smaller and had fewer families. During bitter, winter, cold spells of snow, ice, or rain, houses were drafty. Families built snug skin tents over their bunks to stay warm.

Like all tribes of the Pacific Northwest, Quileute clustered in winter villages composed of such cedar plank longhouses located along waterways. A few houses were also located on inland prairies to safeguard a particular resource or sacred site. Two leaders of equal status, known by a term that meant both "primary" and "rich", directed each village. Each community also included a few people with Eagle powah, which allowed them to take anything from the wealthy that they wanted. Descent was traced bilaterally, but residence was patrilocal, giving kin relations a patri-emphasis.

---

2. The Ozette village has since become an important archaeological site where woodworking and other fragile items were preserved under a mudslide about 600 years ago. These artifacts are well displayed at the Makah Tribal Museum in Neah Bay. The skeleton of their recently hunted whale, taken on Monday 17 May 1999 just before 7 am, is also there.

A Day

The typical day began before dawn as the women prepared food. The household head preached to the awakening children to be honest, chaste, truthful, diligent, brave, generous, and considerate. Any child who failed to conform to these standards was ridiculed in public. The rest of the household was reminded to help the old and poor, to bathe every morning, to emulate their wealthy ancestors, to avenge the murder of any kin, and to excel at fishing so their family would never want for food.

Men spent the day fishing or hunting. Women harvested plants and prepared food by sun drying, smoking, roasting, boiling, steaming, and broiling. In the evening, a household gathered around for dinner, followed by entertaining stories, games, and conversation.

A Year

Quileute recognized five seasons. These were winter, spring, summer, early fall, and late fall. Activities in the winter villages were largely devoted to rituals, potlatching (high status give-aways), and guild matters, but the men did some fishing for fresh cod and sea bass.

During spring, women gathered fresh roots, such as camas, and tender shoots, along with sea gull eggs. Later in the year, they collected berries, fruits, and seaweeds. Men gathered bearberry (kinnickinnick) to add to their smoking mixture.

The pace quickened with each arrival of five species of salmon.[3] The first appearance of each resources was greeted with a return foods feast. Summer was spent fishing for salmon, steelhead, halibut, snapper, cod, trout, flounder, octopus, and other marine foods; digging for shellfish; and hunting deer, elk, beaver, seal, sea otter, ducks, geese, and whales. Men took all of these species with the help of weir, trap, net, hook, dibble, bow and arrows, spear, snare, deadfall, and harpoon. All of this technology could only be used effectively, however, after the proper ritual purification and mental conditioning had been performed.

Quileute were justly famous as seal and whale hunters. These Tasks required the most rigorous ritual preparations. Before whaling, a harpooner avoided all contact with women, and bathed in the icy sea from winter until June. As the moon waxed, he bathed in the ocean nightly at his own isolated spot, swimming like a whale. When he was thoroughly numb, he went to the

---

[3] These five salmon species have a confusing variety of local common names, but all belong to the genus called Oncorhynchus as further designated by species.

A. O. tshawytscha (chinook, king, spring, quinnat), up to 80 pounds, spawns in large streams or rivers, sometimes with spring and fall subspecies.

B. O. kisutch (silver), usually 6-12 pounds, up to 30 pounds, runs in early fall but may not spawn until late fall, in smaller streams far from the sea.

C. O. gorbuscha (pink), 3-10 pounds, spawns early fall, smaller streams near the sea.

D. O. keta (chum, dog), 8-18 pounds, spawns late fall, smaller streams near the sea, lean and smokes well.

E. O. nerka (sockeye), usually a few pounds, fattest species, spawns upriver in lakes; when landlocked, known as kokanee.

In addition, steelhead (Salmo gairdneri) is a sea-run rainbow trout, up to 36 pounds, that, like Atlantic salmon, spawns and returns to the sea. Pacific salmon spawn and die, nourishing local carnivores and generally poor soil (Suttles, Northwest Coast 1990: 24-25).

beach and vigorously rubbed himself with prickly hemlock branches. During the whole time, he prayed to the Universe itself to send him a whale.

The whaling crew prepared for a shorter time. They sang together accompanied by a rattle. Then they dragged a line attached to human skulls along a beach – imitating a harpooned whale dragging sealskin floats. The dead could supply food for the living, so these skulls served as an appropriate focus for the ritual. A human skull cap also decorated the prow of each whaling canoe for the same reason.

A full whaling canoe had eight members. The harpooner was at the bow, six paddlers paired along the sides, and the steersman in the stern. For safety, whaling crews generally joined together in a flotilla, but the harpooner with the highest rank always made the first strike. Then others moved into position and plunged their harpoons. Each was attached to a long line of inflated sealskins. These floats resisted attempts by the whale to submerge and so hastened its exhaustion and demise.

Once the whale was dead, a man jumped overboard, made holes in the lips, and tied the mouth shut – so it could not swallow water and sink. The whale was joyously towed into the village beach, and butchered according to strict rules. The first harpooner to impale the whale received the hump or saddle – the choicest piece, as his due. He also received a flipper to keep as a part of an ongoing tally recording his prowess. The whale was primarily rendered for its oil, but nothing was wasted.

A sealing crew had three men who also made special ritual preparations. Through the years, ones analogous to those for whaling replaced those unique to seals.

A Life

During pregnancy, an expectant couple restricted their eating and other activities until two months after the birth. When the elite parents ended their restrictions, their baby was laced into a cradleboard and presented at a potlatch. Parental discipline expanded to eight months in the case of twins. Throughout the Northwest, twins were equated with salmon, probably because the double birth represented the endless two-way return of the salmon. Runs were believed to be the same Salmon souls with new bodies offered as food.

A mother kept track of her due date with a string knotted in eight places, untying one knot for each month. She delivered sitting up, helped by midwives. A newborn was carefully washed, than massaged with shark oil. The afterbirth was believed to represent Old Woman, the source of children. After wrapping this placenta up with beads and gifts; it was hidden in a salmonberry bush as an offering to her.

The cradleboard was used for a child until he or she was able to walk. Shredded cedar bark served as diapers. In leading families, a board and cedarbark cushion were added to the top of the baby carrier to put pressure on the forehead to make it slope back.

Children played at adult tasks as a way of growing into later careers. The bestowal of successive names and the piercing of the ears and nose, allowing ornaments to be worn, celebrated increasing maturity. Children were taught to be clean, moderate, generous, considerate, and dexterous so they would be admired and bring honor to the family. With the onset of puberty, boys began quest training, trying, until middle age if necessary, to gain contact with an immortal. Particular partnerships conferred specific careers, as indicated by this chart.

Quileute Allies

Career   Ally
Shaman = *Snake, Lizard, Screech Owl, Mink*
Whaler = *Whale, Seal, Porpoise, Spear, Rainbow, Lightning*
Hunter = *Wolf, Owl, Elk, Deer, Horned Owl, Bow, Arrow, Elk Leg or Horn, Cougar,*
    Robin, Two-Headed Dog, Forest Monster
Warrior = *Bear, Sea Lion, Knife, Sword, Sky, Stars, Bow, Arrow*
Sealer =   *Otter, Kingfisher, Bird, Spear, Dragnet, Fisher, Trap, Fish, Duck, Salmon,*
    Cormorant
Rich Man =   *Wild Goose, Warbler, Surf Scudder, Grey Swan, Summer, Whitecaps,*
    Ravens, Sun, Moon, Dentalia
Runner = *Fog, Wolf*
Wrestler = *Bear, Forest Dwarf*
Gambler =   various *Double-Headed creatures*
Beggar = *Eagle, Shark*
Rich Woman = *Ocean Waves, House Dirt, Salmonberry Bush, Red Huckleberry, other kinds*
    of Berries
Canoe Maker = *animate Axe, Wedge, Adze, Cedar Tree*

At menarche, a girl was secluded in her home. Her training include abstaining from fresh and bloody foods, staying awake for five days, and using a scratching stick (instead of her hands to touch her body). While most women did not have contact with the supernatural, some girls from leading families did. As indicated by the chart above, they received Wealth Powah from things that naturally occur in vast numbers.

After puberty, children were ready for marriage, which had at least ten different forms. These included levirate, sororate, and polygyny among the rich. Premarital chastity was desired, especially in high families. Parents of a boy took the initiative in negotiating his first marriage. Both sets of parents then exchanged food, gifts, and wealth. This was done, first, at the home of the bride; then, several days later, at the residence of the groom, where a feast and dance were held. Exchanges among poor families were much less elaborate. If the couple divorced after a few years, their wedding gifts were returned.

Both men and women were shamans, each possessing five or six immortal partners. The most powerful ones had as many as 20. Each partnership was represented by a six foot pole topped with an effigy (or decoy) of that immortal. To sort out their relative positions in terms of differential powah, shamans held competitive displays for demonstrating their control of fire, handling of hot rocks, and consumption of vast quantities of whale oil.

Like other Northwest tribes, Quileute were stratified into three classes of leaders, commoners, and slaves. High families based their prestige on appropriate spiritual partnerships, generosity, and hereditary claims to "crests". These art forms were legitimated by epics enumerating songs, dances, resource areas, designs, and names. A leader was also a member of one of the guilds (below), which were most active during winter.

Each of the bilateral kindreds formed a corporate unit. It was and is localized into households, sharing a set of "crests" nominally under the care of the corporation sigers. These men were once able to call upon the assistance of slaves, acquired by trading or raiding, and of several wives to fulfill expectations of generosity.

Around the actual leaders there was a penumbra of notables. They were linked to them by close ties of blood, training, access to spiritual partners, and inherited prestige. Membership in this paramount class was physically represented by high sloping foreheads. As noted, these were the result of being bound into a cradle with the top of the head pillowed between angled boards to shape the skull as it slowly grew and hardened.

Commoners were average people without claims or pretensions to greatness. In some cases, ordinary children could elevate their status and gain prestige by becoming successful warriors or shamans. As warriors, they had the opportunity to capture slaves, who performed extra labor to produce wealth for their owners. Shamans earned wealth, gratefully given as payment by the patient and his or her family, every time they cured successfully.

Crimes included murder, adultery, and hoarding. These were considered inhuman behavior. For murder, close kin were compensated by wergild (blood money), otherwise they led a revenge raid on the murderer, his or her family, and household.

Everyone had an inner and an outer shade, and a soul, which left the body in stages leading to final death. A week before, the outer shade went directly to the afterworld. A few days later, the inner shade began visiting favorite places before rejoining with the outer shade. At the moment of death, the soul became a ghost, which remained with the body until the instant that the shades recombined. Then it joined them in the afterworld. If the shaman could trap the inner shade while it was visiting familiar places, the outer shade would also return to the person and the illness would be cured. Otherwise the patient died "for good".

Sickness resulted whenever these spiritual components of a person left the body. If they could not be retrieved by a shaman, death was inevitable. Only shamans with powah from a Dwarf could safely journey into the beyond and return with the missing shade or soul.[4]

This was an underworld, a large valley divided by a river flowing down the middle. Recent dead lived on one side and ancient dead on the other. The trip there took a soul two days and nights along a trail that led down from the surface through a resthouse and a lake. If the shades or a pursuing shaman drank from this lake, they immediately died without hope of reviving. In general, time and conditions between the living world and the afterworld were reversed. What was summer in one was winter in the other, high tide in one was low tide in the other, and what was broken in one was whole in the other.

After death, a body was taken out of the house through a hole made into the back wall so that ghost would be confused if it ever tried to haunt the house. Wooden sculptures representing the immortal partner of the deceased were destroyed, but any designs were inherited within the family.

The wealthy were placed into canoes with many grave goods. These were deliberately smashed so they would be whole in the afterworld. This canoe was used to cross the river in the underworld when the person was accepted by the ancient dead. The poor were buried in logs that had been hollowed out. They crossed the river in the afterworld by walking over a

---

4. Among Lushootseed of Puget Sound, similar dwarfs, called Little Earths because they are said to "own" the land, took a crew of shamans to the afterworld to retrieve the lost soul, mind, or spirit of a patient who was wasting away in winter (Jay Miller, <u>Shamanic Odyssey</u>: The Lushootseed Salish Journey to the Land of the Dead 1988).

communal fish weir. A dead child was put in a cedar box that was then added to the canoe containing a dead relative.

Mourners cut their hair. A surviving spouse and children also applied red ocher to the face and body. A spouse could not lie down to sleep for five days, so he or she slept huddled in a large basket. The family had to move very slowly and deliberately during this mourning period. To help them do so, they carried small black stones in their mouths and armpits to curtail their speech and movements.

The name of the dead was not mentioned for ten years. Doing so was a grave insult to the family. If anyone had the same or a similar name, mourners paid them to substitute another one. Words similar to that name were discarded in favor of circumlocutions invented by the family.

The ghost remained on the earth. Each had an elongated human shape, moss covering, long nose, round yellow eyes, and peculiar gait. It was constantly recrossing its legs, moving in a crooked fashion with the left foot moving to the right and the right one to the left. People knew how to avoid it because ghosts also whistled while they ambled along – warning the living.

Recombined shades stayed in the afterworld, continuing any activities their body had done in life. In other sections of this underworld were the shades of whales, fish, animals, birds, plants, and so forth. Quileute and other humans visited these areas to collect food. Dead babies had a place of their own south of that occupied by deceased grownups.

History

The Chemakuan language family includes the Quileute, Hoh, and extinct Chimakum, who once lived around Port Townsend at the northeast corner of the Olympic Peninsula.

Several hundred years ago, Klallam, Straits Salishan speakers, arrived on the north coast of this peninsula, forming a wedge between the Chimakum and the Quileute. Both of these tribes account for their separation, however, with a flood legend. At the northwest tip of the peninsula, the northern neighbors of the Quileute were five Makah villages, speakers of a Nootkan language from Vancouver Island. They have since resettled on a single reservation at Neah Bay. Makah also recognized Kwati as the transformer. Their relations with Quileute varied between intermarriage and the transmission of the Whaling cult, to occasional battles.

All Chemakuans had the reputation of being fierce warriors. Though a tiny group, Chimakum fought off many larger tribes until they were decimated by epidemics and other hardships. Hoh massacred landing parties of Spanish in 1775 and English in 1787. Quileute maintained a stockaded fort nearby on James Island, as protection from retaliatory attacks. La Push, at the mouth of the Quillayute River, took its name from the Chinook Jargon term, derived from French, meaning "mouth."

Quileute signed one of the series of treaties negotiated in 1855 to legalize American title to Washington State. They attended another treaty conference at the state capitol of Olympia in 1856. At that time, they were expected to leave their ancestral lands and relocate on the neighboring Quinault Reservation. Once back home, however, they decided not to move. They remained as illegal aliens in their own land until Grover Cleveland signed an Executive Order to create a reservation for them at La Push. The closely-related Hoh were given a portion of their homeland, noted for its spectacular rain forests and coastal beaches, for a reservation in 1903.

In addition to the return foods feasts for salmon, whales, and berries, Quileute had a complex series of guilds and festive displays at potlatches.

Guilds

Much of winter was devoted to religious activities such as guild initiations, potlatching, and displays of powah. In order of their prestige, these guilds were the Warriors and Fishers (both derived from Wakashans), the Hunters (original to the Quileute), Whalers (from the Makah), and the Weather Workers (from the Quinault). Membership in these guilds could either be purchased for a child by parents hosting a potlatch, or be personally acquired. For the latter, the person encountered the necessary partner during a quest, which led to an illness whose cure was formal initiation. All members of these guilds were considered "ripe" as opposed to everyone else, who was "raw."

These five guilds followed the organizational features of the largest Warriors. Its officials included two fathers, two firemen, a doorkeeper, a water carrier, and a woman face painter, who applied the color distinctive of that cult. These were Wolves = black with white or red highlights, Hunters = brown, Fishers = red, Whalers = dark brown, Weather = tan. This color also appeared to a shaman when he was diagnosing which guild a patient needed to join.

People who met a partner appropriate for a guild took sick and were cured by becoming special members. They were entitled to wear its headgear and face paint, to dramatize its ritual, and to act as father, also called starter. Membership, though a less intense form, could also be purchased for children by their parents so they could share in gifts given at subsequent initiations. Ideally, membership was said to be open to all, but, in actual practice, it was a prerogative of the elite.

The guild with the most members was the Warriors, also known as Wolves and Blackfaces. Its rites derived from the elaborate Wolf Ritual of the Wakashan Nuuchanuulth (Nootka, Westcoasters) and Kwakwaka'wakw (Kwakiutl). Some families claimed descent from Wolves who were transformed into ancestors, as Kwati did locally.

Initiations went on for five days, using the songs inherited by each candidate from their family. The drama included embodied Wolves, Wild Men, and an Eagle, together with some tests of strength and stamina. Finally, two Buffoon dancers entertained the crowd.

Hunters began and belonged among Quileute. Its initiation enacted a quest to and from a mountain top. For someone with a proper partner, this took six days, but, for a purchased membership, it lasted only two days.

The Fishers, Whalers, and Weather Workers were more strictly occupational. They performed dramatic enactments of their activities in a ritual context, such as that already described for whaling.

Potlatching

The most sweeping and integrating institution among the Quileute and other Northwest tribes was the "potlatch". Thus term, meaning "to give", filtered from Nootkan Wakashan through Chinook Wawa trade jargon These elaborate give-aways were public displays of family pedigree. They were held to commemorate births, namings, marriages, initiations, assumption of crest privileges, and memorials. As such they served as periodic reminders of claims to property and rank. According to legend, the first potlatch was held to give birds the colors that distinguish their many species. Ever since, these feasts have been occasions for colorful giving and sharing.

A potlatch was given by families in the name of specific members. Usually, if old enough, they had amassed gifts, contributed by family and friends, to be distributed. When the event was held, though everyone else was welcome, important people were specifically invited, feasted, and gifted. The reason for calling everyone together was stated in public. It was dramatized to show family claims to appropriate songs, dances, masks, and costumes. Then, everyone was given a gift proportional to their rank to serve as a reminder and pledge. In case any disagreements later arose, these compensated witnesses were expected to testify to the legality of these proceedings.

Summary

The Quileute language marks gender by indicating female forms with a k- affix. Thus, "s" means "the (for males)" and "ks" is "the (for females)". Moreover, the term for "right" has associations of priority, men, and all of the directions except south; while "left" relates to other combinations meaning "second hand, southward, and women's way". These and other forms of marking indicate that Man was inclusive and Woman exclusive for the Quileute.

Sources

Quileute are discussed in slim works by James Swan, Edward Curtis, Albert Reagan, Alice Ernest, and Livingston Farrand. Major sources include an ethnic history by George Pettitt (1950), done while he was stationed there in the Coast Guard, and several detailed articles and a manuscript by Leo Frachtenberg[5] based on close cooperation with a shaman. More recent linguistic and ethnographic works, including a dictionary, by Jay V. Powell[6] and Vickie Jensen were done under the auspices of the tribal government. Harry Hobucket published a collection of legends from his tribe.

---

[5] Leo Frachtenberg, Eschatology of the Quileute Indians,1920; The Ceremonial Societies of the Quileute Indians, 1921.
[6] Jay Powell and Fred Woodruff, Quileute Dictionary, 1976; Jay Powell and Vickie Jensen, Quileute, An Introduction to the Indians of La Push, 1976.

Famous as traders of the Columbia River, at the emporium at the Dalles (Long Rapids) along the Columbia River, thousands of people gathered to fish and trade during summer salmon runs. Set at the gateway between the lush coast and the dry interior, this fishery intersected routes along the sea, upriver, and across land in all directions. Small items as exotic as pipestone from Minnesota, turquoise from the Southwest, galena from Montana, and copper from Alaska and the Great Lakes were traded there.

The bulk of the materials were regional, however. From the coast came dried shellfish arranged in standard units by being impaled on two-foot long sticks of salmonberry wood. Upland hunters provided mammal furs and dried meat in tule rush bags of standard size. Dried berries provided a variety of tastes and condiments. From the interior came dried roots like camas and the potato-like wapato. From further east came the skins of elk, deer, and occasional buffalo, along with dried meat. From California and Oregon to the south came slaves raided from small villages.

Local Chinooks, who managed this trade, provided dried salmon, pulverized salmon flour, dried sturgeon, dried smelt, dried seal, and canoes, which facilitated this water borne exchange. Occasional beached whales provided blubber and exceptionally large bones for tools and weapons.

Most valuable of all were tusk-like shells called dentalia (<u>higua</u> in Chinook WaWa or jargon) from the West Coast of Vancouver Island. Ordinarily these shellfish lived deep in the ocean. Off this shore, though, they were only a few hundred feet below the surface. Traders had marks tattooed on their arms to measure standard lengths of strung shells. They carefully appraised the quality of each.

So significant were these shells that they had a supernatural aura. According to Chinook, the insides were the food of people so tiny their mouths could only eat dentalia. After sucking out the meat, they gave the outer shell to their tiny slaves, who strung them in standard lengths to be traded by their noble masters to humans.

Practicalities of gathering these shells were much more ingenious, however. Important families of the Nuchahnuth (Nootka), over centuries, had closely guarded the secret location of dentalia beds. Landmarks along the horizon were used to triangulate a canoe so a round brush could be lowered over the side. Many handles were added on, one joined to another, until the tips rested on the bottom. Stone weights with a hole in the middle were fitted over the end of the handle and allowed to sink until they forced the bristles to close up. Then the entire apparatus was laboriously lifted to the surface, as each handle was detached. If the collector were lucky, a few shells were clutched within the brush.

In this way, dentalia were gathered for trade across all of western North America. The further from the source, the more mysterious was their origin so that they became truly wondrous items.

Even so, their mystery conformed to cultural expectations of a stratified society. The tiny people, like all other communities, were divided into ranks of freeborn and of slaves. Throughout the region, the shape of the head physically distinguished these classes. A freeborn baby was bound in a cradleboard with a sloping plank pressing against the forehead so that the skull would grow into a wide, wedge shape.

The skull of a slave child grew normally. As dentalia were the measure of standard value, slaves were the units of prestige. Every important family had several slaves, as much to indicate their social standing as to perform drudge work. Most slaves were children purchased from their captors, and raised within the household of leading families. They did tedious, sometimes distasteful, work such as getting water, firewood, and clams. If slaves had children, then they too were slaves. Most slaves were commoners taken in raids. Important people, invariably adult women, if captured, showed by their conduct that they would not perform menial tasks. They were more valuable if ransomed by their kin. In some cases, captured noblewomen married into the elite of their captors, forming a diplomatic alliance between their two communities.

Local people might also end up as slaves under unusual circumstances. Inability to pay debts, murder, or other failures to compensate would generally mean that a person had to forfeit his or her freedom, either for a stated period or for a lifetime. Orphans without kin to protect them also became slaves at the insistence of their chief, who used the purchase price for his own needs.

A slave had no standing in the community, nor any distinct identity. Their only designation was that of their tribe, which also served to insult and denigrate all these other people. The life of a slave could be forfeit at any time. Alternatively a master could free a slave or accept a price for his or her freedom. In a few cases, devious owners had male slaves act as henchmen, ambushing, poisoning, or killing rivals in secret.

When European ships arrived on the coast, slaves were sent to taste their strange food and drink their mind-altering alcohol. Since they survived the experience, and some even liked it, their masters knew that these new items were reasonably safe.

Slaves were traded far from home so that escape was virtually impossible. Most were well treated. Those who lived in elite households were well fed, although they ate by themselves because of their tainted status. Slaves who ran away only to be recaptured were punished by having their ears cut off. Even when he or she reached home, however, they still carried the stigma of having been a slave. Unless some form of rehabilitation, like a feast or potlatch with lavish gifts, were held, such a non-person would be shunned.

At the other extreme of these communities were the elite families with molded heads and prideful bearing. Their influence was only limited by their ability. Some governed because they were kind, generous, and skilled arbitrators. Others were feared because they were haughty and suspected of controlling reserves of great puwah that could render their enemies maimed or dead. It was such chiefs who had their slaves act as henchmen and poisoners.

An effective chief managed a vast network of kin, trade, and alliance, in a few instances backed by loyal warriors and bodyguards. This "muscle," however, was otherwise out of keeping within the region. Profitable free trade required wide access and unrestricted transport. Injuries or murders were quickly adjudicated by chiefs to dampen hostilities. Deep-seated antagonisms more often led to secret sorcery than to overt attacks.

Leadership passed from father to son, though Chinook kinship was characterized by considerable flexibility. People claimed as many noble ancestors as possible on both sides of the family. Only matters of residence restricted these linkages since members of a household cooperated more fully than did other relatives. People might live in several households during a lifetime, thus cementing ties of kinship through a large network of birth, domestic, and marriage relationships.

Prestige factors influenced succession because an important leader had both slaves and many wives, and their children inherited certain privileges and restraints. A chief added to his influence by having a large family, not all of whom had the same status. The children of the senior wife had the best chance of assuming leadership roles, unless other factors and abilities intervened. Women from coastal villages outranked those upriver because coastal communities were more cosmopolitan, wealthier, and better connected. Personal ability also played a role. A wise and patient child was often groomed for leadership. An older sibling who was angry, sloppy, or careless was passed over.

Prestige was a key to successful leadership. Thus, the son of a chiefly coastal mother and a father from upriver was more entitled to lead than a man of distinguished but lesser ranked parentage. Some of these women were quite powerful, controlling vast trading privileges.

Chinook leaders coordinated activities, more than directed them. He or she would announce when the villagers would move to resource areas to take seasonal foods. Generally, a man of chiefly family initiated moves to fishing and hunting camps. Elite women led berrying and plant gathering tasks. When a beached whale was found, nothing was done until a chief indicated where the first cut was to be made and what slices would go to which people. While commoners and slaves did the actual work, they could not commence until sanctioned to do so by the chief or his representative. More a manager than a martinet, the chief and his family set the tone for transactions between people, land, and spirits. His ability was judged not so much as due to his pedigree and training, though this was important, but rather to his special relationship with tahmanawas via immortal allies over many generations. Indeed, the Chinookan word taa<u>x</u> for supernatural power ~ energy ~ force entered Chinuk WaWa as the all-purpose word for anything spiritual ~ involving spirits ~ wondrous ~ mystical.

Reliable information from local native sources was begun by George Gibbs and culminated in the work of Thelma Adamson, though both sources remained long in manuscript. Throughout this region, fluency in many languages was a hallmark of high status fostering a complex linguistic context.

George Gibbs (1815-1873)

In his summary report for the northern route for a national railroad, Gibbs presents early and accurate data. His 1853 handwritten list of villages providing place names is archived in Washington, DC at the National Anthropological Archives (NAA). He wrote down this material while he served as the secretary to the Cosmopolis treaty commission (below), until it was dismantled and Isaac Stevens tore up the warrant naming one man the Chehalis chief.

At the council held on the Tsihalis in February, 1855, an opportunity was offered of ascertaining with sufficient correctness, the numbers of these Indians …. The name Chihalis, or Tsihalis, strictly belongs to the village on the beach at the entrance of Gray Harbor. The word itself signifies *sand*. It has, however, now become applied to all the bands inhabiting the bay and river. The Lower Tsihalis, or those from the mouth of the Satsop down, including the villages on the Whishkah and Wanūlchi, and the few on Shoalwater Bay, numbered in all but 217. These differ very little in anything except language from their Tsinūk neighbors. There were formerly five principal villages of the tribe on the river, seven on the north, and eight on the south side of the bay [15 on Greys Harbor], and even within the recollections of American settlers the population was very considerable. Ka-kow-an, belonging to the Tsihalis village, a very old man, seems to have been the principal chief, and his son, Tū-le'-uk, now claims, in his place, to be the head of the tribe (Gibbs 1855: 171).

Figure 2. Cosmopolis Treaty Scene, James Swan, 1855 (Miles 2007, 57).

This aged chief (with another spelling of his name) said he saw Captain Gray on his visit to the bay.

The Tsihalis Indians retain a recollection of Gray. Kau-kau-an, the old chief of Tsihalis Point, informed me that he had seen him. Gray gave them a musket and some cartridges, first, however, cutting off the balls. They did not know its use, but supposed it was intended merely to make a noise, and fired it off until their powder was gone, when they broke it up. Afterward they found out Gray's object. He also gave them axes and knives, the first they had seen. A few years after him came Captain Tomlinson, with whom they also traded. Gray and he used to give them a "small blanket", probably a piece of coarse cloth, for a dressed deer-skin (Gibbs 1855: 238).

Important razor clam beds and a corduroyed portage (*oyhut* in Chinuk jargon) were located on the northern (Brown's) peninsula, where the Johns family had a homestead and cemetery deeded to them in gratitude for their efforts at rescuing shipwrecked sailors.

Thelma Adamson (1901-1983)

Ethnographic details for Chehalis and Cowlitz mostly exist in manuscript. Thelma Adamson concentrated on stories in 1926, which were edited for her 1934 collection and republished in 2009. In 1927, she focused on ethnography and her typed up field notes survive only as a carbon copy in the University of Washington Special Collections. Adamson joined the faculty of the University of Washington in 1928, suffered from TB in 1930, but after 1941 spent the rest of her life in a Vermont asylum (Seaburg 1999).

The photocopy used for the 1999a publication, 2009 reissue of her 1934 texts, as well as the 1991 dictionary, belonged to Dr. Kinkade, who numbered the pages in pencil. Miller (1999a) rearranged her data by topics, cited according to a page number in the consecutive series as well as the initials of the elder~source, usually followed by her initials, e. g. {initials page# ThA} to assure that the native sources of information are highlighted. The initials were taken from the *Upper Chehalis Dictionary* by Dale Kinkade (1991a), which reproduces all of the linguistic forms attempted by Adamson in these notes and in her 1934 published collection of texts, *Folk-Tales of the Coast Salish*, memoir of the American Folklore Society, Volume XXVII. Indented quotes herein are verbatim from the notes, and sometimes need comparison with other sources for clarity. In general, the narrative summarizing the topic provides context and sense for the rough extract.

Personal Initials (Kinkade 1991a: xiii-xiv):

bd	=	Bertha Davis (aka mmd Mrs Marion Davis)
ds	=	Dan Secena
gs	=	George Sanders
mh	=	Mary Heck
ph	=	Peter Heck
jp	=	Joe Pete
js	=	Jonas Secena
jw	=	Jack Williams
ly	=	Lucy Youckton
md	=	Marion Davis

mi   =   Mary Iley
pb   =   Pike Ben
mpw   =   Mrs. Pete Williams
msc   =   Mrs. Simon Charley
sh   =   Silas Heck

The most visible differences between the carbon copy and this rearranged work are the removal of dashes (replaced by commas) and most of the parentheses. Gaps left for native words are marked by double question marks [??], as are uncertain or unclear terms. Separated stand-alone listings of variant native terms, centered on a few lines, have been combined and moved into connected paragraphs. Square brackets [ ] indicate clarification, instructions, and commentary.

In all cases, the Kinkade dictionary is the most reliable source for the native terms. Although Adamson's lacked a firm grasp of Salishan grammatical and phonological complexities, gaps in her typed forms include not only spaces for handwritten diacritics to be added later, but also partial letters (particularly the "a") due to sticky keys on the manual typewriters. It is also obvious that she was an unskilled typist.

By way of further clarification of these extracted notes, in her published introduction, Adamson (1934, ix) noted that the largest group of tales came from Upper Chehalis, living on reservation at Oakville, Washington. Prime sources were Peter Heck {ph} Marion Davis {md}, Jonas Secena {js}, and Pike Ben {pb}. Peter, then about 60, sometimes served as interpreter for his mother Mary Heck {mh}, over 90 years old.

Living at Oakville, Mary Heck (*kwil'inut*, Kinkade 1991a: 336 B1) had six children: Peter, George, Emma, Silas, Lizzie, and Adam. Emma was the mother of Bertha, who married Marion Davis (Kinkade 1991a: viii). Peter Heck said that his mother's ancestry included Tenino and White River (Muckleshoot Lushootseed). His father's included the Westports and a group just above Elma {ph 24 ThA}.

Silas Heck, Peter's brother, was married to Lucy, who had lived both near Montesano and at Damon's Point. Those at the portage there, called Oyhut, were related to many of those tribes {sh 149}. Though Silas thought she was mostly from the Wynoochee, Adamson (1934: xi) traced her downriver, reporting that Lucy Heck, about 70, lived at Oakville but her ancestry was Grays Harbor and Humptulips River. She was raised along Chinoose (Chenois) Creek. Her tales were learned from Pete Simmons, her step father, who died when about 100. He only told her stories prior to her marriage. She told the tales in the Harbor dialect, with Silas Heck, her husband, interpreting. She died in the winter of 1927, with an expensive funeral using funds she saved for that purpose, before Thelma returned to study ethnography and general culture.

Similarly, Jonas Secena, about 40, interpreted for his blind father Dan Secena {ds}. Franz Boas recorded hundreds of pages of stories from them in 1927, now at the American Philosophical Society, and published with young Chehalis commentary in 2018.

Joe and Maggie Pete also supplied Thelma with information. Joe had spend his youth among the Nisqually. His mother was a sister to Dan Secena's father (Kinkade 1991a: viii). Maggie Smith Pete was sister to Ed Pete and mother to Blanche Pete Dawson, who had aided Boas's fieldwork while she was a school girl, writing out a few stories for him in Chehalis.

Marion Davis was born at Centralia. His grandfather and father were Cowlitz {md 50, 229}. His mother, Liza, related among the Cowlitz, Puyallup, and Nisqually (Kinkade 1991a: viii), moved to the Upper Chehalis from the White River when she was five and she taught him some Lushootseed Puget Sound tales recorded by Adamson. His daughter Katherine taught the Chehalis language class with Kinkade and was interviewed for the tribal newspaper. Her son Wayne Barr is an active "eeler".

Marion Davis and Pike Ben were older than Peter Heck. Mr. Ben told a group of Mink tales that Thelma did not regard as properly Upper Chehalis. Mrs. Ben was a Puyallup and several elders insisted that "Mink belongs to the Sound".

Bertha Heck (Mrs. Marion) Davis was the daughter of Emma Heck; her mother's mother an Upper Chehalis, and her father and father's father both Nisqually {mmd 222 ThA}.

At Montesano in 1927, Thelma (Adamson 1934: xii) collected tales from elderly speakers, Jack Williams for Wynoochee and Mrs. Simon Charley for Satsop. Jack Williams was from Grays Harbor, his mother from the coast across from Astoria on the Columbia River, and his father was from the Wynoochee Valley, Montesano, Columbia River, Willapa, and Grays Harbor {jw 91 ThA}.

Mrs. Simon Charley was 60 years old. Her mother was Satsop, her father was Grays Harbor (from Montesano down), her mother's mother was from Squaxin, her father's father was Humptulips, and her grandfather's father was Satsop through his own mother and mother's father. Her father's father belongs to *Wapu:ttci*, who lived near the bridge going to Aberdeen {msc 87 ThA}.

While the ThA notes refer to George Saunderson, the family is known as Sanders (Kinkade 1991a: viii). George Sanders was born at Cleber [Klaber], but left there when he was 5 years old. He spent most of his life at Rochester. His mother and both her parents were Lower Cowlitz, his father and father's mother were from the Scatter Creek people [A34], his father's father was Nisqually {gs 112, 113 ThA}. George was also the source for a remarkable collection of interlinked texts about the Changer, drawn from the Nisqually and Chehalis, called <u>Honne, Spirit of the Chehalis</u> by Katherine Van Winkle Palmer (1918, 1925, 2012). Its publication made Adamson's 1926 fieldwork more difficult because some were suspicious their stories would be sold for a money that would go to Thelma. His daughter Helen was interviewed for this study, and identifying her father's father as Nisqually Jim.

Queen Susan (Kinkade 1991a: 336, A20] was mentioned several times. She was an outstanding example of advantages of a high ranking woman. She belonged to the "best family" as the sister of Chief Yawnish, but relied on her own capabilities. She was one of the very few women to be doctors with the power of a spirit ghost ally that allowed her and her spirits to retrieve "souls" of people, especially children, from the Land of the Dead. She also had luck power [qép- K1441], and a third one unnamed. Because she was so powerful, she was suspected of poisoning people who disagreed with her {sh 141, md 153 ThA}. She was middle-aged when Marion Davis was still a young man.

From the beginning of time, natives knew their lands best. Researchers, usually from New York and DC in the early years, conferred with leaders and elders to record this crucial information, and fortunately often named their sources so we can honor their sharing. For this area, we are especially grateful to the Cultees, Secenas, and Haydens.

Cultees

At Bay Center, Franz Boas (1894, 1901), father of academic American anthropology, collected texts from Charles Cultee, a fluent speaker of two Chinook dialects, who was married to Catherine, a Chehalis woman, and using her language in the home. Boas's research, therefore, spanned the entire Chehalis River, coast to upriver, while Thelma Adamson, his student, never went downriver. Boas later worked with members of the Secena family at Oakville in 1927, recording texts in both English and Chehalis.

Charles Cultee

Using Chinuk Wawa, Boas worked with Charles during the summers of 1890 and 1891, and again in December of 1894, collecting texts in Chinook proper and in Kathlamet. Charles father's father was a Swaal Willapa Athapaskan.

Henry Cultee

Henry Cultee lived in a "fishing shack" a few miles up from the mouth of the Humptulips River of Grays Harbor, at the place the Lower Chehalis who had fished here for generations called *Samamanauwish,* which was also Henry's traditional name, inherited along with his luck in fishing from his grandfather's brother. It meant "between two channels," and nicely described the channels of the Humptulips that ran on either side of his cabin (Holden ms).

From long experience, Henry knew where the "fish trails" were through Grays Harbor, some leading into its streams but others sweeping along the shore. At Cosmopolis, "Henry Cultee's mother's father obtained his Indian doctor power that was as famous as it was dangerous. After he found his power, his grandfather took the name of the place where it lived: *Khaisalomish.* He had a white name too, but he never dropped his Indian one. Thus he was known as *Khaisalomish* Pete – or as pioneers anglicized it, Cosmopolis Pete" (Holden ms., 2).

Henry Cultee is fondly remembered, especially his role in safeguarding off-reservation lands and resources, and providing safe haven for native fishers during the time of the Boldt decision.

Secenas

Boas collected many bilingual texts from Jonas B. *Seseneẋan*, who wrote a note saying "I thank you my people, Jonas B. Seseneẋan, Story teller of Chehalis" (Boas 1927 Notebook 14: 885). Jonas was the son of Dan Secena and the brother of Murphy, who was away in a TB sanitarium for much of his adult life. Dan's wife was Alice, who, though blind later in life, was famous for her pies (berry, apple, peach), made every day to serve to people from all over who came to her as a healer. Murphy was married to Nancy, a strong and independent woman. Copies of these Secena texts from the APS archives in Philadelphia have recently been provided to the tribe as part of this project.

John Hayden

An elder and leader well remembered is John Hayden (15 August 1879 – 5 February 1973), one of several of that name who carried on Tsamosan and Shaker traditions.

John Hayden III was a master of all he undertook, especially involving woodworking, harvesting skills, and seafood. Weighing about 240 pounds, he was agile, big, and strong. He spent time both at Oysterville and Chinoose Creek. He married Bertha Walker and they settled on the Walker homestead at Oakville. Hayden's brother was Charley, of Tahola, who was crippled and ornery. His sister Nellie was married to Walter Walker; they lived at Tahola and had three daughters, born in the following order, Martha, Anna, and Rosie. The Haydens and the Walkers were Shakers, who traveled widely.

As a boy, John Hayden played around James Rock, using smooth log rollers and planks he found there as construction materials. At a young age, John's ears were damaged when he dove after slain seals to attach buoys to raise them to the surface. In his later years, he would bring (gift) seals home to Chehalis to butcher and smoke the meat for winter use.

Seafood was his staple. He fed the family on crabs, razor clams, salmon, seals, and waterfowl. They took mussels and razor clams at Point Grenville, using a tire or flat iron to pry off the mussels. The family had a Model A Ford, with four cylinders and gravity fuel feed. A washtub full of bivalves was cooked and eaten at the beach, or preserved at home over a 3- to 4-hour span.

Over his lifetime, Hayden carved a canoe and constructed a barn, large enough to hold 12 cows and 5 horses, plus a hayloft. The barn, built on his wife's family land, usually sheltered 8 milk cows and 3 horses. Inside the barn, he built two boats, a large one of 20 feet and a smaller skiff of 8 feet. John was a logger, especially a bucker and skilled saw filer. He worked his fields and garden with two plow horses. They grew hay and had chickens.

In October, he would transport his 20-foot set-net boat to Chinoose Creek where he fished salmon and sold them to the fish buyer there. He would smoke silvers for the winter and salt down layers of fresh salmon in a box and a crock. Members of the Chinoose family who moved to Taholah (Quinault Indian Nation [QIN]) included Clyde Chinoose, who married Eva Williams (Satsop, Wynoochee); and Dan Chinoose, who married Edith (Oregon Siletz).

Hayden's aunt was Mary Pete, who was allotted at QIN under the name of Sly. She was married to Circus Jimmy Sly, a carver whose poles are restored for a park in Aberdeen, and she had some connection to a Simmons, who may have been the storyteller (Pete Simmons) who taught Lucy Hayden Heck the stories she told to Thelma Adamson.

Summary

Notable for its wealth, complex societies, and trade routes, this confluence has many historical, linguistic, and anthropological sources, both native and foreign. Native ones include the Cultees, Heydens, Secenas, Youcktons, and Hecks. Over two centuries, European sources include Vancouver, Work, Douglas, Wilkes, and the Luark and James families. Scholarly contributions were made by Gibbs, Boas, Adamson, and, especially, Dale Kinkade (Appendix F).

RELIGIONS

Religious topics include: genesis, specific powers, quest stages, dreaming, visions, inheriting spirits, insignia (manifestations), personal encounters, spirits, Shakers, luck, sky, and earth.

Genesis

In the beginning of the world, when someone tried to steal a hoop, a fog was made and all the beings got lost. This was a time when all animals were people, just like humans. These beings made a home wherever they got lost and became the *tahmanawas* spirit powers that give help to humans {45 ph, 41 sh ThA}. Just to the east [of Grand Mound] are many small mounds that once were porpoises [qʷsiyu' K1612] before the Flood.

More thorough information from ThA and elsewhere indicates several epochs. The world was populated by bird-like spirits until a Flood. Muskrat brought up dirt from the sea bottom, a mountain was made and expanded into a new earth. A Changer made improvements, often for selfish reasons that worked to the better good, until the Fog came. Two girls married Stars and one gave birth to a boy who was kidnapped and rescued. He reunited with this twisted twin and mother to avenge their wrongs. Then they burned up the world and remade it closer to that of today before the brothers went into the Sky as the Sun and Moon, who was the more important. Spirits separated from species until the world capsized and humans appeared to live in the present world.

After a human died, its spirit would try to join up with another member of that family. All of these spirits, therefore, belong to the earth. They live in this world, but in places that are remote and unsullied by humans. Spirits were around all the time, but ghosts mostly came in the winter since it was then reversed as summer in the Land of the Dead {js 339}. Shaman's curing spirits were always near, but ordinary career spirits were strongest in winter, when visionaries met to sing their songs in large houses like that at Rochester, which was large enough to hold foot races inside {js 340, md 195}.

Some people got more than one spirit ally, questing until they were satisfied. Spirits gave success either for ordinary careers such as that of leader, fisher, hunter, gambler, singer … and so on; or for curing as a shaman, although this work did not start until much later in life. A shaman was not paid for the first few cures until people were confident in his or her success {mh 219}. Any power could be used either to help or to harm someone, so people were careful how they treated those with spirit powers.

Specific Powers

Peter Heck {ph 42} listed these basic types of *tahmanawas* abilities [Chehalis Tsamosan: ʔə́xtkʷliš K93, Chinuk from *tah* ~ taax̱ = spirit power] and the usual gender of their recipients:

1) doctoring the sick, both men and women

2) dancing, including the ghost familiar, more women than men

3) going to the Land of the Dead, mostly men

4) hunting, mostly men but at least one Cowlitz woman

5) fishing, gifted from something of the water, mostly men

6) owning property and attracting more, mostly men

7) inheriting from a close relative, mostly men

8) borrowing from an ancestor {ph 245}, perhaps a ghost, mostly women

Quest Stages

A spirit ally is acquired through the stages {md170, sh 142, mh 219} of trance, dream, vision, and song, when the personal link between a spirit and human is confirmed by a special tune. Each of the first three stages can occur several times before the song is ultimately given once and for all.

Sometimes, a spirit will send a messenger to make sure the quester is nice, clean, pure, and willing before it comes as itself {ph 393}. The spirit chief helps decide if the boy or girl will get an ordinary or a special spirit. If the youngster is satisfied and does not object, that will happen, otherwise another spirit will come. The quester will act according to the power wanted. If he or she behaved like a doctor, a curing spirit appeared. If he used a bow and arrow, a hunting spirit came to help.

Dreaming

Spirit dreams provided access to powers. They were never forgotten. Common dreams did not come true, only spirit dreams did because a *tahmanawas* talked to the person {js 131}. Every native was born with such a dream to be shaped by life and training to come out well. In a spirit dream, the person was semi-conscious or aware of the special circumstances because his soul was involved. Even day dreams might come from spirits, especially if someone got into the mood by smoking a pipe. A shaman would both smoke and drink alcohol to get in touch with his spirit dreams. A dream might reoccur several times until it led to a vision, when the youngster actively sought contact with the spirit and received a song.

From the time she was eight years old, Mary Heck had a dream of living poles painted black or with red and white strips {ph 396}. She would sleep walk when the dream came and awake in a canoe beached along the river. Once two men came to her, one all black and the other in broad red and white stripes, holding a snake. He thrust the snake toward her and said to take it as her "food." She escaped from the dream by sleep walking. Finally, her father took the dream away.

Some dreams are premonitions. To dream of dead relatives means that you are getting closer to them, especially if you are old. Spirit dreams mostly come to the young, although an old man at Gate City did dream of the arrival of Europeans and their goods, especially kitchen utensils.

Peter Heck {ph 79} dreamed that one of his sons was dying from a broken leg, so he hit him with an ax to end his misery. A week later, that same son was hit at the exact same place by a sweep [metal cable] while pulling stumps. Routinely, just before Peter gets sick, he has a dream of being in boarding school with severe indigestion.

Silas Heck {sh 137} dreamed of a pond among cottonwoods and the sound of a flute made of a thistle stalk. He felt a buzz in his head and became dizzy. Looking into the pond, he saw a deer looking back from the bottom. Then he awoke. Some days, he would wander to that pond, hearing the sounds of someone chopping out a canoe, but there never was anyone there. He finally told his mother, but she scolded him for thus forsaking a potential power for carpentry. In another dream, he was wading out toward a shark he could not see but he knew was there.

Marion Davis {md 157} dreamed that a shaman was coming to make him sick and thus was prepared for the spiritual attack when it came, as from Squally Jim. Davis dreamed that he hid on the bottom of the Nisqually River and so was saved. Such dreams were a protection. Another time, he dreamed how to win a bone game at Puyallup. An unusual dream came when he was coming from Centralia and took refuge in the James family barn. It was late and he was wet and cold. He went to sleep but was awakened by a song. He went to find out who was singing and saw a rooster jumping on the ground and singing. He learned the song and went back to bed. Another night, he listened to a pig speaking in the Grays Harbor or Lower Chehalis language about Davis being a carpenter {md 161}. His gambling song came to him when he dreamed he was riding on the back of a Wolf.

Mrs. Davis was once so sick that only a shaman from Hoquiam could cure her. He found that her soul had been hidden in her stepfather's coffin. Later, when she went to the industrial school in Forest Grove, Oregon, [forerunner of Chemawa federal Indian boarding school] her mother married that same shaman, but when they divorced, he took revenge on the daughter. After local physicians had given up on her, she dreamed what was making her ill and thwarted the attack. Soon after, the man burned to death in his home while smoking in bed.

A man at the mouth of Scatter Creek predicted the location of a deer that was hunted to feast everyone {js 343}.

Visions

Training for a quest in earnest, a youngster of about 10 years old applied paint and fasted in preparation for entering a trance [tcɬaq*um* K477], fainting or passing out to become as though dead. In a dream, the souls showed him or her their kingdom, often a house inside a lake or mountains, until a spirit decided to stay with that person, giving him or her a song to use before undertaking the activity of their successful career. In this vision, the spirit appeared as a human but left in the outer shape of its animal or other form of being. Thus, for example, a woman was visited by a man who gave her a song and then left as a Bear.

In Mary Heck's father's vision, a doctor spirit took him on a tour of "the other side," always moving higher to get more power. The spirit explained how he would cure and gave him two sticks for his first child, who would be a daughter, to hold when he had a difficult case. He was also given songs while going up a river in a canoe toward the spirit's house. The audience sang along with these songs, "like frogs". He had another vision and song near Satsop, in addition to a spirit ghost who took him to the Land of the Dead.

Spirits best liked young and clean youngsters, before marriage. A young man might start to get a spirit ally near a trail only to have it go away if an old person came near. Sometimes, the ally will meet the boy again at another place. Sometimes, it never returned. Spirit powers could still be inherited after marriage when a relative died.

After getting the first power, others were easier to lure. Most powers were acquired before marriage, while the youngster was chaste.

A man could only begin using a career power at about the age of 20 when he showed maturity by handling a canoe, hunting deer, and starting a family {js 342}. Warrior power was something special, but apparently a kind of # 4 [in the list above]. It can only be used to defend the town or tribe, never to benefit that person. Gambling power was a kind of # 6 [in the list above], usually with a fine song. Warriors and chiefs were often big gamblers.

Other spirits could become attached to that person later, either inherited from a deceased relative or attracted by the grief caused by the loss of a baby. Often the spirit of that infant itself would offer to help the father while he was in the sweat house or bathing in a cold creek for 10 days {md 163}. The spirit promised to be reborn into another child, provided the father followed instructions. A miscarriage would sometimes come to the mother as a spirit and offer the same help. The person had no control when a spirit came. He or she got more and more sleepy until the dream began that ended with the vision.

At the least, a close relative would try to lift the grief of the parents by teaching them the use of certain dicta, compelling magic words, to improve their lives.

A human acted as master to his or her spirit allies. Any spirit could be sent to harm someone else, but the danger of this malice was that it could always ricochet back to hurt a weaker member of the person's family {md 162}. Sometimes, the intended victim was so strong that the power reverberated back to kill the sender.

Whatever happened to the power also happened to the human. If a spirit was maimed or weakened, so was the human "master", only the spirit could recover but the human might not survive. For example, two spirits once fought too near a fire and that of Peter Heck's wife's father got burned. Later his daughter got sore red eyes from this, not her father, and had to be cured by Queen Susan to overcome partial blindness {ph 278}.

If a family strongly suspected that a person had sent his own spirit, or hired someone else to send one, to kill one or more of its members, they might hire a shaman to send a counter spirit, a warrior to waylay the person, or add poison to his food {ph? 79}. The choice was up to the family, not the chief.

A doctor had stronger spirits than an ordinary person. He or she could hide someone's soul under a roof to lure a rival shaman {ph 277} to their death when attempting a cure. Only a native doctor could cure soul or spirit sickness.

Inheriting Spirits

When a person died, his or her spirit tried to reconnect with a younger member of the family. If the child did not know what to do, the spirit poisoned it to death. Sometimes, many children died in the same family until either the spirit was sent away or a youngster accepted the power.

For example, a boy met his grandfather's spirit ally but ran from it. That *tahmanawas* became like poison inside his body. He could not think right and never got over it, but how could he accept it when he did not already have a power of his own [to help manage control of it]. He was an orphan, though, and such are favored by the spirits. The old people said that the world took pity on orphans and protected them {sh 141, md 170, ph 264}. The boy was about 25 in 1927, but he had disappeared two years before.

In important families, children were carefully told not to be afraid of anything strange. It might be a spirit power they could get. Sometimes, a father or uncle would deliberately forget something in a remote place and send a child there to retrieve it. Though afraid, the child went in hopes of meeting a spirit. The proof that he or she went was to return with the object.

Such children were clean and had "pure hearts" because they were related to chiefs. They did not have to go far to find a spirit.

Insignia ~ Manifestations

Sometimes, the spirit ally specified an emblem for the human to make and use. Silas Heck's great grandfather had a cane that helped him get wealth {sh 145}. Questing in the hills behind Gate City, another uncle got a cane to symbolize long life if he would live by the rules {sh 137}.

Peter Heck {ph 46} recalled a slave who got *axayus* [horned snake] and made a figure 7 feet tall to represent it during a potlatch at Elma, where it was unwrapped from blankets after everyone was seated. Other people painted images of their spirits on boards or parts of a house, such as planks that the beams rested upon.

Every winter, people with spirit powers gathered in a house to help each other sing their songs. A special repeater made sure they got the words correct. Afterwards, the singers gave gifts to everyone. First time singers in public had to be very careful that no shaman stole their spirit or mixed up their song to cause them pain.

Spirits could also be summoned up briefly. Jonas Secena's mother's stepfather went over the mountains toward the Yakamas and prayed to see a rattlesnake {js 339}. Three came to the trail and then left. This man was a Nisqually and they, like the Puyallups and Yakamas, have a special relationship with snakes.

Personal Encounters

People also have personal encounters with spirits. Mary Iley, as a girl of about 11, was lost picking strawberries. A white woman came and showed her the way home. The woman told her to put on all new clothes once a year. Again, just before she became M1, she met a boy wearing pretty clothes, who said she would have a son just like him. When she turned back to look, there was a snake where the boy had been {mi 6}.

Marion Davis's stepfather, who was a shaman and odyssey doctor, died in Olympia and the agent sent his body home. Marion's mother and older brother wanted to put some things in the coffin, so Marion opened it and threw them inside. The man had been dead for some time. A native doctor stood behind him and willed Marion's soul inside the coffin too. It got buried inside. Marion got very sick. No one could cure him. Finally, his mother took him to Cedarville where her own doctor was, but he said the situation was bad and Marion was beginning to smell like a ghost. He suggested the doctor from Hoquiam, and Marion's brother brought him back three days later. The Hoquiam doctor had a spirit ghost ally who went after the soul in the coffin. Marion got well and the doctor was paid a horse {md 56}.

A man predicted that whites would come with tame elks (cows), metal fires (stoves), pots that did not burn (kettles), and things to ride in (wagons). People called him crazy, but he was right {ph 47}.

In 1927, most Chehalis were Shakers, members of the Indian Shaker Church. Peter Heck was the elected bishop for the entire region from California to British Columbia. At that time, Shakers were expected to reject their tribal traditions. Whatever spirit powers and other possessions they had were believed to convert to Shakerism at the moment they themselves did. Nonetheless, Heck provided ThA with a wide range of important traditional information.

Today, spirits have been hurt and taken away from the people by the combined actions of slaves, those of low class, and white governments {js 339}. Instead, they gave people bad blood and disease like tuberculosis. Mary Heck {mh 219} thought that the spirits had been driven away because books and schools have made children forget.

Spirits

Thunderbird {ph 46}. When a storm moved from east to west, people said it was Thunderbird going to hunt whales in the ocean. People used to find whale bones on White Mountain, so that was a place where he ate his catch. Lightning belongs to Thunder, shooting out of its mouth. When thrown at a tree as a bolt, an agate could be found at the base to bring good luck.

Yelm Jim, a Nisqually, had Thunder power. When he got hurt, he prayed to Thunder to cool things off so he could not get a fever. After he fought in the Stevens Treaty War of 1856, he was set to be hanged, but a thunder storm scared everyone away and he escaped {ph 46, md 184}.

Warrior power came from Otter, Mink, Cougar, or Wolf, who often fathered twins. Mary Heck's husband had Wolf power that came to him in the form of a woman {ph 100}.

Leschi, war leader at Nisqually, had power from bees called yellowjackets that also made him a marksman {ph? 76}.

Hummingbird gave power to doctors and to warriors and gamblers. Though tiny, he was strong because he moved so quickly by the power that was in his mind.

Fishing power came from Fishhawk, Kingfisher, Otter, Raccoon, and Mink spirits {js 343}.

Gambling power was given by Bluejay, Flying Squirrel, Wolf, Coyote, Chicken Hawk, or Hoot Owl.

Sharks were put in a certain place in Puget Sound by $X^w ane$. Anyone seeking them as a power went into the woods, cut a two-foot length of hardwood, and sharpened both ends. When he dove into the Sound, holding on to a basket full of rocks, this stick was held in the teeth. As a shark came for him with open mouth, the boy used this stick to hold the jaws open {73 ph}. The shark's wife came next and asked him not to hurt her husband. The boy passed out, gained power, and revived safely out of the water. Sometimes, as proof, people found the dead shark on the beach with is mouth propped open with a sharpened stick.

Recovery power gave ability to go to the Land of the Dead and retrieve souls. It could be anything associated with the dead, such as a rotten canoe, old bones, or a graveyard {ph 41}. Queen Susan, sister of *Yawnish*, had this power {ph 75}. Hers was called "moldy face." Women's ability was exactly the same as men's for this. When these shamans went together to the Land of the Dead, they did not look at each other because they were afraid that their spirits would fight each other.

Humans would contest with each other using their powers {ph 81}. The one who lost got sick and died unless someone with a stronger power cured him or her. Shamans were very jealous and so fought each other through their spirits.

Only women, such as Elsie [?], had Bear spirit {ph 249}.

Sqeip, looking like a person painted on the chin and each shoulder, lived on the Earth, but flew and gave a good song to partially heal {md 56}.

A very powerful spirit for a shaman was *ayaxos,* which had a body like a snake and a head like a deer with antlers {ph 256}. Men away in the mountains to hunt deer or elk would see five *ayaxos* go in profile along the slope. A man who wanted this power would chase after them to the other side of the ridge and have them go, one at a time, in front of him. They got smaller every time he saw them because the smaller they got, the more power he received. If one of them opened its jaws like a crocodile and showed the red inside, a boy could get great power by shoving his arm down its throat. Sometimes, a man would catch and kill the smallest one, taking the ribs and hide off to keep for luck. No one must know about his having this power. It had to be a secret. *Syk'amen* was a man who had this power.

Other powerful spirits looked like a tall man or like a woman with huge breasts who raped men and covered them with slime {ph 256}. She lived in the dark timber near the town of Chehalis. In a swamp near Montesano, a spirit woman lived with a crying baby that scared people. Certain families were visited by a crying, old, grey-haired lady just before a member died. Spirits in the hills confused people so they would get lost. Many remote locations at mountains and lakes also had *psa* (dangers in human form) who killed people.

A Sturgeon power lived in a lake across from Independence, but not many young men could endure the ordeal of encountering it to receive fishing success {ph 258}. A woman spirit with long hair lived in the Black River. A whale lived in a crooked-shaped lake near the town of Chehalis.

Siyikwwvlx was the power to be well off without much effort. It was like whites who go to college, set up an office, and live well off half an hour of work {ph 264}.

Little Earths lived near water sources and made people crazy. People who were alone had to be careful when they took a drink. They had to ask these Little Earths for permission. To be safe, they blew out puffs of breath and squirted out some of the mouthful. Their power helped doctors go to the Land of the Dead.

The journey to the Land of the Dead involved different kinds of spirits. A doctor needed a personal power and spirit ghost ally to take him or her there, along with a ghost familiar (literally called "stays there") who lived with the dead and "told out" [revealed] where the patient's soul, spirit, or essence was. Marion Davis {md 195} said the familiar "kind of phoned" the shaman with this information, perhaps by telepathy. Sometimes the familiar would bring it part way back ("like from one stage stop to another") to make it easier for the doctors to retrieve, particularly in earth's summer time when the Land of the Dead has winter snow.

Shakers

The Indian Shaker Church was founded when John Slocum, at the head of Skookum Bay, died and revived in 1882 (Amoss 1990; Barnett 1957; Richen 1974; Ruby and Brown 1996). Slocum went into a trance and visited God, who sent him back to reform his own life and others {ph 47}. He taught people to kneel and ask for a blessing. A few days later, people in a room began to get the shake {md 170}. A woman (John's wife Mary) gave them this special trembling as medicine for getting well.

Mrs. Heck joined the church at Mud Bay, the mother church, in 1883 and Peter Heck joined in 1884. He came to believe in Shakers when he envisioned a woman with 5 duck feathers in her hair. He was made to see his own father's power. In 1911, he became the Shaker Bishop {ph 47}.

John Slocum. Heck {ph 42} does not know if Slocum ever had a *tahmanawis*. "He may have had some, but I do not know about it." Heck never heard it said. Shaker Church has been here since 1884. Heck joined then. Mrs. Heck joined in 1883 at Mud Bay. Heck was appointed Bishop since 1911.

Shakers now find lost spirits, like doctors used to do, but they see ghosts as lighter and better dressed than the doctors did {mh 218}. Shakers believe that candles help out. Five candles were as good as 20 people curing {msc 91}. Bell ringing also helps. Shakers forbid sin, lying, killing, adultery, stealing, and badness.

A young man joined the Shakers and tried to be a missionary, but he "got back on the powwow way" with his *tahmanawas*. His family had to tie him up so as not fly away {ph 399}.

Luck

The left shoulder, hand, or side of the body will twitch or shake when a relative dies or gets bad news. The back part of the arm will indicate that it was a distant relation {md 61}.

If you find a snake eating a toad and kill the snake, the rescued toad will give you good luck {js 256}. Two boys abused their power by using it to keep a snake from giving birth {js 255}. When thousands of snakes came to bite the mother, these mean boys laughed. Then a toad came and the snake gave birth. As the boys turned to go, they fell over dead. They were too free with their *tahmanawas* and used it wrongly on animals.

An agate found at the base of a tree struck by lightning was secretly carried for luck. Tiny fungus from the salmonberry is also kept for luck, not carried around. A hummingbird nest kept in a bullet pouch brought good luck when hunting {ph 262}.

Sky

Movements of the stars and sun were used to tell the time and seasons.

A piece of star broke off and plunged into the earth to make Grand Mound {md 59}. Some stars were [had been] people before the earth capsized. The big dipper was an elk with three or four people and a little dog hunting after it. A falling star is off to meet a lover. A comet meant the world was close to ending.

Morning [Moon] was a baby stolen by two women at Lequito and taken west before being rescued by Bluejay to become the Moon {58 md}. His brother became the Sun. Everything bad was burned {js 386}. This is the story of the founding of the chiefly lines {js 345}.

Rainbow was never pointed at {ph 275}.

Earth

Shooting an arrow at night was dangerous because a boy might hit the eye of the earth, who would pinch and kill him by winking {md 153}. When the earth winked its eye, a life was shortened [crushed].

NATIVE DOCTORS
Shamans

Most people want *tahmanawas* for hunting so as to eat well, or for wealth to live well. Getting doctor power was dangerous because other doctors wanted to kill you or, if your patients died, their families took revenge.

Parents would send their children out to some remote location before puberty to fast, pray, swim, and suffer to attract a spirit ally. Cougar, Mink, Shark were good for doctoring {pb 73}. If a child got power at 10 years, he or she could not bring it out in public to doctor until 25 years old or more.

First time the song is sung, a repeater, someone with the special ability to catch the words and tune, said them out loud for others to learn. The singer started out crying and sobbing until the repeater could make out what was said, clapped his hands, and sang aloud for others to follow and help the singer {ph 74}.

Women doctors got power to help with childbirth. George Sander's aunt, a Scatter Creek raised at Nisqually, would dip her open hand into a basket of water and sling it across a big room without splashing any of it {gs 113}. Then the baby came easy.

Each doctor had a specialty, such as birth, wounds, or gun shots. Some sucked out bad blood, diseases, or intrusive objects.

The Cowlitz came to Chehalis to gamble. The Chehalis sent a messenger to a young man, Mary Heck's grandfather *silac?*, with great power who was still a virgin. He came and watched the game all morning until two boys were sent up to the roof to move some boards to let in more light. Suddenly the man looked up and his power was unleashed. Many people passed out and blood ran from their noses {mh 220}. The game ended. The man was concerned because the probation period set by his spirit was not yet over and already he had abused its power. He recalled a woman who was menstruating and very sick. He went to look at her. He plucked a hair from his head, tied one end to a pole, and attached a bead to the other end. Using it like a fishing pole, he caught her sickness and used it to weaken his own power. The woman was suddenly well, so the man knew he could now safely go among people.

When his aunt became ill, the man decided to begin his public career as a curer. He called people together to pound on boards and help him sing. He doctored his aunt twice, then she recovered. His great power had been weakened enough to help people stay alive. After he cured a few more people, he accepted pay and became rich. This man had the second greatest power. If he also had had the highest one, he could have brought the dead back to life, like the story of Bluejay's wife [below]. He was kind and good, never using this power to kill anyone.

Doctors who kill can also call the rain {ph 245}, like Yelm Jim did with thunder storms. Peter Heck's father once "borrowed" this power to make it rain so Peter would get well from a bad illness.

When a doctor killed someone, the victim sat up just before dying and spoke like his or her own killer, sometimes gloating over achieving revenge. That was how mean doctors claimed their own. Of course, then the family knew and hired someone to get the doctor, or a warrior would feel sorry for the family and do it for them.

If another doctor got to the patient with stronger power, however, he or she could lift off, remove, or kill the mean spirit and so kill the other shaman. The removed spirit could be drowned, put into a gun and shot out, or burned up. Then the spirit's owner would suffer a fatal accident.

Once, while men were building a potlatch house, a Wynoochee doctor took an Elma man's soul and stuck it into a tree. The man was proud, loud, and boastful. Another doctor found that soul before the tree was cut down to kill that man.

Sometimes, an ordinary person would get hair or clothes from an enemy and place them with a dead person, in the mouth, on the body, or in the coffin. The enemy will then sicken and slowly die, unless the objects could be removed.

A doctor could project or "shoot" sharp objects into persons to make them sick or die. These had to be sucked out by a more powerful doctor in order for the patient to live.

A doctor could send his soul on the trail to the Land of the Dead to see who was there and predict the coming deaths of people. A Quinault doctor even knew when a famous race horse would die. He sat, closed his eyes, and sang while his soul went along the trail for four or five days, resting in a soft bed every midnight. When he met someone singing, he knew their body was on the way to death. When he came back, he warned the family and tried to cure the person before they took sick.

Even though a doctor is called to cure someone, he or she might decide to worsen them instead by inflicting a grudge disease [təčtmani K1920].

Odyssey to the Land of the Dead

Sometimes, a person's soul or pulse would wander off or be stolen to the Land of the Dead. While the human fainted, its soul walked along a marked trail, crossing a river along a foot log. Once there, the person's body would die unless a doctor went to get the soul. It was really his or her spirits that made the journey, but the doctor went through the motions of imitating ("mocked") the actions of each spirit inside a specially prepared house, showing an audience what and how the spirits were doing {ph 44}. Sometimes a doctor would pick something up from a perfectly clean floor and show it to everyone, indicating what the spirits had found along the trail {mh 217}. It might be grass from a basket being made by a woman in the audience. Then they knew her soul was gone, too.

A doctor found out that someone's soul had gone to the afterworld by shaking in a trance. He sang and danced while a carved wooden effigy of his spirit ghost ally went to the Land of the Dead to find out who was there. Whenever this effigy was near someone with a lost soul, it shook violently. To recover the soul, a doctor simulated the journey.

If confident, only one doctor would go, but, usually, a group went for greater safety. A single doctor might distract the ghosts by turning into a Wolf, Bluejay, or other spirit animal. He or she would howl or act like the animal, then snatch back the soul.

Every doctor who went to the Land of the Dead had three spirit helpers. These were a curing spirit, a spirit ghost, and a ghost familiar who actually lived among the dead. Mrs. Heck's father had this power. His three spirits included a little woman, a man represented by a hide cutout, and another man carved in the form of a wooden cane. He always held the cane at the top, above a necklace of shredded cedarbark.

To start the journey, the doctors faced west and jumped into a hole or loosened soil because the dead went underground. Then they came to the foot log across a raging river. Mrs. Heck's father used his cane to vault over the log foot bridge. All of the doctors were very vulnerable to spiritual attack as they crossed this bridge. The next obstacle was a log fastened only at one end and moving up and down to crush travelers. This levering log was along the river bank. Beyond was a crooked prairie where two sisters, who were like Cranes, watched constantly. The spirits spoke well to them and the women let them pass. A huge headless snake might block their path, but the doctors used dicta (powerful words) to strike its heart and make it disappear. They met a perpetual first menstruant and used dicta to make her forget their arrival.

In time, they heard the sounds of the village in the Land of the Dead, beside a second bubbling river. (When a preacher came and talked of the "beautiful river," Chehalis thought he meant this one.) Hidden by the sounds of water, these spirits stopped to confer and decided to made a deer or elk decoy, telling it to run in front of the village.

One of the dead saw the deer and called out so everyone ran after it. If it were night, the familiar sang to make the dead sleep more soundly.

The spirits peeked through cracks and went into the abandoned houses until they found the waylaid soul and any others. As Mary Heck said, all the ghosts looked the same so the souls, who looked like their humans, stood out {mh 217}.

The spirits and doctors now faced east and took the souls back to this world, returning from the Land of the Dead by a "short cut" that took less than a day. The spirits and shamans rejoined early in the morning. They sang and danced in the house, returning the souls to the people who had lost them. In preparation, these people had washed and cleaned themselves. During the moments before the soul was restored, patients had to stand still. If they looked back, their soul would rush away forever. These patients gave gifts and money to the doctors in gratitude. Otherwise, a patient would shortly die or suffer an accident.

Doctors also made predictions about the coming year, based on what they (their spirits) saw in the Land of the Dead.

Mrs Mary Heck Aug 1st '27 Oakville, Wash [Her] Indian name = kwili.not. {mh 217} somuk!wt = name of doctors who go to the Land of the Dead. It is not many of them, just 2 or 3 who know how to go down to the Land of the Dead. When they are ready, those parties always count each one 's smuk!, that is, how many each one has. When ready, they will call their smuk!, each one 3 times.

They make a big board like, to show the people how they are going to cross the levering log XwaniXwani; they always name themselves when ready to go jump over. All the people don't see what the smuk! are doing. If there are 3 doctor s, each has 3 smuk!, they jump 3 times from the board, those with 2, jump 2 times, those with 4, jump 4 times, and so on. They jump from a board in the house. When the smuk! start now, they'll go dancing right here, then they'll find something in the road, it is nice and clean, the road. Will find straw which are using for basket. Will show to the people in the room what woman lost it. "You lost it." A doctor will say that to her and point to her. They go back to the Xwanixwani. The x_anixamix_ are afraid of it, a *Psa*, dangerous. They jump. If the stawen breaks in two, it is dangerous to them. When they start after they find it [the path?], they will go, don't know how far.

Then, they will come to a great, large snake lying across the road. They don't know how to pass it. They use kits!stani to "hit" the snake right away. The sx_anixamix_ who hits the snakes' heart will make the snake just disappear when [it] hits the snake's heart and will go off from the road. Don't know where it goes. This is the great Danger to the novice who has never been there before. When the x_anixamix_ pass the snake and go on, then they will come to a prairie which increases all the time in size. They are afraid of it because they can not get over it. All use their Kits, just as they did with the snake. If can't hit it, will grow bigger and bigger. It is a *psa*. When this smuk! pass the prairie, and not very far from there, watches everything now on the road going. Pretty soon, they will get to a maisx [M1 first menstruant], been maisx in first monthly a life time. [She] has been there all the time. She always tells to the dead Mak!wt what is coming. They'll use this Kits to the maisx to make her forget herself, and never tell about them. Her name is tipulEmai!ln. When the smuk! pass her, they will go on, not very far, when they will come to the village. Now go secretly from that time, so the mak!wt will never know. Sneak in where [they] keep the skwa_u_ku_tEns.

Any house with [a] little crack, they will peep in there to see if any [are] there, because the mak!wt are all alike and all the skwa are different, like pastens [whites]. But when this person died, would become like mak!wt, but when the skwa get there, they are different. When the x_anxami&_ gets through looking in and knows where many are inside, he goes to work and calls the skwa to come out and [he] will then keep them. After the skwa who are from there, then will go a little ways and camp over night in that place. And when the mak!wt [are] all asleep, about morning, the x_an- will get after the mak!wt, when try to scare them off. Toward morning, the x_an will say to one another, "What shall we do to the mak!wt ?" Pretty soon, one will start hollering, and all will holler, "Elk, Elk, Elk," and the mak!wt will hear and it will wake them up. "The Elk are coming!" So all will go and hunt for them. When all [of them are] out, will go inside the houses and will get everything. Then took with them when they went, baskets and so on, before the ghosts get back. When the ghosts get back, they find the spirits gone. They go to bed again, for they never found the Elk.

So {mh 216}, it is early in the morning when the ghosts are asleep that the doctors get after them. Maybe the doctors will bring back fifteen or twenty. Will bring [them] back all standing, facing the sun, [in] two or three rows, double. They must never look back. If one of the rescued people should look back, his soul will be there still and he will soon die [for ever]. He wanted to stay there, that is the reason he looked back. It is near morning, now, when they are finished. [They] will all sit down. The doctor man will tell them: "Tomorrow morning, all of you that have been brought back, women and old men, must go and clean yourselves early in the morning." When they get through bathing and cleaning themselves, they all call them to go to the same house, and the doctor man will start singing his x_an- . Again, he will work on them and clean them, remove all that [from] the ghost. When [he] got through, will begin to get all the souls. When they finished, [it took] about three-fourths of the day to work on them, before they finished [after] they had come back. Mrs. Heck has been brought back many times from the dead people. All believe it, even those who don't have smuk!, because it all seems true to them.

River. Went to, took them 3 nights to go, all night travel. Foot log does not reach across, will jump from the end of a board which has been raised on one end, and then will jump with their cane.

First River. Because it always changes every which way. Sometimes will be higher or lower, in order to fool the people. This is the first river and over which the XwaniXwani crosses.

Second River. At the ghost place, there is another river. There is a nice sound on the river. It is something moving up and down all the time which makes a very nice sound, our souls hear it and not us, that is the reason it likes to go to the ghosts. The xan did not cross this river.

Second Death. When the dead people die again. Cross over the ?? to the second death. Mrs says that Bluejay says it is one end of the prairie and she does not know which one is true. (See Bluejay Visits the Land of the Dead. [ThA 1934: 21-29])

Snake in the Land of the Dead. Name of snake, has no head. Just cut both ends, no eyes, no tail, and his body. His skin is just like the night eel, and when find this kind of snake here on earth, the small ones, it is dangerous because it is a *psa* from the ghosts.

Mountain in the prairie of the Land of the Dead. It only known by ?? a manure pile on the prairie. A large one is called the same thing.

Basket Straw found on the trail to the Land of the Dead. "1 fellow", this is Peter Heck talking, "as father used to tell me, used to clean the trail as clean as anything, but pretty soon the people would see the doctors pick it up from the solid ground. Always wondered how could find it." Father always said the ground was so clean and smooth, that he believed it must be so. But the doctors would stoop down and pick it up."

Soul. The old lady says she does not know what soul is, but she claims it may be "out breath". The old lady claims this. She volunteered that it was probably just natural appearance. The Shaker Religion claims that the dead person is lighter and dressed better, are changed from the old way that dead people looked. Peter continued. Does not know what the difference in looks was between the ghosts and the souls, but supposes they were very much in appearance the same as now. "Just the same as the dead people one dreams of."

When ghosts died in the Land of the Dead, they went across to the "other side" of the river (or town) where they were forgotten by the living. Anyone who died by falling out of a tree went immediately to the Second Land of the Dead. [Like the bones from an abandoned tree burial {ph 397}]. If a grave burned, that ghost also went across and moved upside down from then on. They walked on their heads. Some said those who were long dead went to the end of the town, not across the river {sh 142}. No one ever revived from this Second Land of the Dead.

Dead babies went east not west back to their home, waiting to be reborn with a sun rise. In ancient times, dead infants were placed in trees in the mountains so their souls can return. These unborn babies walk head down so they can be born more easily.

Ghosts exist around the living. They are very close whenever a fire goes out for no reason. To drive them away, people sing with a drum of elk or deer skin.

In the Land of the Dead, time and circumstances were reversed from the ordinary. Winter here was summer there, low tide was high tide, clothed is naked, and broken vessels were whole {sh 144}. This made an odyssey in the summer especially difficult.

In ordinary summer, the trail to the Land of the Dead was frosty and deep in snow. A doctor learned that a soul was there because his or her spirit ghost or ghost familiar "phoned" a warning {md 195}. When the doctors were ready to leave, the familiar managed to get the soul part of the way back along the trail. Then the spirit ghost will help, but only if it is not too cold. The doctors came the rest of the way, took the soul, and restored it to its human body.

> Only Thing Fierce. Only a fellow who has a fierce *tahmanawas* will be want in his heart a good meal, venison or salmon, if not get it, will leave his bad *tahmanawas* and will give the people a short life.

> One man had that here. His name was sis&mɫki. They were afraid of him all the time. When he came to their house, he would not say what he wanted. They would have to guess. If did not do it, so would get sick.

> When he got sick, he had smuk! He had the Bluejay. He died one time, his soul went to the dead village of the dead. He came to a place, where the dead people were gambling and some w&xq'xat of this friends saw him coming into the gambling house said to him "Well, the looks of yours, how's it come that you come in without clothes? You'd better go back again." So he came back again and was about 2 weeks after fixed. Hang up in the canoe and those now, down the river, probably above Grand Mound, old lady Heck's cousin, another man, a cousin, was down to the river where he was. Was weeping for this man. Was coming to the river to wash his face. No one above the river but themselves. Saw someone coming, paddling the river, saw it. Just look like the one he was weeping for. {md 153} Knew his manner of paddling. Waded out, recognized that it was he. On part of his body maggots were walking around on him. they sat down and talked. Repeat. It is shameful to go to the Land of the Dead naked, so relatives in the Land of the Dead told him. His smuq [smuk!] brought him back. If he had not had smuq would not have come back to life.

> People were always afraid of him. Note: can this bad *tahmanawas* be an outgrowth of the secret society farther north. Note: can not determine exactly the nature of *sqeip*.

> Queen Susan. Sister of Yawnis, had sqeip *tahmanawas* Sqeip might say, "I am the doctor's sqeip." She used to poison people too.

> Kwmtoloɫtsin. Another woman doctor cured everyone about. She had all kinds of *tahmanawas*. That is the reason she could cure so well. Had doctor smuk! and sqeip, and another. Have forgotten the name of it. Had many different kinds of *tahmanawas* Was middle aged when Davis was young man. She was of the best family too.

Among Lushootseed doctors, power from a Little Earth was also required to be able to safely go to the Land of the Dead, but Chehalis believed that Little Earths were afraid of the ghost familiars {ph 258}. Power to go to Land of the Dead came from Raven, a black beetle, a post from an abandoned house, bones, Bluejay, or any scavengers {js 342}.

Medicines

Vomiting was induced with an infusion boiled from the bark of the red wood used to make lal [slahal] gambling disks {ph 38}. Sometimes the white flowers of death camas were used. Vomiting relieved heartburn or internal disorders by ejecting black hard blood. While used as a home remedy, a doctor will also administer it early in the morning and press on the patient's forehead and belly to make sure all of it was expelled.

Roots and leaves were used for sore eyes, along with a nursing mother's milk. A plant with little white balls [snowberries ?] or water lily seeds were also used as a eye wash {md 183, ds 371}.

Love medicine attracted and held a spouse {ph 109}, especially if used with dicta.

Cuts and wounds were washed with the water of boiled white fir boughs {md 154}. Red fir pitch was mixed with bear oil and taken in a dose of 5 tablespoons a day over 6 weeks for consumption [TB]. Boiled hemlock inner bark, mixed with dogwood or bearberry, gave strength for recovery. Pitch was used as a salve.

Colds were treated with ferns, cedar boughs, mint leaves, bear grease, and inhaling strong smells.

Broken bones were set with splints and a poultice of smashed red elderberry stems.

Powdered, year-old ironberry blossoms healed burns, while boiled red elderberry bark helped bruises, such as the backside of someone thrown from a horse.

Something like bearberry, with pinkish fall blossoms, was boiled and drunk to cure smallpox and worked for Mary Heck.

Inner cedar bark, raw thimbleberry sprouts, and nettles relieved monthlies {md 155}.

Wild Rosebush medicines of Puget Sound were learned by Marion Davis's mother, who paid a horse for them. Mostly they helped women and babies.

Honeysuckle, as boiled scrapings, was used to treat a baby's sore tongue. The boiled roots or flowers were a hair tonic {ds 371}.

Eel oil was used for chapped hands, sores, and scabs.

Bear grease mixed with spruce needles was a good cough medicine.

Gunshots had to be treated by a specialized doctor or shaman. Spirit-caused illnesses also could only be treated by specialists. White doctors could do nothing with spirits, they could only treat smallpox, scarlet fever, measles, and other European diseases.

Growlers ~ xədxədib

Important families had their members, particularly children, initiated into this secret sect (*xədxədib* ~ *xidxidib* in Lushootseed, *xinxinim* in Straits Salish) for lots of money, but it was humbug from top to bottom {sh 144}. Members secretly stuck the back of the mouth to make it bleed. Upper Chehalis had it along with other tribes around Puget Sound. (Marion Davis said

Chehalis did not have it, but a woman initiate did live among them {md 151}.) It was not nature's gift, but "made up" by people. It was very secret. You were killed if you told about it.

When a wealthy family wanted a child initiated, they call a meeting. The child was "shot," blood poured out of the nose and mouth, and he or she fell "senseless" to the ground for several days before coming to life with this new power, shouting like dogs in a spiritual way. They acted like a fierce *tahmanawas*, singing and growling like crazy and crawling on hands and knees. They were painted black, and black paint was used only by Growler cult initiates.

The power was stronger than one boy, half Skokomish and half Squaxin, so he revived with crossed eyes. Another initiate really died until his uncle blew into the top of his head through a closed fist. It was strong with Klallams and Skokomishes. A lavish potlatch always was held at the end.

> *xenxenəm* [abbreviated below as Xen], *xedxedəb* {md 151, 25 July}. Never had it here, but had it at Skok[omish] and at Puget Sound. Oh, they think lots of that over there. Heard that whenever a person wants his son to have xenxen m, he'll go and ask the head man to gather the people to come to his home, or special meeting house. The Xen have certain people to shoot the person's body; he'll get senseless and lie down on the ground for 4, 5, 6, or 7 days, senseless, and whenever he comes to life, will give him the Xen. Have to have 2 people near the door to drive people out who laugh or shout with the xedxedəb. Will out the +yp [?] in a certain place. Tell them what to do and give them some way of singing xed [Xen], *tahmanawas* painted with charcoal to make them black.

Would shoot dogs in spiritual way, and eat the dog alive, get sort of crazy like. Some kind of fierce *tahmanawas*. The Klallam and Skokomic are the place for it. Does not think any q'waayivł belonged to the Puget Sound. The one who is trying to get Xen will die dead for that length of time. When want to come to life again, will give him a *tahmanawas* song and some power to come to {md 152} life again. When laid too long a time, would not come to life again. A mas. [?] country man, half Sko squax, cross eyed now. Can not see good. Trying to get Xen, but it was stronger than he. There was a young man from Skok, and a middle aged man and from another house there was a growling sound. He had this man tied around the waist with a rope. The middle aged man was holding him back, because when get this *tahmanawas* would fly away. Was running behind him, holding him with rope. Was running to every house. Fell all at once in one house and died right there. The young man from Skok had some relatives here. The middle aged man from Puget Sound was my uncle. The old man began to blow. Blow through his closed fist. Blow on top of his head. Then all at once he came to life again.

His folks hired the folks to give him the Xen, and once in a while he still got it. When got scared once in a while, would get it again. Were living here with their friends. one woman here had it, but she was not a native of Q!wayaił.

A potlatch was given at the initiation. Does not know how it started. I heard there was one fellow, a chief, when was half way out, got the xed, to give to another one. The same way with Skok.

But here, <u>insists</u> they did not have it.

If anyone does not have it, if goes in where they have it, will get shot, and supposed
to get the *tahmanawas*. If do not join it, will shoot him for good and will die.
Everyone who does not have this kind is so afraid that will not laugh where singing
xedxedəb.

Whenever it comes to them, their nose and mouth will be just pouring blood. I do
not know why. Anyone can belong to it who wants that kind.

Membership was used as a defensive power by people along the coast, by "sea warriors
along the water front" {js 377}. In preparation for war, young members might slash their bodies.
Sometimes they held a sham battle with knives. Other people watched from afar, often in canoes
floating safely off the beach. Chief Yawnish once watched from a ship anchored in the Sound
and attracted too much attention so initiates in canoes chased the ship, brandishing wooden
knives that accidentally killed some boys for whom Yawnish had to pay compensation.

Lummi sect members came to Squaxin Island as a flotilla, the crews standing up and
holding seagulls [ducks] that flapped their wings.

A remarkable text dictated by Frank Allen of Skokomish describes 1870s shamanic
attempts to recover lost and stolen money left along Willapa Shoalwater Bay by a jilted wife.

75. Chehalis doctors try to find lost money
with earth dwarf images (FA) [c1870]

(75.1) In my time, when I was a boy about fifteen years old, a man named Lighthouse
Charley (pała'łc'i) lived at nam'sča'c' in Shoalwater (Willapa) Bay, at the end of Chehalis country
[Ray 1938: 41, site # 30].

Now those Chehalis people have c'a'x̣ʷu. Those are little-earth (earth dwarf) images,
about four feet high, made like a person, of wood, with a handle in back to hold them by. We
Skokomish don't use those, but we call them c'a'x̣ʷu too. And they are *tahmanamis* {>
Chinookan *taax̣* 'spirit power'}, and [243] that *tahmanamis* is little-earths (təbta'baxʷ). And that
is their c'a'x̣ʷu power.

Now this Charley had a wife and he was a rich man, he had three or four thousand
dollars. But he quit that woman and got another woman. So that woman that Charley left took
the money, and she hid it, she took Charley's money and she buried it somewhere. After a while
she moved it to a new place, and she kept on doing that so nobody could find it.

Now this woman Charley left died. And who knows where the money is? Well, Charley
met with his people and they talked about it. And they decided to use c'a'x̣ʷu. So they went and
got a woman that had c'a'x̣ʷu, and they told her they'd pay her when she found the money. Her
name was lɑwiqɑm, that doctor woman. And I was there at nam'sčac' at the time. I saw this.

(75.2) So they built a big fire in Charley's house in nam'sča'c'. And that woman sent two
men off in the woods to bring her c'a'x̣ʷu, and they brought it wrapped in cedar bark. And this
woman that owned the c'a'x̣ʷu said, "I'll do the best I can with my c'a'x̣ʷu. You pick your man
now, whoever you want to go with the c'a'x̣ʷu." She said this to Charley. So Charley appointed
a middle-aged man. This man he appointed said, "hi"! This is hard work for me. This burns my
hands." He had held c'a'x̣ʷu before. And he called for oil, he wanted to grease his hand. His
name was kənɑ'n'łnɑł.

And now that woman began to sing: ha• he• a'aha• / ya• he• a'aha•. That is her c'a'$\underline{x}^w$u
song now. And they had a big fire burning now. And that woman sat in one end of the house
singing, and the man that held the c'a'$\underline{x}^w$u kneeled on the floor in front of the fire, facing her and
holding that image in front of him with both hands.

Now the owner says, "Well, my c'a'$\underline{x}^w$u will have to be heated up in the fire. He's been
out in the woods a long time, and now he has to be heated up." So she went on singing and that
c'a'$\underline{x}^w$u got up and shook and danced around the fire, with kəna'n'łnał holding it and sweating.

And all of a sudden the c'a'$\underline{x}^w$umade for the door and went out to the next house. This
had belonged to Charley's old wife, the one he had left. And the c'a'$\underline{x}^w$u went into that house and
danced around inside, and dug into the floor here and there, looking for money, but nothing.
And everybody followed behind, all excited, and the c'a'$\underline{x}^w$u woman singing, and everybody
beating sticks together and helping her sing.

(75.3) Now c'a'$\underline{x}^w$u gave up inside that woman's house and made [244] for the woods,
and everybody followed, singing. And so quite a way through the woods. And c'a'$\underline{x}^w$u came to
a windfall and went over it and came around to the butt of that windfall. And that doctor woman
went right with her c'a'$\underline{x}^w$u, and when they got to the base of that windfall she began to cry, just
as that wife of Charley's had cried there. And the c'a'$\underline{x}^w$u stopped there and shook up and down
at the butt of that windfall. And people dug down a foot or two there, but all they found was an
empty can and a lot of rags she had wrapped the money in. But Charley's wife had moved the
money from there some time or other.

So now the c'a'$\underline{x}^w$u started off again, right back to the village now. And all the people
followed beating with two sticks and helping the owner of the c'a'$\underline{x}^w$u sing. And she's sweating
now, that doctor woman, and the man that's holding the c'a'$\underline{x}^w$u, he's working hard now. And the
c'a'$\underline{x}^w$u coursed along like a hound, following that wife's tracks. And when he got to the village
he went down to the beach to a canoe there. And c'a'$\underline{x}^w$u went right to the stern of the canoe
where that woman had sat down, and then he got up and pointed across the bay to $\underline{x}^w$a'$\underline{x}^w$oc [Ray
1938: 40, site # 24]. That was where she had taken the money. This was about noon.

(75.4) Charley said to the c'a'$\underline{x}^w$u woman, "You'd better cool down with your c'a'$\underline{x}^w$u
now. We'll have something to eat and talk about this a little more." So they went back to
Charley's house, and everybody came in and they ate sturgeon. And that doctor woman said,
"Well, Charley, I'm not able to do this hard work alone. Now what do you say we go and get
ca'a'$\underline{x}$ɑd, Old Man George Kanoodle. He has another c'a'$\underline{x}^w$u, and we'll work together on this. "
Charley wanted that money bad, so he said, "All right, I'll go and get him myself." Now ca'a'$\underline{x}$ɑd
was a big Oakville (Upper Chehalis) doctor man, married to a woman at nam'sča'c', and he was
fishing down on the Columbia River at the time. So Charley went down and got Kanoodle, and
they came back in the evening, and everybody ate again.

And when they got through eating ca'a'$\underline{x}$ɑd said, "We'll have *tahmanamis* tonight. We'll
try to see what my power says about it." So ca'a'$\underline{x}$ɑd sang his song: "isa təsyalɑqɑm" [Chehalis]
(come and help me)." He's calling his power now. And that c'a'$\underline{x}^w$u woman sang with him,
helping him call his other powers. And after a while they finished singing, and everybody ate
again, and then they slept. And in the morning everybody woke up, wondering what to do.

(75.5) Now ca'a'$\underline{x}$ɑd said, "You go now and bring my c'a'$\underline{x}^w$u." And he appointed a man,
and the man went into the woods and brought [245] back his c'a'$\underline{x}^w$u. And that man showed his

hands when he came back, and they were all blistered. It was just as hot as fire, that c’a'<u>x</u>^wu. And ca'a'<u>x</u>ɑd got ready now, and Charley appointed an old man who knew about holding c’a'<u>x</u>^wu. And this man took hold of the image, and ca'a'<u>x</u>ɑd sang the same song the doctor woman had sung: ha• he• a'aha• / ya• he• a'aha•". And that c’a'<u>x</u>^wu danced around the fire, warming up. Then he danced right out of the house to that woman's house next door. And nothing there. And then he took the same track the other c’a'<u>x</u>^wu had, into the woods he went, to the butt of that windfall. And ca'a'<u>x</u>ɑd cried there, just as that woman had done when she was burying the money. And Charley took the can that was there. And Old Kanoodle's c’a'<u>x</u>^wu looked around there, and then he made right for the village again. And now he ran fast to that woman's house again, and that c’a'<u>x</u>^wu sat down right where that wife of Charley's used to sit. And Kanoodle began to cry again.

After a while the c’a'<u>x</u>^wu got up and went to one man there and shook at him. And ca'a'<u>x</u>ɑd told that man, "You sit down right there." And he told that man. Big Jim (<u>x</u>q^wi'<u>sx</u>), the brother of that woman, "Did your sister give you that money?" "Yes, she gave me twenty dollars before she died." So they found twenty dollars of that money.

(75.6) And now the c’a'<u>x</u>^wu went out of the house. It went down to that canoe on the beach where the other c’a'<u>x</u>^wu had gone, and it pointed across to <u>x</u>^wa'<u>x</u>^woc. And ca'a'<u>x</u>ɑd said to the doctor woman lɑwi'qɑm, "Now you bring your c’a'<u>x</u>^wu too, and we'll go and work over on the other side of the water." So they put the images in that canoe and everybody went across the bay to <u>x</u>^wa'<u>x</u>^woc. That was where Charley's wife had been born and raised.

Now c’a'<u>x</u>^wu doesn't work on the water, those images just stayed quiet while they were on the water. And then they landed at c’a'<u>x</u>^wu. And ca'a'xad said, "Now we'll go into this house and build a fire to heat up the c’a'<u>x</u>^wu." So everybody gathered wood and went into that old house of Charley's wife. And they built a fire and heated up the c’a'<u>x</u>^wu, both of them now, while ca'a'xad and lawi"qam sang. And now the c’a'<u>x</u>^wu started to course around, both of them together now. Where one would go the other would go. And around and around they went, till they came to one of the corner house posts, the rear post on the right as you went in.

And now both the c’a'<u>x</u>^wu stopped there and shook at that post. And the owners of the c’a'<u>x</u>^wu laughed now, "hɛ' hɛ' hɛ' hɛ'!" And ca'a'<u>x</u>ɑd said, "You dig right here. The money is here." So they dug [246] down about three feet and they lifted out another can, all wrapped in a rag, and in the can was gold all wrapped up in rags, and two fathoms of dentalia with the gold. And there were five twenties in gold, that's all the gold there was there.

Now that was an Indian way. When you know you are going to die you put something where you were raised. And that wife of Charley's had put one hundred dollars there with that x<u>ƛ</u>ɛ'ɛč. That was all she put there. And that was done now, that's all they found there in that house.

(75.7) Well, now the c’a'<u>x</u>^wu began to run again. Out of the house and into the woods they went, he'! They came to a big tree and the owners of the c’a'<u>x</u>^wu cried, "Here, here!" So they dug there where the c’a'<u>x</u>^wu stopped, between two big roots. And they found a gunny sack and pulled it out. And in it were that woman's hatchet, and her needle for mat making (sča'pšul'ɑd), of hardwood about as long as a forearm, and her t'a'a'k^waysɪd (mat creaser) blocks of hard wood, maple, with groove on one side. And that was all they found there. No money, just her mat-making outfit.

And now the c'a'x̱ʷu ran again, back to the village they ran, and up and down where that woman had walked. Then down to the beach, to that canoe, and they pointed right back across the bay to Georgetown, to nam'sča'c' again. And they got into their canoes and went back across now. And when they got to nam'sča'c' they were all hungry, so everybody went to Charley's house and ate and talked about it.

(75.8) Now in the morning ca'a'x̱ɑd said, "Well, we'll keep on and do the best we can. So you help, you people, and we'll see if we can find the money." They had only found one hundred twenty dollars now, and they're going to try to find the rest. So they built a fire again and heated up the two c'a'x̱ʷu. And now they're off, outside they go, with the c'a'x̱ʷu doctors after them singing, and all the people following.

Now when something is far off those c'a'x̱ʷu will raise up high and shake. So now they raised up in the air and shook, and pointed toward c'xe'ləs (Westport) on Grays Harbor. So everyone got ready and took horses and went to Westport now. I took my aunt's horse and went too, I wanted to see what those c'a'x̱ʷu were going to do now.

So they got to c'xe'ləs, and they built a big fire there on the point and heated up the c'a'x̱ʷu again. Now that wife of Charley's had lived there when she was a little girl, her people had a house there at c'xe'ləs. And now the c'a'x̱ʷu are at it again, and their owners call to [247] them, "ta'e' wəc'a'! (do your best)!" And around and around they went, smelling the track where that woman went. And now they shot down to the salt water and sat down, and their owners cried and washed their faces in the water, just as Charley's wife had done. And they got up again and moved down to the point and sat there a while and cried. Whatever that woman had done c'a'x̱ʷu did the same thing now. And two or three places they went that way, where she had cried and sat down and washed her face. And now they went back at a trot, back to the village, and right to the middle of where the village had been. There was no village there at that time, no houses or anything.

And the c'a'x̱ʷu stopped there in the middle of the old village, and their owners sat down and cried. And now they started to say, "It's right here! It's right here!" And the c'a'x̱ʷu quit now. Those men who were holding the c'a'x̱ʷu were just boiling hot by now.

People dug in the ground with digging sticks now. And they dug away about three feet down, and now they felt something with their sticks. And they pulled it out, all wrapped with gunny sacks and rags. And he'! They found that money now!

But when they unwrapped it there was only one hundred dollars. And they dug a little more, and found her big horn spoons (dəxʷɬu'bɑɑd), two of them, but no more money.

(75.9) So they got the c'a'x̱ʷu going again, to look a little more. And the c'a'x̱ʷu went up a little hill there on the sand spit. And they sat there a while, and their owners cried. And then they went down to the water and washed their faces. And now the c'a'x̱ʷu raised up in the air and pointed right back to nam'sča'c'. So everybody got on their horses and went back home. So that's two hundred and twenty dollars now, that's all they've got.

Now that's the way with well-off people in the early days. When they know they're going to die, they go back to where they were born and where they were raised and they bury dentalia there. That's what this wife of Charley's had done, only she had buried that money instead.

Now Charley invites us all to eat. And he says, "Thank you, people, for all you're doing, and thank you c'a'x̱ʷu people for trying to find the money." And the c'a'x̱ʷu people said, "Well, we'll do the best we can. It's just up to the c'a'x̱ʷu now." So everybody ate. And then they heated up the c'a'x̱ʷu again before the fire, and when they were heated they went out of the house and made right for the beach. And they pointed right out over the water. Now Charley said, "Get into this big canoe, and bring that little canoe that belonged to the [248] woman." But after they got out of the water the c'a'x̱ʷu took them back to shore again, and down the beach east about a quarter of a mile [cf. 75.6]. There the c'a'x̱ʷu owners sat down and cried. Now the c'a'x̱ʷu went back again and jumped right into that big canoe and pointed out over the water. When they had got way out on the bay, in deep water, the images pointed down into the water, and the c'a'x̱ʷu owners said, "Right here! Right here!" So they all went back to shore.

(75.10) Evening came and everybody talked about it, "Yes, out there in deep water is where she threw the money." And Charley said, "You all stay here, people. I've got a seine net, and I'm going to try to get that money up." This was a year or two after that wife of his had died, and everybody wondered how he was going to get that money up out of the deep water.

Well, next morning they got a long drag net the white men had given Charley down on the Columbia River. So they loaded that net in a big canoe, and the c'a'x̱ʷu people stood on the beach and pointed them the way to go. They put down the net and dragged it in to shore. Nothing but a few fish and crabs. So they took the net out a little farther and dragged it in again. And in came the net, and this time there was a big, rotted rag the gold had been wrapped in, but nothing else but a few flounders and crabs.

Now they gave up. That was the end of it. The gold had come out of that rag and was buried in the soft bottom now, so they gave up. And two hundred twenty dollars was all they got. That woman had lugged that money all over, figuring what to do with it. She biwałwəlk'ʷədəbət as we say in Twana, gave presents to the places where she was raised. And then she took the rest of the money and sunk it in the bay. [Note from Henry Allen: in Twana, swəłk'ʷ are belongings of a dead person that are buried with him or destroyed, not given away. You can wəlɑk'ʷad for yourself before you die. That's what this woman was doing. The idea is to take your valuables with you.]

Charley kept the money they had found, and he paid the c'a'x̱ʷu people blankets and guns, and he gave everybody that had helped something. I got something, but I forget what it was. He let Big Jim keep the twenty dollars his sister had given him.

So that's done now. They worked about a week, but the rest of that gold is still out there off Georgetown.

(75.11) Doctor people here at Skokomish sometimes found lost things with their swa'w'š (doctor power). And they used łu'kʷali rattles for that too, at sxɛ•dəb. That was really a better way. But the [249] Skokomish never used anything like those c'a'x̱ʷu images, that's a Chehalis business. Some here get power from the təbta'baxʷ to go to the ghost land, and other kinds of power can go there too, like Big Bill's tiwata'yın' power, but they never use images. The dəxʷuwa'bš (Duwamish) doctors use boards they call swa'w'š with their *tahmanamis* painted on it when they go to the ghost land, but they don't use them here [cf. 71.2; 73.8]. Here they just have canes and that rope to make their canoe [outline for the vehicle to go to the land of the dead and back].

LODGES ~ CLUBS ~ ORDERS

Although much of Hoh ethnography is shared along the Northwest Coast, a distinctive feature, condensed in Doc's these notes is the six lodges, clubs, sodalities, or orders which drew membership from prosperous Hohs (Powell 1990: 433; Powell and Woodruff 1976: 81, 91. 198, 211, 249, 441). Often called secret societies, they represent special privilege and guarded rank, based on knowledge that is protected and only in that sense "secret".

1	λok̓ʷa•li	wolf, black paint, warriors
2	c̓a•yiq	fishers, sealers , Salmon
3	kiλaʔk̓ʷał	hunters, Elks, "uprivering"
4	sibaxʷola•yoʔ	whalers, "oily-voiced"
5	čala•layoʔ	seers, forecasters, Weathermen, "southern voiced"
6	ʔixʷałolaʔa•ʔlayoʔ	doctors, shamans

Only #3, #6, and maybe #5 have Chimakuan origins. The others have obvious regional links, especially in their songs which feature words from neighboring tribes, including Wakashan Kwakiutlans (1, 2), Makah (4), and Quinault (5). This last, may have come from Hoh at a time when Quinault was the dominant language there. Hoh is call "South River" in Quileute.

In Kwakwaka'wakw the word *tʔsetʔsayeka* means "secrets", being shortened to Tsaykik as the club spread to other communities. A distinct category of family privileges involves *tsasa'a* = love songs.

Tlokwaly = Wolves

<λok̓ʷali> Tlokwaly <2-5> 3 or 4 leading men – bad guys – have small dish of charcoal at door – as soon as you get in there – they paint your face if you belong – if you don't belong, you stay over on one side. Everyone had his own song, all join in & sing his song, go clear around – everyone had short stick & pounded on board – then the 4 leading men start it again – getting rougher <2-7>.

One fellow go & grab fire & threw [through] it all around. One fellow grab big piece & put it on his back – everyone then dances, one foot & then the other. Fireman (a certain man) starts fire again – only one man starts fire.

Women folks get dry fish & cook it & eat it with whale blubber. Whoever want to join they must notify 4 or 5 leading men – paint novice face – if a person wants son or daughter to join – must notify leading men & give a present to each person at gathering – wooden spoons, harpoon point, old belt?? made of dry spruce limb – twisted spruce limb around neck to keep from splitting, canoes. <2-9> Tlokwaly song – Joe Cole – would sing the song before giving presents away.

Elk Club – winter & early spring <2-114>

Tlokwaly – winter time – Molly Caplanaho – has scars on her arm where she was cut during Tłokwaly dance when she was young.

Bill's father <2-115> used to lead in Tlokwaly. Bill knows all his songs, especially 2 good songs. Bill's father had elk bone pin & would run it through his body.

Club colors <3-6> Tlokwaly black paint – a woman usually paints faces. Tsayuq = red & white stripes vertically on both cheeks. Each Shaker has own song.

Mrs. Frank Fisher brought Mary a box of weaving grass & an old coat because of Ross Tsailto's death<3-6> [13 July].

Rules of Tlokwaly <3-67> can't sleep with wife for 5 days – will take you before crowd & bawl you out. People act as individuals. Last one (Tlokwaly) was given by Tylor Hobucket for oldest daughter to join. People <3-66> from BC made special trip to give Tylor Hobucket the mask & song & dance (Tylor poor singer – out of tune).

Tlokwaly – mainly for rich people – to join one must give away a great deal. Rank depended upon – membership in different societies – wealth – family – individual – what he has done for his people. Old man Hobucket was chief – he had no sons – so his nephew was chief.

Tłokwaly – Family had children – they select oldest & 2nd oldest – to give party among the tribe. Younger ones are left until later. Beads &c collected to give to people who have had parties before & now belong. Invite some young men (2 or 3 recent) to get small rocks – they pack those rocks, as much as they can carry (in baskets) around to every house in the village and throw the rocks on the roofs of the houses – make a big noise & the people in the house wonder who is leading – (secret at this time – find out at party). In afternoon of next day, these boys go around to the houses with rattle & Tlokwaly song. Rattle is owned by man whose business it is to go around village & make invitations<3-95> [Stanley Grey, Wed Aug 14 (?) 1949].

The leader & boys go out in brush & pick branches off salal bush to be used by young people. Party held at Captain Mason's house. Young people carrying in all the salal branches. People are gathered at old plank house ready for party. People going in are covered with <3-97> salal brush – obscuring their entire body. Dirt floor in house. Two men with Elk [insignia] tail feather fans – are leaders = younger (1st tso•wɛ•yuqʷəp) (and ya•wəqłəp). Others come to help leading men called (older) = (tła•xʷa•xəd) & (tsuqʷa•tsit) (yaq'la•do) (wiba•xəd).

When the brush dancers come in – each dancer has wooden whistle in mouth – made of bark. Leader sings out a short chant & swings the door open. The (two) wolves come in wearing wolf clothes – ears – long tail – act crazy like – growling. [<3-100> wolves called du•łəb, [have] eagle feathers on the mask.] Then came in the brush dancers also acting crazy & line up around the smokehouse, (25-30 young men).

Had 4 big wooden box drums which 6 men sit on each & kick with heels – 3 men on each side of drum – sounds like thunder. Two boxes on each side of door. Four men are boss for the fires in the house (2 fires) – one man called = wəqaiyso , second = o•biq' [bosses for fires]. <3-94> In giving the invitations those people who are invited are named. Stanley Grey was among young people carrying in the salal brush.

2 water man <3-99> = 1st = ya•wəx 2nd = tsəltcayił . During the dance, if anyone drinks or warms themselves by the fire without asking the bosses, they are fined. Watchmen will take knives & cut their clothes off & then these people must pay food, berries [as fine]. Ladies pay berries & lacamas – men pay dry fish or meat, whale. After the dancers are finished with the brush dances, they go out & throw the brush in the river.

Old man (named = wila•isəb) starts his song with a rattle around big fire – song means dead face – "These clothes which I wear belong to dead face." Starts to act like he's getting crazy around & around the fire – he pulls big logs & coals from fire & throws them into the crowd - he kills the fire. His help lets him kill the fire without being burned – that is what his song means.

After the people <3-101 > had gone home, yawəpłəp & tła•xʷa•xəd , each has a gang of people – all wear masks, deer hoof rattles on legs, & in hands – carry pitchwood torches, start at one end of village (after midnight) – 1ˢᵗ bunch goes into the houses first & are followed by second bunch – four men dressed as wolves from the first bunch.

Four other men wearing wooden masks (like human face & dressed in rabbit skin clothes) [try to make people smile]. These are called = gwaləbəqʷəł – come dancing into house throwing invisible things to one another. People in house can't smile or laugh, leader has black bear hide blanket, had bone pins made of bones of dead people – had hair on one end (dead people's hair), called = tłqe•ləqʷəł – 3 sizes – small for young people, middle size, & large size. Used for punishment – if a person makes some kind of mistake – large pin used. Same men have knives through sides [of body].

Party <3-103> is all done – usually lasts for 5 days & nights – for rattles are passed around from different people to sing their songs. After the party, the presents are passed out. During party, each large family is ready to fight other family of tribe. Last lunch – if non member eats with member – he is punished with bone point through upper arm. After lunch, they give away presents of beads – if a person has put up two parties, he gets two strings of beads – some have 5. Also give wooden spoons away, called = tła•sə' . These spoons used for drinking broth left in kettle after meat is cooked – knives, poles, paddles, bailers, harpoons for salmon. People who do lots of singing, get larger present – for helping people in the crowd. <3-105> Some receive bow & arrow, some get wedges & mauls – the hide of elk from its shoulder is wound around head of wedge.

People want their children to join because of added prestige & also because Tlokwaly is for people who are not afraid of any pain or danger – perhaps connected in old days with warriors. Song – means shaking in head – a bird – their help in killing. The older people who were warriors had Tlokwaly power – mean men – their songs were to typify their feeling & tell of their strength. Songs are obtained through dreams – dreams that they kill a person & receive a song. Members get song around middle age & use it themselves.

Stanley Grey <3-103> noted "the Hoh use own language", occasionally conflict of minor nature between Hoh & Quileute. <3-106> Stanly has Butterfly dance, Eagle dance, Tsayuq. Bernice Jones is head of Tlokwaly. Sintos Ward – willed to Bernice to take care of food – Joe Pullen's wife.

Stanley Grey <3-107> has four Tlokwaly songs, also can inherit songs from father. Stanley Grey Tlokwaly songs sung at Makah Day or other parties. When he is asked by leader to open table to let people eat – he sings his Tlokwaly song. Stanley Grey put up party for his daughter – 300 loaves of bread – cases of peaches cases of pears etc. Ideal is of giving a bigger party than others – some jealous of the party that Stanley Grey [gave]. Bernice Jones receives 1ˢᵗ present at La Push, Emily Cleveland 2ⁿᵈ, Tylor Hobucket's daughter 3ʳᵈ, Lillian Fisher 4ᵗʰ, Jack Ward 5ᵗʰ, Joe Pullen 6ᵗʰ – [Just] one name mentioned for whole family.

56

Tsayuq = Fishers

Tsayuq = All of Bill's brothers and sisters were Tsayuq, Bill wasn't. When they want child to join they gave party – they announce it will be a Tsayuq party <2-113> [14 July 1949].

Each person has own song – when one person stops, the person next sings, left to right. Person stands up and both hands are waved from side to side in front of the person (Neah Bays hold hands up and move them around sides & front of head) person can be young (5 or 6 months) or old. Family gives presents to others. Young people use family song – later on may get song of their own get power by dream or hear it - hear song

Neah Bay <2-113> led by Young Doctor – kwikwał have fans & dance, canoe songs. Young Doctor got songs in sleep when he was sick. Dreamed they were bringing them in canoe around the world & will get well when he gets home.

Tsayuq' dances <2-115> in winter time because power comes in winter time – early – dances at Johnsons Party at Neah Bay – have Tsayuq power – have power with them all the time. Some people have 3 or 4 songs. Many have parent's song.

Mary got very sick & they thought she would die – couldn't move hands, didn't eat – could hardly talk. They covered her face with good silk handkerchief because they didn't want to look at her – she could hear them talk as if in a dream. Lighthouse Jim said he felt bad because he thought Mary would die. "When night comes, I told myself," my mother said, "I wonder if it would help if we got people together to sing – somebody comes & asks if it would help – I'm too weak to answer. They gather 8 or 10 people & they start in singing. There were two persons I wished would sing again – I liked their song – it made me feel better – the other songs didn't come to me. The last person sang – I went to sleep – first time for a long time." The next night they called the <2-117> people again – first time people sang & then I went to sleep & the 4th night I could look around, I felt lots better, I could eat a little bit & got stronger. My mother called people & they sang again. She gave lots of payment. I always like Tsayuq after that. Joe Pullen is Mary's cousin.

Mary never got her own song but a song comes to her occasionally in the last two years. She's not sure whether it's really her song or one she has heard. She is going to sing it to Molly to find out.

Hudsons: Theodore – Elk , Jane – Tsayuk , Floyd – Elk <2-116>.

Adelle Martin <2-116> gave party last winter for her daughter to join Tsayuq & also for her birthday (10th). They gave away lots of things. They live at Queets – they wanted Elk party but couldn't find a leader, so they made it Tsayuq party. During party, Adelle brought out 4 steelhead, 3 gallons fruit, 2 lbs coffee, 6 loaves of bread, & 10 lbs peanuts – had men bring them out & carry them around room & back to door where they came out. She announced she <2-118> was going to give it to waxəb (Floyd Hudson) who had given her some presents at a big party he had years before. Lots of presents were given away – [went] 3 times around room. Bill, Floyd, Theodore were not at party. Food given to person at end of party – extra food called = ła•kwa•tsl [??].

Tsayuq <3-57 [in ink] people receive power [with] distinctive dance, distinctive rattle design, distinctive songs [from Morton Penn, Aug 10 1949]. Face painting – 3 vertical stripes on each cheek – red costume – long headdress of cedar – hangs down, long, colored brownish red.

Back is plain cedar color, covered all over with down of seagull or male fish duck. Color –
baked clay, Can get Tsayuq power at any age. Ceremony lasts 5 days & 5 nights, usually in
early fall or late winter.

Tsayuq <3-66> a fish song, people must bring in a steelhead or salmon. One man about
25 years ago sang a Tsayuq song in which he told about [how] floats on his nets were dancing in
the waves. People didn't like this because they thought it was too modern. But what he really
meant was the floats he saw through his Tsayuq help that helped him to catch fish.

<3-68> Tsayuq headdress – Mrs. Gold – Elk headdress, Elk rattle, Tsayuq rattles, & tokwaly
rattle – made like raven, [also] had wooden masks.

Tsayuq <3-113> "Lots of [eggs] on the coast, I climb up every rock – biggest rocks.
Hunting for sea gull eggs. I pick up enough to use, come to dream I was flying around the rocks
– shirt full of eggs, tied at waist with snake. I can not break [it]. The snake told me song will
come. I land over at Cape Rock with my dream. I saw snake & flew in my dream, two eagles
each side, see nest [one eggs in nest. Offered egg in dream & saw creature inside]. Snake
becomes dragon – see hole in rocks, look down & see lots of white rocks, get song. The song
belongs to the sea coast. High rock with hole – sea goes through from S to NE, lake below. I
look <3-115> SE & there is green grass – big field – there's a man [man named = yawəx] in the
field – he raises lots of boys – makes lots of money – butchering boys. Dragon's home in rocks
– that's why I'm not short of money when giving party because the man makes lots of money
killing the boys and selling them. I was proud and happy.

Dragon home called = xɛxɛxtuya' . <3-114> Dragon makes the lightning, which, when
it bites a tree, makes the bark peel off in a spiral fashion around the tree from top to bottom – 8"
strip Winter salmon – steelhead = titałiłqᵂ .

Tsayuq <3-115> people have different types of rattles – double row of sets around
smokehouse – had two rattles for singing, sounds like roar of surf, sing about steelhead salmon
for winter.

Clubs = Elks, Whalers

Elk Society <3-7> [14 July 1949] each person had his own Elk song – today none of the
young people know songs painted face with dark red – reddish brown color – horizontal strip 4"
wide across face – above tip of nose covers eyes. Only Elks have face painted, one woman does
this at all the parties. When person dances & sings – the others sing with him.

One time I invited Neah Bay, Queets, Hoh, Quileute – for Floyd when he was 12 years
old – had 2 elks. Some used parents' songs. Bill had one or two songs – Got his song on elk
hunt when rolled in fire. [Bill also has Tlokwaly pin from N fork of Calawah <3-8>.] Man
receives power in woods after he does the killing – Comes home & invites friends & sings song.
Elk parties in wintertime. Bill's children & grandchildren in Elks society – June also Tsayuq –
now they have meetings in houses & there is no room to dance – just sing. Ceremonies in winter
because during summer people are too scattered – also <3-9> lots of food to feed people – also
lots of elk tallow = pi'ts & jerked meat. Much work to do in summer.

Whalers <3-38> may have warm black blankets because whale is black. Taft Williams =
g'lo•tciyił = leaf, an old Hoh whale hunter [?? Q or G at start of name ??] <3-39> [drawing of
leaf]

Hoh was recognized as the same group as La Push <3-39>. Hoh & La Push people never had any trouble between themselves – good relations. They attended the winter parties of each other. Invitation sent by one or two (3 or 4) men, who walk down the beach in the winter – too rough for canoe – highest ranking people asked first, given gift, such as

    Hoh – Floyd – takes father & mother $5
    Elva $4
    Scotty $3 or 4
    Herb $3 or 4

Old folks mentioned last

Bernie Jones, Stanley Gray's granddaughter > youngest daughter's youngest daughter = suqsa•yił child. Lillian Fisher as grandmother gives things for her. Peale Penn, Helen Hobucket, Arleen Sailto, Lovetto {Eastman} Black, Lawrence Jackson

    Elk club (1) = tsex^{w}əłayu' <3-43> [35 hours to date, 4/29/49]
    Whale club (2) = tsibałayu'
    (3) tsatsaa – singing group [love]
    (4) Tsayuq –

Elks <3-45> club members have head gear with elk horns on it Hold on to stick. Person has to put up party to join Elks Club – announced that person wants to join – give presents away. Face of new joiner is painted – across eyes. New joiner dances with old members until dance is learned. People must follow the directions of the leaders or they are fined – ex[ample] – if drummers miss beat. Fines – peanuts - things to eat, small calf. <3-47> At subsequent party – the amount of the fine is determined – formerly fines were dry fish & other food stuffs – rest of members eat [it]. At Floyd's party, Bill had it announced that he wouldn't bother their present of $780 – he returned this money himself $50, $55 returned. Party cost Bill over $1000.

Only one dance used "double tail dance" <3-65> If first comes Elk dance, then maybe comes the Tsayuq. It must be announced that it will be a double tail dance – formerly couldn't laugh, smile, look at one another. At Tlokwaly – if a person was seen laughing – the person who saw him would take a burning stick from fire & throw it at you, or lips would be pinned together with bone pin.

Parents have to pay for child membership in these societies – then when the person is invited he is paid – whether he dances, sings or not. If person wants to join – he announces that he is going to give party this winter – before then, people go around & throw pebbles on roof of house of people to be invited.

Elk songs <3-66> sung when hunter gets into a bind – it will mix them up – no hunter can get one – also aid in tracking.

    Stanley Grey
        Whale society = tsibax^{w}łayu   ts'ayuq
        Doctors songs =   tc'la•layu t'łoqwali
        Elk society =   tsi•x^{w}əłayu
        Love songs for girls at puberty = tsas'a•
        Love songs to sweetheart = a•ałits'sis "I am very glad to see my sweetheart."

One time <3-91 >, one of the party at La Push (Harry Hobucket) started dancing for a new 14' canoe that Bill Hudson had built. Bill had built the canoe for a white man & had a check for the canoe ($30.00) in his pocket, but he hadn't delivered the canoe yet. Bill didn't want to give up canoe since it was promised, but Harry Hobucket kept dancing & singing for the canoe & wouldn't stop. His friends were helping him. Finally Bill said alright he could have the canoe. Bill sent the check back to the man who ordered it.   H. Hobucket's father came over & asked Bill when he would deliver the canoe so they could have food ready to receive them. Bill said next Saturday & said they would deliver the canoe on Saturday.

When the time came six dancers danced into the big house carrying the canoe. Bill was in front <3-93> to sing his Elk song & do his dance. Then everyone began to do their dances & finally someone made the announcement that they were delivering the canoe that Harry Hobucket had danced for & that Bill had returned the ($30.00) check. (This made him a big man.) In return, Harry Hobucket gave Bill $1.50 & a thin sheet blanket (black), the total worth being about $1.75. Bill was angry at so small a payment but being a big man could say nothing. People regarded the small payment by Harry Hobucket as being not the mark of a "big man" & although he received the canoe for a small amount – his position in the group was lowered. People say he could never be a "Big Man". He did not have the money to pay for things.

When Bernice Jones <3-115> got married to Casey Jones, she got $449 dollars. Billy Hudson brought several boxes of silver salmon – danced in with them but wouldn't stay mad.

SG's granddaughters <4-9> Bernice & Emily have dance costumes made by Mrs. Grey after design dictated by S Grey. They are used when they put up a party – Eagle style. Arms extended with feathers on them. Tlokwaly dance.

SG has Butterfly Dance, Eagle Dance, Steelhead Dance, Tlokwaly Dance <4-11 >. Stanley Grey was going to put up a flagpole in his yard with an eagle on top – his help – received flag for dancing for cannery owner at Queets – didn't raise pole because his grandson died. Might do for great grandson. Butterfly Dance – SG has 18 costumes – sang for it. SG got song through dream. His help for leading dancing. Steelhead Dance, Tsayuq, SG father's ghost – doesn't go to sleep at night – bothers at night time.

Weather Forecasters

Tc'ala•layu <2-116> a dance & song – they have a good time with it. Some real old people have power for this – a doctor power – they jump around. This is different from Elk & Tsayuk. Always use peanuts at Elk party. Bill Hudson is leader of Elks

tc'ala'layu <4-13> for well off men {such as Dr Obi, Doctor Lester, Esau Penn, Frank Fisher <4-12>}, using songs which they believe are better for getting greater wealth. Dancing by jumping up. Songs say they have lots of property. If man finds five white pups on rock on beach & the pups lick his legs – he receives wealth power. Don't catch the pups – just see them. Dream it first & then go look for it.

People in tc'ala'layu' – after they join they receive help to become doctors. Idea is power resident in the sky – SG father – had ship in sky – Tlokwaly – tc'la•'layu.

Details

Bill Hudson <4-21> White paint made of burned bone which is then ground up & mixed with oil. Mary's mask is Tlokwaly – made by Jerry Jones, Mary's uncle. Masks are shown by people at meeting & give presents away – presents are returned later [at other hosted events]. At Neah Bay last Friday, money was given the family of Jesse LaChester by many people. People sing & dance & then gave money. In old times when a person died, they destroyed a lot of property.

Long time ago, Tommy Payne <4-23> lost a song, 12 years ago – he ~~gave~~ threw away all his whaling equipment – gave his canoe away to Sally Black (he's her brother-in-law). She gave $75 for the canoe & blankets. She invited lots of people (long after death) – she is going to pay canoe off to TP & have eats. Jim Black gets upon floor & talks good to Tommy Paine. Two or three years later, ? Pullen made a speech & asked Tommy Payne to come back to whaling. Dixon Paine his brother made more equipment for him. He went out that summer.

Before person goes to a party, they fast so they will have a good appetite – fast for 1 or 2 meals <4-27>. g'iya' = to fast – tied up . The visitors want to eat all the food if possible. qi•yił = closing song at parties, sang by big shots – use large clam shell rattles. During a Give-Away – when one of the boxes or baskets has been emptied of the gifts, one who intends to give a party at a later time, will walk out & take basket. At Elk Dance when they give-away things – they spread a blanket or sheet on the floor – pile stuff on it. After everything has been given away – they say, Here is a blanket for "our father" (the leader of the Elk club), such as Floyd Hudson, Bernice James.

After Jonas Cole's ~~wife~~ sister died – Bill's wife & Bill got sick – they haven't used the smokehouse at Hoh River. Healer's wife is religious <4-29>. Hoh was looked up to in past years – had lots of money. Theodore was going to put up party for Junior after he got out from training school.   You invite only the head men of family, rest follow [after], ex[amples] are Floyd Hudson, Elva Hudson, Bernice Jones, Herb Fisher.

Old lady Ward (Jack Ward's mother) <4-31> carried invitations [to Elk Party Aug 10]

Bernice Jones is head of Elk Club & Tlokwaly. Mrs. Fred Penn gave Elk party for her granddaughter (married to Taholah man) – party for their daughter (Mrs. Penn's granddaughter) Mrs. Fred Penn is sick & wanted to give the party before she dies. Mrs. F Penn gave the baby (1 year old ?) an Indian name = tsa'osastəb) [Agnes Penn's aunt is Mrs. Frank Fisher]. Food – brought by relatives, such as Fishers – deer & salmon, salmon was roasted around fire. Other food – salmon berries, red huckleberries, strawberries, peaches. Mrs. Penn's relatives did the cooking for second meal had salmon stew. <4-33> Mrs. Charlie [Lela] Tsailto brought berries & fruit. Invitations to Harvey James & his wife.

Invitations <4-35>are handed out in order of location by~for house in the village. Start from far end of village & go from house to house. Go to door & sing 2 songs – march right in & invite head of house by name.

La Push invites:

    Fred Woodruff & his wife Sarah (helped cook)
    Tylor Hobucket & family
    Jack Ward & his mother
    Walter Paine & his wife
    Hazel Bright
    Rex Ward
    Bobby Ward

Floyd Hudson & wife B
Monk Williams
Venny Black & wife
Joe Pullen & wife
Ray Black & wife
Dewy Cleveland & daughter & wife
Annie Hopkins
Grace Jackson & 2 sons
Stanley Grey & wife
Bernice Ames & son

Hoh invites:

2nd Frank Fisher & wife
3rd Scott Fisher
5th Theodore Hudson & wife & 2 older children
1st Billy Hudson & wife
4th Herb Fisher & wife

tsexax <4-34> Stanley Grey brought 2 bags of peanuts for his great grandson – hired Pansy & Elva to spread them around hall. The significance being that the peanuts represent the dropping of the herd of elk.

Songs

No seal hunting songs or power – whaler has power – gets song from inside song sometimes sung at gatherings. Elk hunting song received when in the woods, song comes with power. Bill Hudson tried to get Shaker power – but could never "feel of anything" <1-109>.

Whale hunters society = tsibax[w]layu

Elk Club = tsilig[w]əliyu , songs = tluq[w]ali [Tlokwaly]

Run skewers through skin, had meal after ceremonies, ate dried fish smoked eggs & potatoes [powdered face black with charcoal]. Had big bonfire = wllaisəb - one man grabbed hot coals & threw them around in the house <1-109>.

Indians have lullaby song – Nona knows quite a few songs – Mary will put up 2 dollars to know who has lullaby song <2-118>.

Singing <3-43> Man sings love song in group – to girl – she may rise after words & return the favor by singing her love song = tsatsa'a – have long sticks with which they beat on long poles hung around smokehouse – Love songs usually sung during girl's puberty ceremony – 4 day ceremony – girls don't eat or sleep. Grandfather tell people they can tsatsa'a all they want, so he gives a big party. The girl is secluded behind some mat curtains, so she can hear but can't see. The people sing songs for the things they want & [that] the girl's family must give [to] them.

(5) k̓ ig[w]ał a new dance – brought from Alaska by Sitka George (42 years ago) & others they learned it when they went sealing on the schooners [George = q[w]əwsə] <3-45> Williams *tahmanawis* – <u>Tlingit</u> . k̓ ig[w]ał = only slightly at La Push. Some songs brought from Alaska,

others were received (new). gi•a qi•yił = big shots own private songs, but not many had them –
belong to family. Stanley Grey, Bill Hudson, North fork of Calawah, [always did] closing song
at parties.

Esau Penn claims he received Stanley Grey's father's songs. SG doesn't believe it
because he doesn't use it right. Stanley Grey's father was a great doctor <4-8>.

Society comprises (with subheadings capitalized) Rankings of chiefs, commoners, slaves; generosity, social class examples; Life cycles of birth, twins, training, teachings, stamina, questing, orphans, masking, first menstruation, marriage, adult duties, death, burial, reburial; Interactions of pets, smoking, sweating, hospitality, trading, gaming, crimes, warfare; Adornment of head, hair, paint, tattoos; and Responsibilities of names and dicta.

Rankings (Social Classes)

Like other nations of the Northwest, Upper Chehalis and Cowlitz recognized the three social classes of royal chiefs, commoners, and slaves. The first two were freeborn, but not the third. High chiefs, low chiefs, commoners, and slaves might be further distinguished {js 360 ThA} (Collins 1994, Elmendorf 1971, Miller 1999b).

Royal Chiefs

Chiefs [*ʔals* K20] were royal in the old days. Their line was founded by Moon while he was on earth. Sometimes they were called *taiyiman* from the Chinook jargon word for chief or leader, *tyee*. No matter how much money any person had, they could not be a chief, "not in their hearts". A chief was born not made. A chief, first and foremost, kept things going smoothly within the tribe and dealt with outsiders whenever they came. He had to be smart, know about all the families in the region, and speak many languages {ds 372 ThA}. They also safe-guarded dicta that used a special vocabulary and power given by Moon to his royal relatives when he remade the world, establishing the "laws, rules, commandments" which govern the present-day world.

Chief's Story. {js 256} All chief's stories have the "law" on the end. Anyone who knew the Moon story could tell it. No matter who, the Moon has his own commandment, so chief doesn't have to make it. ?? = was a crooked chief before the Moon. Bluejay was also partly a chief.

Commandments of the Chief. If any one of these rules were broken, would be given a good hard whipping with the hands by the warriors (? ThA). Were supposed to be good to everybody, old or young. Some [examples]

(a) To learn the rules of the people, when you eat, look about you, if you are eating see if there are any who need food served. Strangers, see if anyone is late, if he needs help, please help him. That's the way you just help everyone.

(b) Learn to help those who need help.

(c) If you are the grandchild of the chief, use a pure word, and keep you heart perfect.

(d) Treat the other chief faithfully.

(e) Don't use any slang words amongst the other chiefs. The children of chiefs are supposed to know these things before they grow up.

Treatment of the Old by the Young. [unknown source] Doesn't seem to know the information given by Mrs. Davis and Heck.

Strangers were treated like brothers, if from friendly tribes. One of the chiefs keeps [hosts] him. If he has any food with him, enough to put on the table, if a little chief will make feast, will tell the people what he brought. All the little chiefs will join in and make it larger. Then they are going to eat. the whole tribe, the guest will never eat his own food, against the rules, but the hosts will feed him. Probably a general custom for anyone. "1 should not eat what one delivers," would cause hard luck if eat own lunch which you bring to a tribe. Your house will go on fire as a punishment. Do not pick up anything dropped out of hand while eating, against reg[ulations] of living people, will grow in your heart, will cause you to follow someone who deserts you. Told boys or girls not to pick knives and forks up, or food. Shows that you may become deserted when old. "When deserted, do not follow," the chief says.

Chief. Daren't [sic] marry inside their tribe, or their children. Each chief's family {ThA 348} have 4 [far] connections. Common can marry inside their own tribe, just any old way they want to, don't need to buy their rights.

People gave things, food and presents, to a good chief so he never had to work hard. He was always fed and given the most at gatherings like feasts and marriages. Fur blankets, dentalia shells, and canoes were important gifts, then later horses and trade blankets {ds 364}. A chief also owned and managed a fish weir or trap to feed his people.

Women of royal families had much prestige and authority, and a few became famous.

Women Chiefs. {js 258} Don't like to acknowledge a woman, but chief will take her word. If she does not know anything won't take anything from her. She is respected as much as a man, but the really [break in text]

Yawonish Sister. He had a sister she had a child, a son, they respected him as a chief. He had no more children. He wasn't a chief, but was of their family. Alice Cross of Puyallup, great grand niece of Yawonish.

Family. Were 4 or 5 high families, didn't need to be related, might possibly be. Chief has a sister, she is respected as well as he is. Her word is good if she know anything. She marries a man from another tribe. If her brother has no more children and if she is the only one who has a child who is fit to be chief, her son will be chief. Her son might have 2 names. Might take the chief's {js 350} name. Will give a big potlatch, would have announcers and speakers, to take care for you. The 1s who work for you, other chief[s], will get more than others.

Announcer. Have to belong to the same tribe, and his aides will have to be from same tribe or relations. That is, a potlatch. Her name for chang[ling] names with outside people. Will be so and so after chief. You shall be disgraced for a few dollars, or sister is changing her name. (He really doesn't mean one is disgraced.) It is just a way of saying it, means another chief will come when he is called for present, rather common like. I went to a feast just 2 years ago, to Toledo, a Squally who formerly lived at Camp Lewis. [½ to 2/3 of the Nisqually Reservation was taken in WWI for this army base. Some compensation was eventually paid and part of it was probably used for this feast.]

Those who are working for the host will get the most pay. The big chiefs of the other tribes also get more. The common people just get a "Christmas present to cheer them up."

Warrior Chiefs. Would gamble while a big time was going on, with other tribes or amongst themselves.

Potlatches. If is going to invite in other tribes, cannot give a potlatch by himself. In old days, large chiefs, smaller chiefs, all were doing it.

Interest. Can't find any way of paying friends back, who help 1. Might get ready for several years before giving a potlatch.

Property. Doesn't give away property for his personal use, would always be invited to the other tribes, no way of becoming poor, so much game, deer, ducks, and so on.

Chiefs. Have to be physically strong, but would not have to work. Chief's wives and daughters probably worked so much as the other women.

Royals always married among themselves. By strict rule, they married until death. Chief Taholah at Quinault married the mother of Chief Masin from Scatter Creek {gs 113}.

The chief told people to be friendly and not go against one another. If someone building a house needed help, the chief would ask people to assist {md 50}. After a murder, the chief was the judge deciding on the compensation that would make it even with the victim's family. If the chief could not decide or the families agree, then the murderer or someone in his family was killed to resolve this family feud, provided both victims were of the same class and rank.

Chehalis {md 46} used to have a chief, old *Yawn-s*. He used to tell his people what was right, not to steal and so on, and especially when a murder occurred, tell what was right. So people would be friendly and not against one another. Chief, if willing, would tell people to go to war, but, if not willing, {md 51} people would not go. Houses, sometimes chief would go and tell people to help one another [with building]. Sometimes people would take care of it himself.

Chief would follow father or uncle. Would listen to what the father said and would listen and then act the same way as the father or uncle. *Yawn_s* was chief just to these Chehalis people. The Tenino had their own chief. Cowlitz had their own chief. Black River people were included under *Yawn_s*, but they [also] had a little chief of their own. They [He] would come to *Yawn_s* for advice. Tenino might also come to him for advice, but 2 was "second to *Yawn_s*."

Chief *Yawnits*. {md 57} Born at Grand Mound and buried there. Used to have a class and tell the stories to the boys. *Sikamen* was just a common man, had 3 wives, used to live forth and back from here and Satsop. Used to live close to the river. He used to move in his canoes. All lived in one house, the women's beds were separate, though. He died about 30 years ago, but he only had one wife when he died. The government took the others away from him.

Buys his wife, goes to some place where [there are] royal women and buys her. Last women, he brought was towards Astoria. Thinks she was a ?? *tc vk[+w]* woman. Mrs. *P'ełe masł m* = mother's name, kept daughter, kept her in a box so no one would ever see her, or make love to her, and so made the daughter royal. When go out, lots of slave women to watch her. ? = princess ? = chief ? = chief of *Qwayail* language, others have mixed languages ? = same meaning chiefs ? = Gray's Harbor language ? = for Wynoochee ? = Tehola language ? = Humptulips language ? = lived at head of the river, close to people Ell, ? = lived almost to head of Chehalis River, ? = lived on other side of the mountains {ph 71}.

In royal family {ph 75}, wife supposed to stay with wife's family if husband is dead. Can not get married without man's side. Trouble if she does. Have to marry husband's cousin or brother, so he'll take care of her children and raise them right. If married to a stranger, always have trouble with the children. Law was strict. If woman dies, if has sister or cousin, ask woman or girl if willing to marry the man, always praise another woman for that kind of wedding. Would remain widow or widower for a number of years. Women sometimes for years. She did not care.

Heck Wedding. Mrs. Heck's people came just so far, holding pans and plates in their hands. Mrs. Heck's side sitting down just looking on.

Everybody {ph 76} had flat heads in the old days. Common people could as long as women knew how. Slaves could, no one to look after it. A little pillow, perhaps filled with feathers, little piece of bark underneath to make a hole. Pillow on back of neck so can put the head back, hands down straight [at sides]. Baby bound across chest, bound across knees so as not to have bow legs. When baby wakes up, takes blanket off and rubs across belly, calf of legs, pinches nose so nice shaped, small belly. Flat square back from the cradleboard, shoulders set straight.

Chief also punished thieves. After whites came, a chief could order someone lashed. A jury of wise men helped the chief decide. Of course, if a family did not like the decision, they might hire a doctor to work sorcery to get revenge {ph 274}.

When a chief died, everyone mourned as he was buried in a big canoe. The chief would inherit from a father, an uncle, or a brother. A younger brother might also inherit the wives of the dead chief. Sometimes, the brother was just a regent for his nephew, the chief's son.

[Chiefs]. {ph 268} (1) *Yawnish*, he was out of royal blood, and that is the reason he was chief after the others died. *als tsiniitia* [*Cinitiya*] chief, was the most important chief. Was a well off man, was the Q chief. Had many wives, but does not know exactly. Had a wife from Cowlitz and one from Squally, last wife he bought was the above mentioned one from Astoria. (2) *Cinitiya's* son was (3) *Ananitx*, but was killed when young, was the young chief. Both lived here, but *Ananitx* was killed at the Harbor.

Can't appoint a common man to be chief. If a person is well off, people expect lots of things and he is always giving things, but *Yawnish* was kind of a poor man, and did not expect him to give so much.

Cinitiya was well off, had lots of slaves. When went some place to gamble, would call his young people to go along with him and give them a blanket, each 1. Know he had at least 3 wives and may have had more.

Ananitx was claimed to be a good man but wasn't good when had whiskey. Was very fond of woman and would get after some of his friend's wives.

Cinitiya died before Heck's time, but *Yawnish* was still alive in Heck's time. *Yawnish* wasn't so rich for had so many children to feed. His 2nd wife had many children, *Yawnish* was an *'als*. He was a Boston man, had just one wife. 1st died and he married a young wife and she had babies.

Does not know genealogy of *Cinitiya*, *L'aqai&qł* lived at Grand Mound. Say he had lots of slaves, but I don't know how many. People may have had 2 3 4 slaves each, does not seem to be very exact.

Thinks *Yawnish*'s mother was from Q but Does not know where father came from. too long for Heck to remember. Thinks *Ananitx* was killed before *Yawnish* died. It seems *Yawnish* had not much money, but still he was *tuwała'ls*, hat is, "from royal blood".

Cinitiya's people all died off. Does not know if any of *Yawnish*'s people are living. Thinks that the fact that *Yawnish* had just one wife at a time had nothing to do with the whites being here. Remembers not of the wedding of *Yawnish*'s daughter with east of the mountains man. Does not remember death of *Yawnish*. His house used to be right back of old school building at Oakville Reservation.

A chief lived in a big house with his many wives and owned slaves, who lived "like dogs" without regular sleeping places. Slaves were taken in raids or sold far from home, unless they could be ransomed back by their family {ph 85}. Peter Heck's mother's aunt was ransomed from Skokomish warriors at Port Madison [Suquamish] and cleansed with a potlatch. The children of slaves remained slaves, unless someone royal took pity and freed them. Slaves who married royals had the "taint" washed off with a potlatch, but, behind their backs, people still insulted them, saying they gave their family "bad blood" {ph 256}.

Slaves

A chief wanted his slaves to work so he sold the lazy ones. Slave women [*yaqiṅ* K2454]wore their hair in a bob. They dried salmon like other women. Slaves were treated well as long as they worked [hard]. When they died, their bodies were put out of the way but not otherwise buried or mourned {js 392}.

Cost of Slaves. {ph 269} Always give the highest priced blanket and something else for a slave. Blankets were scarce. Women had no skirts other than cedar [bark] or much except skin on back and coon skin on babies. When blankets came with the white people, they saved them to give away and each person had so many. Dentalia, about a finger long, King George [English] blanket, all wool, red, black, and white were they type used after whites came. What type of blanket was used for exchange? Does not know. *K^cw staimx^u* are small people from the north side, so Heck thinks from the story, the people whom the Ducks fight. (See Jonas's story). 2 men stole salmon from them, saw a man diving and came out with 5 salmon on each finger. 2 men steal it. *Kcw* came out on canoe and peers about. Sees what has happened. Takes them home and keeps them, *Kcw* tells men someone from here was going to fight them. "Here they come." It was *xatxat*, all men no women. Duck went, only woman *svnx-l*. Hell Diver went along when they got there to fly, the ducks flew above the *Kcw* and their feathers dropped. The feathers hurt the *Kcw* "To get shot with an arrow." Hell Diver would say to *Q'letstila*, Ducks when they got down too low, she would holler to them then above, "Down too low." The 2 men beat the ducks with sticks, took the feathers from the wounded and they recovered. Show them how to fight the ducks then the 2 fellows from this side cook the ducks.

A slave was known by the name of his or her own tribe. An enslaved Snohomish was called "snohomish" {ph 243}. They never had a personal name or a separate identity.

Peter Heck's grandfather had five slaves, three men and two women. He sold four of them before he died, but kept a young woman to take care of Heck's father while he grew up. She did this faithfully until she died of smallpox {ph 268}.

Once, when my father {mi 14} was young, he had a nice slave girl. A man, a 1/2 brother, came, saying "I will trade you a boy for that girl." "No, she digs *lackamas* and dries berries for winter." The brother said, "I'll tell you why I want to trade. The girl is pretty, your son is a big boy now. He always goes with her. No, you can't tell. Maybe they [he] will fall in love with her. That is shame to you." So, my father said, "When he was big enough to know anything, his father had just one slave." My grandpa had one. My aunty one, a boy. She liked him so well, she would say to him when we girls came to visit her that "Those are your little sisters. Later, when I grew up and he saw me, he still called me sister."

Cowlitz usually had just 2-3 slaves; Yakamas, I heard, had 5-6. 3 slaves were considered a lot because Cowlitz did not fight anywhere and always got their slaves by trade, while Yakamas were always stealing slaves. I don't think the Taytnapam ever went any place to fight. The great grandfather of George Jack was stolen her[e] from Klamath.

Slaves could get spirit power or be doctors, but their owners could take their pay (Collins 1974, 1979, 1994; Donald 1997; Miller 2002). A fine fur blanket was worth one slave in the old days. A famous chief, *YuliltitsL*, at Grand Mound, had 40 slaves because he was so kind, and they asked him to buy them. He also saved two early white men from frostbite.

Generosity

A chief had to marry a daughter from another royal family, often of another tribe. One of *Yawnish*'s daughters even married east of the mountains among the Yakama. She was one of the very few to marry so far away. Mostly royals married along the coast. A chief gave presents to "buy" a foreign wife, but a commoner did not {ds 362}. They just "lived together" and probably even belonged to the same tribe.

A chief hosted potlatches, and a big chief had a special house built for his own lavish potlatches. John Heyden had the last one built, about 1875, for a potlatch celebrating the piercing of his daughter's ears {ph 70, ly 130}. A chief from another tribe made the holes for this royal daughter when she was about 10. Many people came from all over Puget Sound. About $1500 was given away. This potlatch lasted five days. Jim and Charlie Walker helped Heyden with the expense.

A name was usually given to that person when their ears were pierced. For royals, these were famous inherited names. Sometimes, a power gave spirit names to a father before the children were even born.

Children of chiefs were royal and carefully treated. As infants their foreheads were flattened with pressure to mark them for life {ph 85}. One woman kept her daughter secluded in a box [cubicle] until her marriage so she would be much honored. Slave women watched and guarded her all the time. Royal children were raised to have a good character and to speak well.

Other potlatches were for a reburial or to renew a grave. The body was removed so new clothes, new gifts, or a new casket could be supplied.

A royal woman could not be chief [?!], but she took charge of the other women and knew about picking berries and digging camas. Only men were chiefs. Royal women managed female activities, while their women slaves did the hard work for the chief's household.

Social Class Examples

The Upper Chehalis chief was *Yawnish*, who was born and buried at Grand Mound. He held a class to teach stories to boys and told people what was right to do. *Yawnish* did not have much money because he had many children to feed from the young woman he married after his first wife died {ph 268}. He was a "Boston man" who had only one wife at a time. His house was behind the old school at Oakville.

John Heyden had the bones of *Yawnish*, Queen Susan, and Lizzie Johnson's sister reburied in a single coffin at Grand Mound {ly 130}. *Yawnish* and Queen Susan were brother and sister. Heyden was their nephew.

Tsinitiya was an important chief before *Yawnish* {ph 268}. He had many wives from all over, including Cowlitz, Nisqually, and Astoria. He had many slaves. He subsidized young men when he went gambling. His son was *Ananit'x*, a drinker who was murdered at the Harbor by a jealous husband. [State court records say he was killed for siding with the Indian agent.] After *Tsinitiya* died, a son became chief before *Yawnish* succeeded him.

Teninos and Cowlitz had their own chiefs. Black Rivers had a little chief of their own, but [he] was under *Yawnish* for overall advice. Same applied for little chiefs at Oakville and Skookumchuck {gs 112}.

Syk'amen ("light") was a common man who lived between Chehalis and Satsop, moving by canoe. He had three wives who had separate beds in the same house. When he died about 1900, only one wife was alive after the government took the others away from him.

LIFE CYCLE

Birth

Unborn babies came from the sunrise in the east {ph 98}, traveling through the air along the path of sunlight {sh 141}. [Tillamook of the Oregon coast also had a belief in a land of unborn babies, where they lived and even married waiting to be born.] While the dead lived in the west, the unborn lived in the east. Anyone could see the fire of the dead, but only a spirit could see the dead themselves or help a doctor to see them. People also felt when ghosts were nearby. Peter Heck's father once rushed home from winter hunting near Independence when he sensed the dead.

Pregnant parents should not look at anything deformed or suffering because their baby might come out that way {js 132}. A mother ate slowly and carefully to keep the baby safely small. These parents could not be lazy, working all the time to stay fit and strong {gs 113}. The woman never ate anything that stuck to the sides of a pot or paused in doorways for that would delay the impending birth. A few months before delivery, the mother began drinking a wild rose infusion (of boiled bark) to speed the birth.

The baby was born in a separate hut, assisted by a midwife or kinswoman. The mother squatted with hands on the ground. To make a baby turn before delivery, the mother held her breath and shifted her stomach. Two rocks were struck beside the baby's ears just after birth to make sure it will always hear. The newborn was washed in cold water, sprinkled with ashes, and wrapped in rabbit fur or a soft blanket {mi 3}. For the next year, the baby was carried in a cradleboard, made by the father, to make it grow straight. If freeborn, the baby's forehead was weighted and flattened as a mark of class.

Mother and baby were secluded. Taytnapams waited five days {mi 2}, Chehalis waited ten days with a girl and nine with a boy. Anyone could go near a baby boy, but only women went near a girl baby. The place of seclusion was heated by hot rocks in a deep hole, covered with ferns to steam and smell nice. New hot rocks were added twice a day. The mother's breasts were held over this steam, and rubbed with white moss or shells to improve the milk. The baby nursed on demand, but the new mother still did not eat anything fresh, raw, or bloody.

Bands of wildcat skin, put around the woman's abdomen two months into the pregnancy to hold it tight and keep the baby small, were cut and retied to help her belly to heal. The umbilical cord was cut but not tied. When the stump fell off, it was put into a beaded buckskin bag, sometimes hung from its cradleboard. Taytnapams gave it to the child at about the age of ten to take into the woods and tie to a little fir tree. [This made the child close to nature and "fresh air".] Chehalis burned it completely to ashes.

The afterbirth was put into a tree with an offering of beads or buttons. That of a boy was placed higher than that of a girl {mmd 224}, but if it was too high the child would want to climb all the time. The offerings "paid" the afterbirth to keep the child from getting "silly" or hurt. Some families buried the afterbirth. [Though unstated, Chehalis, like other tribes, probably placed the afterbirth and cord in a place that would benefit the character of that child, such as, a tree for a hunter.]

According to Chehalis, the mongoloid spot at the base of a newborn was caused by the afterbirth hitting the fetus because it was lazy being born {ph 246}. An old woman might use dicta to speed a birth, but men did not know such formulae. If a baby did not arrive after two or four days, a native doctor was summoned.

A Greyback Louse went to "heaven" to report each birth {ph 276} and decide if its arrival would be marked with good or bad weather.

While a first birth was supervised, at later births the mother was alone. Mary Iley was splitting wood when she went into labor, gave birth, fixed the fire, dressed the baby, rested near the stove, and got fresh milk for the baby's older brother. The baby was enticed ("primed," like a pump) to suck with warmed bear grease rubbed on the mouth. Children could be nursed until they were three or four years old. While they were nursing, women did not menstruate or conceive {ly 126}.

An unmarried royal girl killed her baby because she could never raise a bastard. She should have aborted it to avoid scandal.

A baby who was someone reborn would have marks, usually on the earlobes or at the locations of grandparent's scars {sh 141}. A chief was always reborn since they were trained never to die, always returning among their own descendants {js 340}. Mrs. Davis noted that her own eldest daughter seems to have been reborn in her son's daughter, and they intend to give her aunt's name to the grand daughter {mmd 226}. If the person had come back into another but related family, they would give another name.

The new father used the sweat house for two or three days. The new mother went to the sweat house for two days after her 10 day seclusion with a daughter or for one day after her 9 days with a son. If a father wanted his baby son to be a hunter, he hung a tiny bow and arrows from the rim of the cradleboard {sh 138}.

The baby was massaged to shape it. For boys, shoulders and legs were stretched. For girls, the nose was squeezed, cheeks pressed downward, foot arch indented, and buttocks lifted. Some families prayed to Thrush while doing this {ph 246}. Babies were bathed morning and night. A slow growing baby had very cold water poured over its buttocks to cause a growth spurt.

A cranky baby was bathed in cold water and wrapped up warmly to sleep. A neglected baby became sickly and a special doctor had to go to the land of the unborn in the east and coax its soul back [cf Chehalis]. It wandered away along the earth, leaving tracks to be followed, and then flew at tree height (or as high as its afterbirth was located in a tree?). The doctor sang a song that slowed or halted the baby along the way. If the baby stopped to listen, it would be cured; if not, it died.

Twins

Instead of calling twins [čiyuyaʔ K527] two babies, Chehalis used the term for "wolf" [qinunɬin' K1469] since these canines had double litters {mi 3, md 60, ph 104}. Twins were fragile and rarely lived to become adults, unless they were boy and girl. Cowlitz had a word for twins, but also called them "wolf" or "cougar" [wa•wa K2129].

Training

Children of a household were made to get up early and swim, diving away from the bank so they will have plenty in life {ph 105}. An old man was their trainer. If their legs were not red when they stood beside the fire after bathing in cold water, he hit them with a paddle or stick and covered them with cold ashes to make them go and plunge again. They were told "not to lie to their own life." They swam for a long life, good luck, and a good home.

Children played together when small, but after they got to be ten and started questing, boys and girls stayed apart. A boy, rarely a girl, was given a stick to take to some remote place and leave in hopes of encountering a spirit. The trainer went there to make sure the stick had been left and the boy did not cheat. Sometimes the quester was expected to pile stones at a spot to prove he or she had been there. Important spirits lived where there were no other people. While spirits visited humans in the mundane world, they did not give power then.

Teachings

Every evening in good families, children heard "teachings," mostly about being helpful and energetic, particularly with the elderly {mi 4}. "Help out, wherever and whenever you can! When you visit, do housework, split firewood, or get water. Eat whatever is put in front of you. If a woman is making a basket and leaves the room, work on the basket to help her. Also, when you are host, give people good food and a nice time."

People will know the character of children and say, "Here comes that bad one or that good one. Coaxing made a child good. Never make fun of anything or anyone. Never laugh at what you do not understand." A child who listened and obeyed all the teachings led a long and rewarding life.

Children could not eat food stored for over a year or they would become deaf {js 132}. They should be good to all elders in the hope that a grandparent or other oldster would promise them "Since you have been good to me, I will leave my soul to you when I die so that you can live a long time." This made the child proud {ph 262}.

Children were sent to visit relatives when they were old enough to have sense and learn about their relations. They might stay a long time, sometimes years. Even strangers were welcome as long as they helped out with food and chores. [This was also an opportunity to learn another language by immersion.]

Teachings were like the Ten Commandments, but involved all the world of living things. The Earth listened and punished those who did not live right. After hearing a story, children had to swim {md 54}.

Stamina

Some boys were sent out to run naked in hail, rain, and thunder storms to get a strong power and make them hearty, tough, and healthy. They swam where it was cold, but not icy because "ice" also meant "very poor" and was an ill omen. Whenever a boy got home from a cold quest, he could sleep beside the fire.

When snow accumulated on trees, boys and girls charged through them to get cold, wet, and tough. The boldest did this 5 times, although it was very grueling.

Boys and men practiced weight lifting with boulders. Some, as at Lequito, were specially prepared. Towns or tribes would challenge each other at weight lifting, foot racing, or wrestling. Later, people learned boxing and horse racing.

Questing

A questing boy bathed at least every morning and evening, if not more frequently {md 56}. A boy who did not sweat, bathe, or swim was considered dirty and "full of sin". A clean body attracted a spirit because it could see the heart of someone pure and clear. To get a powerful one, boys dove into deep water holding heavy rocks. Diving was an act of courage and daring. To be successful, diving had to be done 5 times. In the salt water, a boy rubbed his arms, legs, neck, and back against the edge of the canoe to chafe the skin before diving {md 192, ph 260}. Older women also chafed the boy's skin to increase their ordeal.

One old man insisted that his grandson dive near Olympia, but sharks ate him {ph 259}. Desire was not enough, a family had to know about using supernatural protection to safeguard its novice questers.

Over a decade after a power was acquired, the man or woman sang in public during the winter. People then were sure that they had a spirit power. In some cases, a young man would prove this by telling hunters where they could find a deer or other game to kill and serve to that gathering. The spirit provided this meat to the people who helped the man to sing and announce his power. At the end, goods and gifts (like beads, clothes, and cloth) hung along the inside walls were given out to the guests {md 161}.

Later in life, a family member might inherit the spirit of a close relative. Silas Heck felt his father's Wolf hunting power following him after his father died in 1915 {sh 138}, but he rejected it because he was a Shaker. Similarly, at Little Rock, Peter Heck saw their own father's hunting spirit as an ugly woman wearing five duck feathers in her hair. A spirit can best be inherited when someone already has another spirit to help welcome and control the new one.

A family might take revenge by imposing one of its spirits as a "chronic" inheritance in another family, where it was unknown, unexpected, and potentially very lethal.

When he was 18, Mary Heck's grandfather died in an epidemic and was buried inside a bark house near Grand Mound. His Bluejay spirit brought him back and gave him the ability to go to the Land of the Dead, recovering souls. After 10 days, his mother went out to weep at his grave and found him. He told her he had gone to a big gathering of the dead, but he was naked, so his own father sent him back.

Orphans [verbatim]

Orphans. {mi 325, verbatim} They get the best *tahmanawas*, the very best ones. Get to be the best doctors generally, become doctors and get rich. Get *tahmanawas* to be wealthy, but seems to think usually wealth through doctoring.

Mask

Taytnapams had a mask like a *psa* [a danger]. If a child was mean, nasty, or always crying, someone would put on this bark mask of an old woman (Basket Ogress ?) and scare the child into behaving properly. Once the child saw her, men tried to catch her to drive her out of the house. The person who wore the mask was paid with dried camas, berries, or fruit.

First Menstruation (M1)

Menstruation first started when some girls made fun of an old man bleeding from the eyes. They laughed at him. He wiped off the blood, threw it at them, and, everafter, women have had their monthlies. The allure of Moon and the Stars remained a concern, as Mary Iley {mi 3} notes below that "For five months, I wore a hood so I could not see the stars or the Moon. I stayed shy."

When a girl became M1, she was taken to a hut near the house for five months. She wore a hood "blinder," with dangling noise makers like deer dew claws, shells, or bells, to warn others away {ly122}. She could not look at small children because they were weak and vulnerable to her power {ph 31}, which might detach their souls {md 54}. The M1 could only look down because paralysis was usually a sign that an M1 had looked, deliberately or inadvertently, at that future invalid {md 169}. While the girl was isolated, often for the first time in her life, she was never entirely alone since older women watched out for her, using protective dicta. If she needed help and no one was near, she pounded on a board. She must never shout or cause any disturbance.

A man at Satsop had a magical bow and arrow that made the elk drop dead by merely holding it up {mpw 95}. When his daughter became an M1 and went into seclusion, a Lower [?] Chehalis shaman decided to steal this girl and punish her father for either lying or bragging. But when the shaman got to that man's house, he found elk lying all over and everyone drying meat. He backed off.

A girl could eat only dried salmon, fresh camas, or anything else from the ground because that came from the work of woman. She could not eat anything fresh or bloody without risking a hunter's luck or her own welfare. She must never drink from flowing water or she would die of consumption when her heart flooded with blood {mi 325}.

A girl who was prepared for the onset of M1 found a white tree out on a prairie and painted it red to highlight her readiness. She also put red paint along the part of her own hair. Her father had a bed of cedar boughs inside a bark-covered hut all ready for her {ly 117}, with a new fire made inside. This fire could never be brought from a house, it had to be started fresh [anew] for the M1 {mh? 203}.

At M1, a girl's face and lower arm, especially fingers, were painted bright red. She wiped this paint off with shredded cedarbark each time before she bathed, which often meant wading into water shoulder-deep. She rubbed hard to scour her skin and toughen it. If she bathed at a place that was dangerous with *psa*, women used dicta to calm them. Once, a woman painted and named three rocks for the water dog *psa* who lived at a place in the Chehalis River.

To keep track of five day intervals, M1 wore five cedar bands around her right wrist, removing one each day before swimming {ly 126}. A new mother did the same thing, using 5 knots in a deerskin cord and untying a knot each day. Some girls wore tight garters at wrists, ankles, and below the knees {mh? 203}. Some wore a tight belt to lessen hunger pains.

To scratch her hair and tend it, each M1 used a tip of horn, a sharp stick, or a comb either of lashed together twigs or carved of alderwood. Unlike other tribes, she had no drinking tube, which was used only by the very sick.

The M1 worked hard, often preparing fibers and making both soft and hard baskets. She gave these baskets to old women so they would pray that she have a long life.

Often, an M1 stayed secluded for five months, but some took a whole year {ly 117}. M1 never ate fresh fish nor meat, only dry camas, dry berries, dry seeds, or dry roots, according to the Taytnapam. A Cowlitz M1 also ate fern-root mush.

If M1 came during berry picking season, the girl wore a bridle, a white peeled stick kept between her teeth, so she could stay busy by helping to pick but did not eat any berries. The stick bridle was inspected each evening to make sure there were no berry stains. If she ate any fresh berries, her reckless use of power endangered the harvest for the next year.

Salal berries were a *psa* to an M1 because they belonged to ghosts, who used the longest stems for canoes {mh? 204}. It was *x̣ax̣aaʔ* [sacred, forbidden K2288] to eat them while an M1.

Seclusions should last 10 days for the first and second times, then five days thereafter. For monthlies that lasted two days, women stayed in a hut three nights {mi 7}. Younger women secluded for each monthly, but older women usually just stayed quiet at home.

Change of life [menopause, *siatsnawł, syaćnaw*] came at about the age of 50.

Mary Iley's M1

When Mary Iley began to menstruate {mi 3}, she was scared and hid until her sister found her, saying "Do not touch your hair. Bend it up and out of the way. Put something over your head like a hood. Stay small. Do not lie down. Do not stretch. Stay compact."

Mary continued, "I made a tiny fire with lots of pitch. Like other Cowlitz and Taytnapam, I made ?? *saletcvn* [seclusion ?]. My hair was braided, looped, and wrapped with buckskin. Beads were tied on the ends. I could not touch my hair or head or I would get headaches. My mother or aunts combed my hair. My father made me two sharp scratching sticks, and I wore them suspended on a long necklace of beads. My face and arms to the elbows were painted red. Someone painted me this way every day.

"I stayed warm and fasting for five days, then bathed. Every morning, I bathed and rubbed myself with five little bundles (half a palm in size) of hemlock sprouts until only sticks remained. This scouring kept hair from growing over my body. I was not supposed to drink, but I got thirsty on the third day. My mother said I had to eat before I could drink.

"I finally slept on the third night and ate on the fourth day. I ate dried rice, a bit of sugar, and two dried pancakes. I ate the same on the fifth day. If I had lasted the full five days, I would have been strong.

"I stayed out of the house for two months. I never saw my little brother or any other small child. The last five days, mother made me pack firewood and pile it beside the house. I kept busy so I would never be lazy.

"For five months, I wore a hood so I could not see the stars or the Moon. I stayed shy. I only looked at girls, never any males. Men were afraid of M1. I never ate fresh salmon or bloody meat. My food had to be roasted on a stick and then dried. I could eat fresh berries because they were women's work.

"If I had to wade across a stream (even though I was forbidden to go near running water) I threw dirt or dried leaves upstream so it would float down and hide my passing, otherwise the salmon would never return to that stream.

"After five months, I could eat fresh salmon. During every later monthly sickness, I went outside for five days [in a shelter] but after I married, my husband would not let me go out, so only one of my babies was born outside."

Marriage

Families exchanged goods at a wedding. The parents provided half of the gifts for their side, the other half coming from their relations {mi 2}. The exchange was not equal; the groom's side gave more then the bride's since she went home with them. Gifts were mats, blankets, baskets, elk skins, beads, and foods. The boy's family gave more household goods, and the girl's more foods. Important families gave slaves to help the new couple. Cowlitz gave horses {ly 120}.

The boy's parents began the negotiations for a marriage and continued giving gifts for the duration of the marriage. When the husband's mother came to visit her inlaws, she wore a fine dress and hat, which she removed and gave to the other mother-in-law. The mothers-in-law should be like sisters, and the fathers-in-law like brothers.

Boys married after 15, girls after 10. A chief gave permission to marry into another tribe, but people had to be careful. Satsop and Skokomish women had "easy minds" and did not stay faithful {ph 82}.

When Taytnapam saw a boy who was a good hunter, they wanted to marry their daughters to him. People who were lively in work and life were preferred as spouses.

Important families would betroth their children while they were small to become inlaws. Personal likings were not important, only the family rankings. If a boy or girl were opposed to the match, he or she could only run away and hide. If an approved boy and girl were devoted to each other, they ran away and hoped for forgiveness after they had a child. When the couple returned decent and well-behaved, the parents gave gifts to each other and became inlaws. If one of the couple was a slave or low class, the parents never reconciled to the mating. People who married relatives, of whatever degree, were called "dogs" because they could not recognize their own relations {ph 272}. Brothers and sisters would sometimes swap or take spouses from each other {ph 270}.

Royals always married among themselves. By strict rule, they married until death. Chief Taholah at Quinault married the mother of Chief Masin from Scatter Creek {gs 113}. A royal wedding was expensive in order to show who the children were. Gifts from her family covered the path the bride walked between the two sides. After these were given away, the groom's family laid down more gifts along the same path for distribution. Then the families displayed their inherited dances and songs before giving new names to the bride and groom and hosting a big feast {ly 120}. Sometimes, hostilities were settled by having the offspring of the feuding chiefs marry, forging an alliance.

A common marriage signified only common children "born to the dust," while royal babies are "born on top of the heap" piled with treasures {ph 272}. Children of poor or slave families were called "bastards" because their "fathers were unknown" in that they had no pedigree or ancestry.

Before a marriage, the inlaws gathered to get to know each other. At the ceremony, the bride's side and the groom's side sat about 200 yards apart {ds 364}. Women of the bride's side tossed beads, blankets, and gifts for all to take. The bride, wearing a cap covered with beads and earrings down to her shoulders {mi 3}, was led across by two old women and seated on the groom's left side {ph 82}. Old women from his side removed the blanket hiding the bride, finalizing the marriage when the wife and husband actually saw each other.

If the families were royal, their chiefs spoke about the consideration needed for a good marriage. Inlaws exchanged food and gifts as long as the marriage lasted. After children were born, the families were linked and an aunt or uncle was expected to replace [re-wed] a spouse who died. A sister married a widower or a brother the widow so the children would be cared for by a relative who became a step-parent.

After a husband died, the wife was supposed to stay with his family and marry his brother or cousin. If she married a stranger, the prior children would always have trouble because they had no "real relatives." If the wife died, her sister, niece, or another girl in the family was expected to marry the widower. She felt it was a duty to her family {sh 150}. A special kin term applied to these re-wedders [*smaKtuln* K1042.10a]. The parents and family of the deceased could decide if they would allow the widow or widower to marry someone else. If a widow did, the former inlaws gave back some of the dowry. The widow mourned for a year, wailing loudly each morning if she truly grieved. Her hair was cut off above her ears and she re-wed when it grew back.

Women were not to tap their feet or seem distracted. If a jealous husband saw his wife wiggling her toes with her legs crossed, he suspected she was thinking of a lover and might stab her in the heel with a knife.

A man without character ("bad in his heart") might marry his step-daughter, but most men would not do so. A woman never married her step-son. An unlucky man who married a dutiful wife, who bathed and prayed, would become lucky.

Shamans often could demand a wife. A girl might be given to a doctor in payment for a cure {mi 15}. She either was married to the shaman himself or to his son or nephew. She had no choice in the matter, but she could desert the marriage after an honest attempt over a year or so. A doctor envious or jealous of a pretty girl about to be married might kill her for revenge {mi 16}.

Marriage Examples

Lucy Youckton's father had three wives who lived with him, but he was left with one after the oldest one died, and the youngest one got mad and left {ly 120}.

John Smith was a young man "not thinking of women" when his father or uncle died, leaving a wife named Maggie, whom they had "paid" a lot for so the families forced them to marry. John refused, so they put them in bed together, but he ran off. Maggie waited for days until John came back, and they became congenial {ph 272}.

Syk'amen ("light," sickman) had three wives, an old one from Scatter Creek Prairie and two young ones with many children. He favored the middle one, a Satsop woman, and always took her in his canoe. The other two wives had their own canoe, but always quarreled. After *Syk'amen* died, the youngest wife (Satsop and Puyallup) married a sailor from Chile and learned Spanish. They lived and died in Oakville {ph 271}.

Two first cousins ran away and married. They had three children, one of whom was Mary Heck's father, when Mary Iley's great grandfather found them among the Upper Chehalis and welcomed them back to Newaukum {mi 1}. Thereafter, the Ileys and this family called each other cousins.

Chief Tsinitiya, half Cowlitz and half Upper Chehalis, married the daughter of a Lower Cowlitz chief, giving 10 slaves, 10 horses, and beads. Her family kept her well hidden all the time because she did not have a flat head marking nobility so someone might make fun of her. She could not cook or work, but she was royal. Since she never went out, she did not know how to ride horseback. At the wedding, she fell off the horse. Her mother immediately scattered beads all over the place where she fell for everyone to pick up. Tsinitiya already had 7 wives, but this girl was the only one to have children {mi 4}.

Mary Iley's mother's father (a Taytnapam named *watatanx*) had four wives, only two of whom had children {mi 11}. The oldest wife had two daughters and the other one was her own grandmother, whose daughter was Mary's mother. The oldest drove one wife away and fought with the others, who were cousins. She beat them, and cut up baskets they were working on.

Once, her grandmother had worked on a coiled hard basket that she kept hidden, but the oldest wife found it and cut it up. The grandmother shouted, "You treat me like a dog. You slashed my hard work. Now I will beat you for good." The women fought while the husband had Mary's mother in her cradleboard. Her grandmother struck the oldest in the face, getting the best of her. The husband tried to separate them but her grandmother knocked him down. He took his knife and slashed her arm to the bone in three places.

The youngest wife, who was childless, took Mary's mother in the cradleboard and medicated the grandmother. Then they left, walking across the top of the fish trap. They wandered all day long for five days in a row, only coming home late at night. Finally, the grandmother decided to move to Mossy Rock, joining her sister, Lewey's mother. [cf. Melville Jacobs (1934: 239) worked with Lewey Costima, an Indian Shaker in his sixties at his farm at Bremer near Morton in August of 1927.].

Soon, the husband began to seek his wife. He was out of gun powder and wanted to hunt along the way. He got to Mossy Rock, but his wife hid for 10 days waiting for him to leave. He knew that if the cuts healed before he got her back, she would always get her way for her spirit was very strong.

At Mossy Rock, the husband was refused powder by his nephew (actually a second cousin), who was a brother to the cousin wives. For this insult, two days later, this man died, speaking like the husband at the end, which confirmed the uncle as a sorcerer.

The youngest wife heard that they were coming to kill her husband and she tried to protect him. She slept with him every night. One morning, the hired killer named mo'oɬ found him and shot him with four loads of shot, like they use for grizzly bears. Blood and flesh covered the youngest wife, but she was not harmed. She washed and prepared the body for burial, wrapping it in an elkhide. No one else would help, so she had to bury him in a hole left by a huge fallen-over cedar. She placed two guns, three brass kettles, and other goods in the grave. Then she filled in the hole and disguised its location.

The other wives divided up his goods, but would give her nothing. She threatened to tell what they had done and so was bribed with a buckskin and a blanket. They burned down his house and pretended that the husband was lost and they were looking for him.

The youngest wife moved to Mossy Rock and married a series of her murdered husband's brothers, but none of these unions lasted. Several of them beat her and left scars, others died. She had several children, but they all died while still young.

A Cowlitz married a beautiful slave girl, who worked very hard. In time, however, a slave man named qa'os took after the girl and she yielded. The Cowlitz let them marry because qa'os also worked hard, taking care of the horses, getting water and firewood.

Sometimes a man traded away a slave girl before his son entered puberty to avoid temptation {14 mi}. To be polite, young slaves were sometimes called brothers or sisters.

Adult Duties

A carpenter had a special craft, assured by his spirit power. His tools were elk horn wedges, stone hammer, scrapers, and knives {pb 73, ph 290}.

Hunters left without eating and were gone all day long. They sweated or bathed for about 5 days before to purify their bodies and remove human smells. They never hunted at night, except when trapping eels {ph 106, sh 150}.

Women mostly managed their households, but some females got spirit powers to doctor or to excel at basketry, berrying, or tanning {ly 121, 128}. Women's work was to get plant foods, tan deer or elk hides, make mats or baskets, shred cedar bark, and sew clothes.

A husband or wife could own separate things, but they shared and helped each other. A wealthy family would own the land where their house stood, canoes (later, horses), and maybe a fishing site {ph 99}. Berry, camas, and hunting grounds were common property, even used by Nisqually and Cowlitz.

Death

When someone's soul left forever, he or she died. Sometimes an owl, lizard, snake, beetle, comet, or omen warned the family in advance. The body was washed, dressed, and wrapped in cattail mats and an elkskin. A wake was held for 2 or 3 days to allow friends and kin to gather. Children were sent away for their protection. The body was never taken out the door, but instead through a hole in the wall made by removing boards {ph 97}.

In the old days, corpses were put into canoes placed in trees, such as one at Gate City when Marion Davis was young {md 53}. Sometimes the canoe was cut in half to make a bottom and a top {ph? 76}. Once secured among tree limbs, other family members who died might be added to the canoe, which had holes bored in the bottom for drainage. Any grave goods put with the deceased were broken or damaged, sometimes by nailing them to the tree, so their connection with the family would be broken and they would be whole in the afterworld {ph 244}. A woman's favorite basket was put on a pole to wave in the wind {ds 370}.

Once people became Christians, they buried the dead and hired a grave digger, who chewed white fir while working {ph 245}. Then he had to sweat and fast for a time.   In the old days, grave diggers had special power, as from Wolf, to allow them to do reburials.

Beliefs. {ph 85} Snakes. When find coiled up, way [up] in a tree, just coiled there and lying, then someone is going to die. That's why he stays up there, as people who put the dead in the trees. *loq!wa* = snake. All of those he remembers. [that is, burial canoes were put up into the branches of a tree, foretold by a snake coiled up in the same situation.]

After the deposition (or burial) early in the day, a feast was held and everything movable the deceased owned was given away. If a woman died after picking fresh berries, these were given away or, if no one wanted them, burned up. The family gave all these things away so they would not have reminders of the loved one, who might lure them to the land of the dead. In the old days, non-related people took everything as soon as someone died.

The house stayed in the family, unless its owner died, then it was torn down and the pieces moved {sh 149}. Houses were expensive since it took two weeks just to make a plank, but it was fumigated and cleansed after each death.

A doctor might look over the close family survivors to make sure no ghosts or spirits were clinging to their grief. If any were present, he or she removed them {ds 370}.

If a royal person died, the chief spoke at the wake and funeral to remind everyone of his or her deeds and family connections.

Before the funeral, people gave money and gifts to the chief mourner to spend on new clothes for the deceased, a coffin, or food to feed those who attended the funeral {md 193}. At the dinner after the burial, the mourner announced the donations and paid back a token amount (a few dollars) to those who prepared the body, dug the grave, acted as pall bearers, cooked the food, or gave money. If there was money left, some was given to all who attended. In 1927, Joe Pete usually did the talking as "em-cee" (master of ceremonies) at these events.

The name of the dead was never said in public, and words that sounded like the name might be changed at the insistence of the family. Years later, the name would be revived and handed on. Rob Choke's grandmother did this for a relative named "noon" [in Tsamosan] so everyone used [this] English word.

After her husband died, a widow used a sweat house for 10 days, scouring her body with sweet smelling hemlock. She avoided fresh meat for three months or so because the blood might settle in her liver or other organs, causing her to spit up blood later.

After a hunter's wife died he had to be very careful to sweat and fast for 10 days to keep his luck. Lastly, he rubbed his face with punk from a rotten log.

A long-married pair was especially close, and the survivor was vulnerable, so dicta was said to break the bond. After a year of mourning, the surviving spouse was expected to re-wed into the same family.

The ghosts of the dead come closest to the living during the winter, when it is summer in the afterworld. If they took someone's soul, doctors had to go after it. If they touched someone, that person went crazy. Only doctors can see the dead with the help of their spirit ghost ally, but ghosts always smell moldy to anyone close by.

The dead person's spirit power would look over the survivors to locate the person who would inherit it, unless this was settled before the death.

Newborn babies were treated differently because they came from the east and went back to the place of the unborn. After they were a year or two old and capable of "sin," babies were buried with their families in the tree graveyard.

Slaves were dumped into the sea or under a log, without any ceremony at all.

Burials

When Lucy Heck, Silas's wife, died after a long illness, he burned down their house with everything in it, due to his sorrow {ph 98}. His wife had set aside $15,000 for her funeral. Her coffin cost $800.

Mary Iley knew of children who had taken beads and a copper bracelet from a moss covered-canoe burial. That night the ghost came in a dream, so they threw the beads away {ly 123}.

In 1927, the agent allowed only caskets worth up to $150 so that funerals would not be lavish. Peter Heck often made caskets for people, whether or not they paid him.

Suicide was rare, usually an angry act by a rejected spouse {ph 101}. Few people became crazy, and the Shakers cured them before they caused trouble. Some were crazy from being touched by ghosts; others from meeting *siyatko* (wild men, sasquatches) who were tall, whistled in the woods, came from the north, and had a dope [used a drug] to make people crazy {ph 106}.

Reburial

If the graves of a family were falling apart or threatened with erosion, the family had the remains removed, cleaned, redressed, and buried. Sometimes, an old person will arrange such a reburial as a gesture to ancestors before they meet again {ph? 77}.

Interactions

Pets

Dogs and horses were the native pets before whites came with cats {ph 48}. Other people said that the first horse came from the French and was seen at Tenino, brought by the Nisqually from the Yakamas {ds 368, ly 129}.

The Hecks had a pet raccoon, which begged for food and was treated like a person {md 192}. Youcktons made pets of young deer, beaver, wild cat, and owl {ly 119}. Young beavers were also kept, but not bear cubs because they were too mean. Children used to catch a mud puppy (water dog, salamander), dress it, and put it on a tiny cradleboard like a baby.

Every single bone of the first fish caught each Spring was carefully placed in the fire so animals could not eat them {ly 119}. In the fall, some families mashed Chinook salmon bones and mixed them with berries to eat like hash.

A dog howling at night meant that someone was going to die. People did not like the sound {ph 287}.

Dogs and babies talked to each other. Dogs were like people and so could eat the bones of hunted elk and deer {js 380}.

Smoking

Old people merely enjoyed smoking, but some spirit powers insisted on it for doctors, who drew in the smoke "clear to the toes" until he or she passed out {md 60}. After people got tobacco from the traders, they mixed it with kinikinnik [bearberry] leaves. A pipe was called *lapip*, from the French word, and was sometimes passed around a circle.

vSome powerful people competed at smoking, drawing in more smoke for longer periods. A man might have the power to light the pipe without using fire, just by willing it so. Young people did not smoke, nor did most women {ph 285}. [Klallam men and women smoked yew leaves in pipes with duck wing bones for stems (Gunther 1927: 279). ThA used Gunther as a model for her own research.]

Sweating

Sweat houses were built near a creek, so people could plunge into the cold water when they were too hot. Women used them more than men, especially as M1 when she had to bathe daily for a year {md 54}. A new mother or father sweated for 10 days. Water was sprinkled on hot rocks in a basin-like depression to create the steam. Soothing those hurt, sore, or tired, a few vomited in the sweat house to force a cure {ph 260}.

Hospitality

Guests were always welcome. Good hosts fed and entertained them well. Indians never had hobos {ph 84}. Meals were served morning and afternoon, with snacks throughout the day.

Upper Cowlitz visited the Taytnapams to fish for smelt or pick huckleberries {ly 125}. Smelt came twice a year, in February and late March.

Trading

Ocean foods were traded for land foods, coastal for interior. Blankets were much in demand {ph 105}. Upper Chehalis traded with the Quinault, Nisqually, Puyallup, Muckleshoot, Squaxin, Cowlitz, Yakama, and many others.

Gaming

Girls always had dolls and cradleboards, then younger siblings, while boys had tiny tools. A favorite children's game involved placing a shell on a pole on the beach and having members of each team walk up to take it while the other side used words and gestures to try to make him or her laugh. Sometimes, a member of one team was supposed to carry the shell across to the other side, withstanding jeers and taunts. The game taught self control, dignity, and coping with public recognition, but most children broke down, laughed, and ran back.

Children also tested their stamina by hopping in place {ph 111, md 188}. The winner was able to do this the longest. Boys ran far as part of their training. Before dawn, a royal boy should swim and then run from Rochester to Lequito and back.

Guessing Games used verbal clues to find something hidden.

String Figures or Cat's Cradle were made using cattail strings. Peter Heck could name 11 such figures {ph 330}.

Teams formed for a tug of war using a long pole {ph 261}. Sometimes adult women pulled against adult men, or different tribes, or towns. The women's trick was to sit down so they could not be budged. Sometimes two men sat across from each other holding a stick until one of them was pulled up.

Boys staged mock battles using stump grass arrows and small bows {mh? 201}. Popguns were made, probably as a recent idea. Before a sneak attack, each boy told what his pretended power was in case they needed help along the way. Seeking girls for slaves, the boys rushed an encampment, whose campers fled into hiding. Any captured girls were ransomed by their families and the boys feasted on the proceeds.

When geese [bird flocks] passed as a V overhead in the fall, children ran outside, clapping, dancing, and singing "Leave me some backbone!" to change the weather.

All gambling was a contest about the relative strengths of the powers involved or invoked. The side that won had the greater power.

Slahal was played with a pair of tubes made of horse bones, just long enough to hide inside of the palms. One was plain, called woman, and one had a middle black band, called man. Two people each have a pair of bones. Teams and sides would match bets so a winner got double. On the ground, a fire burned in the middle and long poles along each side marked where the teams sit. People used sticks to pound on the poles when they sang lively bone game songs. Leaders sat in the middle of each line and took turns guessing the location of the plain bones. [Klallams said that the game was originally played with only a single plain bone (Gunther 1927: 274).] Swaying, two hiders on each side moved their arms with fists clenched. Every correct guess earns one of the 10 counter sticks, but a game usually goes to 30.

Slahal players were mostly men, but one woman at Chehalis had power (from a large Crane) to do this and people came from all over to play against her. It was wonderful to watch her play when "she was in business" {ph 109}.

Cheaters could effect the outcome of a game by hiring a recent widower or a M1 to stand near the other side and make them unlucky {md 188}. This work was done in secret, or the other team took offense and kept the bets. In more severe cases, a doctor was hired to hex a team or a race horse.

Hoop Disks was played at night with lots of betting before the two sides sat on mats. These disks were eight black and red, one black, and one white. Each side had five and hid them inside shredded cedar bark. They play to a count of 40, using split sticks for tallies, guessing for the solid color.

Beaver Teeth, used like dice only by women or children, were decorated with circles and dots on a side. Those with double rows were called "man," while the others were "woman." One of these "woman teeth" also had a black middle band. Various combination and arrangements of patterns were scored differently. For example, when all four teeth were decorated-face up, it was called "all are laughing" and counted two tally sticks. When all four red backs showed, that was another two sticks.

A hoop made of hazelwood was rolled by boys, who tried to thrust spears through it as it reached a specific spot. Sometimes teams formed. One side rolled the hoop and the other threw spears until it matched a certain agreed-upon count and the sides changed. The winners took away [won] all the spears. Sometimes they threw the hoop up and tried to catch it on an arm.

Arrows were used in shooting matches with a large fungus target set in two opposite directions {md 187}. Players shot at one, turned, and shot at the other. The winner got all the arrows used. Arrows were also shot for distance, the one that went farthest won.

Ball Game ~ Shinny was played with a carved white fir sphere and hooked sticks [like field hockey] to get the ball across a goal line. Games were held at gatherings where teams could be recruited during dry weather since play was rough and wet ground made it dangerous.

Horse Races were held after these animals were traded from east of the mountains {ph 110}. Both horse and rider fasted and thirsted for a few days before a race. Heavy bets were made, including slaves and clothes. There was a race track near Centralia {ph 297}. People rode bareback, but they did use a homemade pack saddle of crooked roots for transport.

Prairies were deliberately burned over in the spring so the horses would have fresh grass. In the winter, horses knew how to dig under the snow for grass. If winter conditions were severe, an owner might cut fresh reeds or rushes to feed his horses.

Strong men wrestled, grabbing the hair if they were from Quinault or Grays Harbor. Mostly men used the back hold.

In the Myth Age, Animals gambled among themselves. Bear, Cougar, Wolf, and other meat eaters played against Elk, Deer, Beaver, Fisher, Rabbit, and other plant eaters. Of course, the meat eaters usually won {jw 91}.

Crimes

A murderer had to sweat, fast, thirst, and pray for 10 days while his relatives negotiated a settlement or payment. Then he could eat sparingly using a pointed stick or drink from a skunk cabbage leaf. Any plate or cup he used had a hole in it. For about three months, he could not directly touch food or water {mi 5}. Like the M1, murderers could not touch things with their fingers until the blood was "wiped from their hands."

A murderer had to fast and swim to purify himself or he would die. He would only hold a bite of food in his mouth briefly before spitting it out {ph 274} during 10 days. He would drink only a tiny amount of water. While he was fasting, his own family negotiated compensation and settlement with the family of the victim. The best go-betweens were royals.

Unless purified, all the murderer's family would die and brush will grow over their houses {mh? 204}. At Satsop, the family of Stout, who killed Tenas Pete [who reburied graves and so had ghost power {ph? 77}], died out because the murder was not settled with payment and a feast.

Certain doctors had the power to stick a knife or probe into the footprints of a thief, who then would be identified by a foot injury and confess {ph 244}. [Klallam had shamans who could find lost or stolen goods (Gunther 1927: 299).]

Warfare

Warriors prepared by sweating, then plunging into freezing water. Sometimes, they stood in such water for half a day until numb. A warrior was driven by a fierce spirit who demanded a short life in return for great fame {js 256}. Successful warriors could marry into the royalty. Some [mean] warriors picked fights for the fun of it. He had fighting "in his heart like Teddy Roosevelt".

They trained for stamina, endurance, and strength by running, suffering cold, and holding mock battles. They ran through snow-filled trees and dove into ice water.

Strong warrior powers were Wolf, Fox, Coyote, Otter, Cougar, Bear, Eel, Pygmy Owl, Condor, Eagle, and Snake or Lizard, to get through tight places. The greatest of all was Thunder, like Kitsap, Jonas Secena's grandfather, had at Suquamish. A warrior never ate the animal form of his power.

One power, an antlered snake, was so strong that it twisted the unready bodies of those who encountered it. If a lucky boy of good family found it, however, he would always win at war, though his life would be short. Jeff Secena saw it and his life became golden until he died in an accident {js 259}.

Women might get some of these powers, but never at full strength. It just enabled them to be brave enough to carry weapons and serve behind the battle lines {js 259}.

Local warriors never scalped like Satsop and Nisqually. They cut off the whole head and stuck it on a pole in front of the town. The Snohomish did this to Peter Heck's great grandfather's son {ph 243}. The Snohomish came to Mud Bay to counterattack for an Upper Chehalis raid and found this boy courting a sweetheart there.

The Squaxins at Mud Bay had been warned by the sounds of cranes flying at night and fled their homes, but this boy was found close by. A Snohomish who had been a slave recognized who the boy was and they killed him, taking his head away.

Once, at Grand Mound, someone threw a bone into the brush and knocked senseless an enemy wearing buckskin clothes and white paint around his eyes like an Owl {js 257}. Using pitch torches, they found his body and burned him up.

Upper Chehalis would fight the Westports or Skokomish. Mostly warriors wanted children to sell or keep as slaves, many from Grays Harbor. Good families would try to locate and ransom their captured relatives as soon as possible.

A woman and her son were taken from Black River to the Columbia River. Her husband asked his relatives at the mouth of the Cowlitz to watch for his son, who had a scar on his cheek. These relatives found him and ransomed him, after some bickering, for a slave and a fur blanket, itself worth a slave. Thus, the warrior doubled his loot and the boy was freed.

His mother was taken to Oregon, where she worked hard. Everyday, she saved some food until she had enough to escape. They searched for her with the chief's dog, but she hid in a log and fed the dog dried salmon. Near Centralia, she met two men, but one was an enemy. The other man used lip gestures to warn her to stay off the main trails. At Black River, she waited for her son to come to the well and made sure he was safe. Then she went back to Jamestown because she was born a Klallam. She never wanted to see her husband again because he gave up on her.

Upper and Lower Chehalis fought 300 years ago after the Lowers raped and pillaged upriver {sh 145}. The decisive battle was fought at Oakville and thereafter their common boundary line was set at the Satsop River. [Silas Heck told Dale Kinkade this boundary was Cloquallam Creek near Elma.]

Adornments

Reshaping Head

[verbatim quote]

Head Shaping. {ph 212} Does not know how long head padding would be kept on head. Mrs. Heck said perhaps a year. *L'aqaiis* = the flat part of the head above, is called this, only the saucer below is called *ats[+u]kaq'was* is OK; *atsukaq'wais* = a dish shaped place in head. Mrs. Heck's father's {ph 212} was just above his nose. Her mother told her that this place would hold water. East of the mountains people means [they were] different from people here because all [everyone there] have round heads [without flattening to mark those of high status].

Hair Care

Hair was parted in the middle along the crown of the head. Women put theirs into two braids, men into a ponytail. Using tweezers or fingers rubbed with ashes, men plucked out their facial hair; women their eyebrows, covering the location with dark red paint.

Sometimes bear grease was rubbed into the hair to keep it soft and glossy. A special plant medicine was used to thicken thinning hair {ph 277}. Combs were carved of yew or oak; one per family. Thin sticks were also interwoven to form comb teeth. Hair combings were hidden or burned so they could not be used for sorcery against that person.

Mourner's hair was cut after a death. For a son, everyone in the family had their hair cut. For a husband, the widow had her hair cut to the ears {ph 275}.

Paint

Some paint was traded from the Yakama. Another, like a reddish bread dough, was dug from the riverbank, baked in a pit over night, and mixed with elk tallow. Faces were painted all over to prevent chapping from exposure to wind or sun. The part of the hair was painted to appear attractive, particularly to a spouse.

Painting Part in Hair. {ph 212 verbatim} When Mrs. Heck's father got a wife from Cowlitz, he had the part of his hair painted red. Does not know what it meant, "unless it was to make the woman think more of him." Women also, young and old, painted the parts in their hair. When it was gathering time, the women painted the parts of their hair and they painted their faces at the same time. Doesn't seem to have any significance to Heck, except that it was the style and they looked pretty. Does not know if M1 painted their parts because was "never allowed to go near them" but knew they braided their braids very tightly in "order that their hair would not fall out, perhaps." Thinks girls also braided their hair before M1 (ThA would doubt this) but that braided it much tighter during the period, and again, so that it wouldn't fall out.

An M1 painted herself with red paint and washed it off, cleansing her of sin. Paint was also applied to make dicta more effective. It also improved love medicine, which had to be purchased from other tribes.

An old man once painted his face to court a young girl (Marion Davis's sister) at the agency school, but he was sent away by the teacher, Mr Bell, and threatened with jail {md 55}.

White paint was made from cottonwood ashes {js 254}.

Black paint was only used by Growler cult initiates.

Tattooing

A few people had a tattoo [séc' K1722.9] applied as dictated by their spirit, such as a Skokomish and Upper Chehalis woman who had a small circle tattooed on each cheek. Mary Heck's mother had tattoos all over her legs, which showed below her skirt, and an elk and deer on each breast. Her cousin Kate had hearts on each cheek {ph 282}. Some women had tattoos on the legs and lower arms, done with a gooseberry thorn and the ashes of burned raspberry canes.

Tattooing. {ph 212} [verbatim] Women wore it on their legs. Legs showed bare beneath their skirts. Mrs. Heck's mother had it all over her legs, stripes running up legs, all around. Her mother also had an elk and deer on each breast and her cousin, Aunt Kate, had small pots on each cheek shaped in heart[s]. Only person knew who had it on their face. Women had it on legs and on arms to elbows. Stripes of dots, it was just women folks' style. Men never had it unless their sweetheart put it on. Mrs. M has small mark on right arm. Mrs. Davis also has small mark. Girls had it done for them when they were young, in each case would use gooseberry thorn and alderwood and would burn red raspberry *m&tsqwnł* bush and use the charcoal from it on the needle. Would smash it very, very fine and then push it in with the needle to make the design. Thinks there was no particular time when tattooing was done. Thinks it was done at the preference of the person. Doesn't remember what kind of designs were preferred.

Men did not tattoo in the old days. Now, sometimes, a sweetheart "will put it on" out of devotion. Marion Davis had a tattoo saying "Tillie" on his arm {md 55}.

Responsibilities

Names

Family names were inherited {mi 6}. Royal families owned important names and gave a feast and presents when each was bestowed in public, singing family songs to everyone.

Names. {js 258} Each family have their own names, for example, not one family name, nearest relative would use it, in case of death of other names [holders]. My grandfather was 2nd Secena name. Was from Quinault. My grandfather's grandfather was the 1st Secena. Just one person could take the name, my grandfather was a Q but he had a slight connection with Quinault.

Sometimes spirits gave names to someone before they were married or had children. Such a name would "warm up" the baby so it would get a good spirit and song later, like its parent {mi 15}. *Tahmanawas* names might not be potlatched since they were personal, unique, and specially given.

A doctor who could go to the Land of the Dead might be given a name for his or her child by a spirit ghost, perhaps to have its own former name continued {md 163}. Jack Knoodle was given such a name for his son George.

Mary Heck's father's spirit singled her out from her sisters to help him cure. Her spirit name was *misal&mx*, her name when she was young. She got another one when she married {ph 395}. If she wanted to "condemn" this name, so no one else could use it, she could take another final name for the end of her life {ph 285}. Mary Heck's husband, the father of Peter and Silas, was named x̱iq^wimał [x̱ekwimł K:337 B15] and then *kuqla* [k^wuq^wła K: 336 B4], after his father's father.

At his wedding, Peter Heck was named *yanm* after his father's father, with the announcement that "the dead man has now returned" {ph 82}.

Some names were nicknames. George Jack was called "raven" to tease him. His father had three or four wives in a row like his Raven power {js 132}. Lena Heck was called "lake".

When someone died, the family might remove [retire] a word that was like that person's name. The dead were sacred so it was an insult to continue to use such words. For example, when a man died whose name was "ax," they made up a new word for this implement. When a woman died whose name sounded like "iron," they used the chinook [Chinuk] jargon word *chickamin* for "metal, money, and iron" instead {ph 37}. The Lower Chehalis changed their name for "deer" to "jumper" or "grey face," because a man died whose name sounded like the old word {sh 140}. [Thom Hess used concentric wave-like distributions of these different words for deer to show historical aspects of Lushootseed language change.]

After a few years have passed, they will bring back a name by giving it to someone in a younger generation of the family – a grandchild, nephew, or niece. Names were changed throughout life.

If a Chehalis woman was married at Quinault and wanted to give her grandfather's name to her new baby, "naturally" [of course] she came back to have that name called out among the Chehalis, who would hear it at a potlatch. Those who accepted gifts would be acknowledging as witnesses the bestowal of that name or giving up their own claims to it {sh 140}.

White names could also be inherited. Mucy Bill Simmons was the third one in his family with that name {sh 140}.

Some families even had names for their dogs or other pets {ph 72}.

Anyone could be insulted by calling them a "slave" in public {js 132}.

Dicta (power words, formulae, spells)

Compelling words or formulas were known in certain families, jealously guarded, and used in a variety of situations (such as love affairs, childbirth, illness, or grief) to determine a favorable outcome. [Other Salishans also passed down such dicta, but not much is known about them. ThA was confused by Erna Gunther (1927: 247), who worked among the Klallams and mistook such forms of "mind control" for a kind of wishing.] Though usually transmitted through family members, training in dicta had to be paid for to make it legitimate. To be effective it had to be very secret and very expensive, but using it "could make a person in New York change their minds" {js 253}.

For example, a jilted woman could use dicta to either lure back or harm her husband or lover {md 51}, reciting it as the sun rose to attract him, or at sun down to kill him {sh 145 }.

When used to cure, dicta were said while hands rubbed with bear grease touched the afflicted part of the patient {ph 247}. Other kinds of dicta were used with red paint. The woman who cut the hair of mourners used dicta to lessen their grief.

When gathering medicines in nature, dicta was used to talk to the spirits of these plants and places. Someone who learned a great many dicta quickly was sure to live to a great age. One who had trouble remembering any of the lessons was doomed to an early death.

People could influence the weather {ph 276}. It would rain if the father of a newborn looked at the mountains or waded in a creek. Playing with a shuttlecock made of arrowbush stuck with white duck feathers caused snow. Working strings for cat's cradle or a bullroarer caused bad storms. Teasing tiny fish in a stream near Gate City caused rain. It was expected to rain after a funeral to wash away the dead person's tracks. A hard wind blew after someone drowned in the ocean {js 373}. Pointing at a new moon caused rain {sh 151}. Pointing at the moon in winter caused snow {md 170}.

Dicta used a special vocabulary and power given by Moon to his royal relatives when he remade the world.

TECHNOLOGY

Technology considers houses, woodworking, clothing, tools, fishing gear, hides, basketry, and, more recent, horse gear.

Housing

Houses (Suttles 1991; Waterman and Greiner 1921; Waterman & others 1921), with walls of tied-on standing cedar planks (without pegs or nails), were built so their length ran parallel to a river or stream with doors at both ends. [Early travelers noted this up and down placement of native house boards, and Fort Chehalis (1860) was built the same way (Van Syckle 1982: 36, 152).] (At Grand Mound, because the Chehalis River ran east and west there, the houses happened to be oriented to the sun, but this was a secondary consequence of their following the waterway {ds 365 ThA}.)

Firewood was stored just inside the doors. During a freezing spell in winter, a mat tent might be made inside these doors to keep out the cold. Sometimes, there was a double door. An outside one hung like a pendulum so it could be moved back and forth to allow passage. The inside door was fitted, longish and squarish, so it could be locked with a cross bar.

Planks, wedged off cedar logs, could take two months to finish an adzed surface. Those with knots were used for the sides, while those without knots that let in the wet were used for the roof. Gaps were left along the peak of the gabled roof line to serve as smokeholes.

Most houses had two fires, used by four families (two families share a fire), but a house could be as much as 80 feet long and 40 feet wide for a six-fire house for 12 families, about as large as houses got {sh 150}. Their doorways could be fastened closed using a string that hung down {ph 267}. In colder spots, houses were dug deeper {mh? 205} and had a thick layer of dirt piled along the outside of the walls as insulation. The area outside the house was bare, no platforms like those of the Kwakwaka'wakw [formerly Kwakiutl] of British Columbia {ph 39}.

Inside each house [xáš K2280] was a packed dirt floor, fires, and beds. Built as platforms along the sides, these bunks were four-feet high, surfaced with cedar planks, and covered with (2-6) layers of mats about six feet long and 3 or 4 feet wide {md 154}. They were used as seats during the day and as beds at night.

The man who built the house, or managed and paid for the construction, was regarded as the [primary] owner. After his death, it was inherited by his close relatives, beginning with his wife, then his sons, but it was the family home so all of them shared it {ds 364}. If a family died off, anyone could move the house to another location that was regarded as safer or more lucky for the living. Once the house was moved, anyone saying he or she belonged to the owner family had no claim to the prior site {ph 295}. Anyone could move there. Ownership consisted of occupancy.

Houses were swept daily using a broom of bundled buck brush {ph 286}. Blankets were hides, but wealthy families had bed spreads woven of dog or mountain sheep wool {ph? 81}. The woolly dogs were raised locally, but the sheep hides were traded from the Klickitat [Yakamas]. Large mats were used as inside walls. Dried salmon and other food hung from the rafters above the fires.

The house of a chief was larger and dug deeper {md 184}. Slaves slept inside, without assigned locations, ready to work. Contrary to the Skunk story [below], there were no little outbuildings where slaves lived. That was a literary device of Marion Davis, who told the story. A chief might also build a large house just for a potlatch and leave it standing as a monument. A potlatch was like Christmas, with someone standing in the center of the house and telling the helpers to whom to give presents {ph 39}. Chief John Heyden built the last one in back of where Secena lived in 1927. It was torn down only when it began to collapse.

Villages were clusters of these houses along a shore associated with a particular band of people. For example, Upper Chehalis were from Cedarville to Lequito {ph 296}. Teninos had Scatter Creek, Skookumchuk, and a section of the river {ph 99}. Remains of a village at Gate City are now gone {ph 108}.

During the summer, people moved upriver to camps where they used flat-roofed cattail mat tents. Smaller sweat houses were also used all year long {ph 256, 269}. Unlike the Klallam, fish were never dried in these summer homes because they would spoil quickly. Rather, they were hung from the rafters of the winter plank houses.

Woodworking

Every family needed the firewood of two or three trees every winter {md 186}. Both women and men packed wood. People would find a dead or dying tree and set a slow fire to burn it down. Several days later, they would go back and chop up the wood, load it into a canoe, and bring it home. Backpacks and, more recently, horses were also used to carry wood.

Firewood was stored inside the doors, while bark and twigs were kept under the bunks. People did not like to have to get wood in the rain.

Fires were mostly small, except when a chilled hunter or fisher came home. Then bark, wood, and limbs were added to the fire. To increase the flames, pitch or seal oil was added.

A firedrill was used to make a fire. A glowing punk was made of braided willow root {ph 101 ThA}, carried inside a large clamshell only by women.

Cedar bark was pried off trees in June and July when it was loose. Strips should be wide, up to six inches or the width of two hands for use as soft baskets, women's aprons, and shredded towels {ph 286}. Women mostly did the work, but men helped if needed.

Every woman was busy making mats, which were used for walls, padding, plates {ph 84}, and covers. Small round mats were used for playing the disk game {md 154}. Shredded cedarbark served as towels, skirts, pads. Shredded cedar was sometimes dyed red using alder bark. Spoons were selected clamshells or carved from yew or alder wood. Dishes were made of hard wood, often maple.

Canoes

Because they had to float well and keep passengers safe, canoes were the epitome of woodcraft (Carlson and Hess 1971; Olson 1936; Waterman & others 1920). Everyone preferred to travel by canoe, although there were trails {ph 102}. When whites were taken downriver to the harbor by native guides, they came by wagon to Little Rock, where they loaded into river canoes. The harbor canoes, for saltwater, were too "wild" [erratic], too sharp pointed to keep straight in a riffle. Sometimes they hitched a horse to a canoe to drag it overland to the Cowlitz River.

Chinooks on the Lower Columbia and in saltwater had war canoes with sculpted and painted shields on the bow and stern, equipped with portholes to shoot arrows. Built in something like the long-abandoned head design for war, they were striking as described by Lewis and Clark, Cox, and Henry.

The bow and stern are about the same height, and each provided with a comb reaching to the bottom of the boat. At each end are pedestals, formed of the same solid piece, on which are placed strange grotesque figures of men animals rising sometimes to the height of five feet, and composed of small pieces of wood firmly untied with great ingenuity, by inlaying and mortising, without a pike of any kind. The paddle is usually from four and a half to five feet in length; the handle being thick for one third of its length, when it widens and is hollowed and thinned on each side of the centre, which forms a sort of rib (Cox 1832: 110).

Many of the largest Chinook canoes were of fine design, the bow and stern frequently mounted with tall sculptures of Coyotes, Eagle, Bear, or man-like creatures. Fur trader Alexander Henry saw a Clatsop headman pass up the river one February in his new war canoe (Rubin 1999: 152)

about six fathoms long and wide in proportion, the stem [bow] rising perpendicular about six feet, on the top of which was a carved figure of some imaginary monster of their own rue imagination of uncouth sculpture, the head of a carnivorous animals with large ears erect, and arms (but no body) & legs clinging to the upper extremity of the stem, grinning most horribly, as it ploughed through the water. The large ears are painted green other parts red and black. [K153]? The stern also rises perpendicular about five feet in height and has no carved figure on it. On both sides of the stem and stern are broad strips of wood of the same piece as the stem and rising about four feet, and holes cut through them for the purpose of shooting arrows through.

Many canoes at Kelso that were bought from the Chinook had a front painted black or red, same as their paddles.

Clothing

The woven cedarbark skirt overlapped at the back and was made more sturdy in front {mi 7}. It came below the knees and was longer in back {ph? 78 ThA}. Other skirts were also made from strips of muskrat, badger, wild cat, mountain beaver or raccoon hide, twisted while they were wet. A cape made of cattails kept off the rain.

Blankets were made by sewing together 6 or 8 such pelts. These animals were so easy to catch that a woman could make two or three blankets in a week. For these blankets and warm clothing, the fur was left on the hide. Deer and bear pelts were used full size {md 191}. Chehalis traded with Puget Sound tribes for a blanket woven of duck feathers {ph 333}.

To make leather, fresh hides were soaked overnight to loosen the hair, scraped, and rubbed with mashed brains as a tanning agent {ph 26 ThA}. The next day, the hide was rinsed, wrung out, and rubbed with an abrader to soften the fibers. Mrs. Youckton and Mrs. Secena were very skilled tanners. Some men knew how to tan, but mostly women did it. In 1927, soap and lard were used for tanning, along with deer or cow brains.

To color the leather, a slow fire of rotten logs was built in a pit and two deer hides, loosely sewn together, were tented over it to smudge into a yellow tint. After many hours, such smoked hides shed water and always remained soft.

Both men and women wore buckskin leggings when they went into brush, for example, to pick berries. The word used for leggings [*mitas*] in Chinuk Wawa derived from Ojibwa, Great Lakes Algonkian, and was spread via fur traders.

Dentalia (tusk) shells, dangling in strings, were used for earrings and other objects of wealth {ph? 78}. As elsewhere along the Pacific coast, natives did not know that their source was Nootkan traders from the West Coast of Vancouver Island, where the shells were ingeniously dredged up from the ocean floor several hundred feet deep. Instead, a race of dwarfs with tiny mouths, used to suck out the insides, was believed to supply the shells to the trade.

Women made beads of clamshells and wore them in necklaces {ph? 78}. Young men gave strings of such beads to their lovers.

Men sometimes wore a shell through a hole in the nasal septum, as did a few women. Winter was the time for head coverings, which were not worn in summer. Men could use the head of a deer or other animal as a hat. An otter hide, beaded and decorated, made a hat that was "too high toned" and likely to cause jealousy {ly 122 ThA}.

Some used a basket hat [cap]. Taytnapam women wore nice basket hats that were all white, all yellow, or white and black, made by Cowlitz matrons {ly 122}.

As undergarments men wore something like a diaper [bikini, briefs] made from leather. Some women also wore them under the skirt {ly 119}. The leather for these was particularly nice and soft.

Girls at Grays Harbor liked to wear beaded strings just below the knees, along with another three bands above the ankles.

People wore moccasins, stuffed with fur in the winter. Deer hide was used for moccasins because elk hide did not last. A toe [ThA has "tow"] strip was sewed to the moccasin and wrapped over the arch and around the ankle {ph 292}. In deep snow, snowshoes and snowboots were used {js 380 ThA}.

Tools

A woman owned everything she earned or made {ph 281} and took it with her when she divorced. The same applied to a man.

Stone tools included a hammer, about a foot long, with a rounded bottom and a tapered top to use as a handle {ph 102}. Made of grey stone, such hammers were used to pound stakes or wedge off planks by men, and to make flour of dried fish or meat by women {ph 284}.

Each woman had a dibble (digging stick) made from yew with a handle of elk horn. Women twisted string and chord on their hips and do not seem to have used spindle whorls.

Spoons were made from boiled and shaped mountain goat horns {md 61 ThA}. Suitable clamshells were also used as spoons. Cowlitz got large spoons from some kind of ocean being {mi 8}. Oblong basins were carved from curly maple. Stirrups were made from oak, boiled half an hour and bent to shape. Mary Iley's father knew how to make all of these. Round wooden water buckets were traded from Canadian Indians who made them.

Cowlitz {mi 8} traded horn spoons from a Boogey in the ocean. [winaw' K2162.5] = large horn spoon. Also made a horn receptacle with a handle on each side. [ta'nasłoł K2019] = oblong maple dish. Curly maple, pretty but very hard to make. My father made them. He made stirrups from oak. He would boil it for half an hour, then bend it to shape. He knew how to do this.

Copper was found near Toledo and used for paint.

Bow strings were made from sinew taken from along the backbone of deer. Bows were made from carved yew, arrows from fir or from arrowwood. The use of armor was uncertain, but ironwood slats might have been worn over the chest and back.

The only musical instrument was a long pole used to keep time by pounding on the roof during a dance {ph 102}. Only the Puget Sound tribes had musical instruments such as [square] drums, rattles, and whistles. [Yet drums did have a special use since "Ghosts exist around the living. They are very close whenever a fire goes out for no reason. To drive them away, people sing with a drum of elk or deer skin."]

Deer, elk, bear, and other animal bone was used for beads, needles, and awls.

Fishing Gear

Before salmon came up the river, fish traps were put up. Certain people always had a trap in place in time for the spring [c'awł K324] salmon, using it through the fall salmon run in October {ph 27}. As many as five people could be involved with making such a fish trap [cupi- K272], helping one another cut lots of little sticks that were needed and lengths of vine maple [p'áni K1362], maybe 5 feet long and about an inch or more in diameter {ph 28}. These poles were sharpened at the bottom, stuck in a line into the stream bed, and tied together with willow bark every yard or so. This fence was braced with slanting poles set against the water flow. Basketry cylinder traps, made of interlaced hoops, were set in the water to hold salmon until they could be gathered up.

A whole tribe might build a trap together, but the chief had the most of the say about it {ds 367}. A trap could be built in a day, ready to catch fish that night. The first-caught fish was roasted on sticks and everybody was invited to eat so that the trap would be lucky. Even lazy people were welcome. Similarly, when fish were distributed, everyone got a share, regardless of what, if any, work they had done. There were never quarrels or disputes for that would offend the salmon.

Spring runs were from February until the last of June. The water was high, so a net was not used. All of the salmon was dried. To roast any, it had to be soaked overnight.

Black salmon [q'ʷəlí K1662] was the first one in the fall, maybe in September; then came red [čan- K428, pink] or dog [núnxʷ K1212] salmon. They were speared [cf. pɛttcēks K1340] and cooked by being boiled or roasted on sticks. These fish always dug into a riffle and so could be speared in the backbone sticking out of the water. Steelhead [qíw'x̱- K1473] came up both the Black and Chehalis Rivers.

Suckers [x̱ʷuqʷtm'š K2419.12] were in the rivers all year around. They were speared, using a small net to make a drive for them since they always went in a bunch. Men in canoes floated on both sides of the river and hit the water with paddles to drive the fish toward another canoe with a set net.

Chub, another fish, were also in sloughs or in slow, still water [łaq'ʷ- K833]. In the spring, fat ones were caught on bone fish-hooks or with a little set net [yúmt'i-K2515]. They are caught at night when there is no light.

Red mouth, plentiful all year around, were caught in the spring when they were good and fat. Trout [pak'ʷawš K1235] were taken with a fish-hook any time of the year, while steelhead or salmon trout [čám'cš K493] come only after the salmon in the fall. People looked for salmon eggs to use as bait, particularly from a white salmon with a small mouth caught below a riffle, where they stay waiting for the eggs [to be deposited in a redd].

While local nettles, carefully gathered because they sting, were used for fish line {ph 28}, nets [q'ai ts- K1557] were made from nettles [qʷən- K1592] traded by the Yakamas {ds 369}. The dried nettles were soaked in water, then women used a finger cap [thimble] of coarse white material to scrape the bark off, remove the fibers, and twist them into double strands on the hip. This cord was spun fine or coarse, depending on what kind of net was intended {ph 28}.

Nets [K1557] = [K1592 = nettles?] {ph 23-4} comes from east of the mountains because they spin it to make it awfully strong. Women would make the nets. Spin it fine or coarse, depending on what kind of net was intended. Scrape the bark off and take out the insides. Use a finger cap of coarse white material to scrape the bark off. Twist it on the hip, 2 strands [together]. Nettles which grew here were used to make fish line, my father said. Perhaps also used for nets because it was strong. nettles = [K1592] because something stings you when you touch it. When it is dry, in the fall, gathered then because all of the poison is off. Dry it, soak it in water to soften and then twisted.

Night fishing was done from a canoe with a fire burning on a bed of dirt in the middle. The spear was made of split fir, tapered nice and smooth, with 3 hardwood prongs attached with cherry bark {ph 107}.

Hides

Cougar, badger, and mountain beaver fur was greased and buried so the oils would soak in, and then strips were knitted into blankets. Each was worth one slave or much of a bride price {mi 8}. Elk skins were traded for bison hides. Blankets were made of squares of bear or beaver fur {mi 5}.

Whole elk skins were used to wrap a body for burial or reburial. A tough elk hide was used to test the strength of a boy's hunting power. If his arrow went through, he would succeed {gs 114}.

Deer hides were smoked [smudged] through in half an hour, but most were left for half a day {md 167}. Saved brains were mashed and mixed with hot water to soak into the hide as a tanning agent.

Tanned bearskins were traded from the Mossyrocks and Yakamas.

Bear. Used to tame them. Hide was cut square and stretched before whites came. Hair left on. Put grease on a stick, bury it in the ground for 4-5 days. Agate tied on to stick like a little shovel and then scratched hide until it was soft. Men and women worked too. [?? unclear fragment] The later for int. Beaver made into a blanket. Hide was dried square, 4-6, 1-3 made into a wide blanket.

Badger and Cougar. Wild cat buried under the ground so it was air tight and the grease would soak in. [Whole] mountain beaver was not buried. Badger would be cut and rolled all around. They made a "quilting frame" of sticks and worked just like darning stockings. A stick needle did not take long to make by either men or women. 1 blanket traded for 1 slave, or to buy a wife. Price could go over or under 1 blanket.

Mountain beaver was just scratched [scraped], not buried. Squared off hides sewn together in blocks. Hides could also be cut up into strings, like badger. Buffalo hides came from east of the mountains. My father traded elk hides he tanned himself for buffalo [hides]. Elk hides never smoked. [soaked then] Oak sticks as long as a forearm from elbow tied with string [in bundle] and used to hit the hide. After father had wrung it out, he hit it until it was dry. Elk hide moccasins do not dry as quickly. Rots soon, so deerskin better. Elk hides kept to bury people in. Every 2-3 years, loved ones bones exhumed, wrapped in elk hide, and put back into a burial canoe.

satskawst n = cemetery [m'ák'ʷt cf. K1042] If too far from the house, wolves would eat the dead. Body wrapped up tight to keep wolf away. Wolf bad for this. {mi 8}

Baskets

Upper Chehalis made soft and hard baskets {mi 7}, along with mats. Soft ones, with a bottom woven of roots and grass sides, were used to pick berries in the mountains (Jones 1977; Nordquist and Nordquist 1983; Thompson and Marr 1983). Cowlitz women's hats were woven of grass and willow bark twine [for Taytnapam].

Hard baskets were used for cooking [qʷasúqʷa' K1576]. The Upper Chehalis only began to make hard baskets with imbrication after they saw that whites wanted to buy them. They copied Wynoochee and Lower Cowlitz baskets {ph 36, ly 125}. Mrs. Heck learned to make them from Minnie Case's mother. Hard spruce [hemlock] twined baskets [kʷúl K728] may have once come from the Grays Harbor or Satsop region, but spruce does not grow in the Chehalis neighborhood {ph 37}.

A quick pack basket for firewood was made of little cedar limbs, split and twisted into an open weave. Other hasty baskets, assembled as needed for berries and such, were made with any flexible bark {md 191}. Either men or women could make such an emergency basket, according to Mrs. Youckton.

Women made small mats [lačáw' K735] of cedarbark or cattails to use for drying food, such as berries, or for a table cloth on the floor when serving food {md 190}, also baskets filled with shredded cedar bark to sell to gamblers {ph 286}.

Sweet grass itself [*qaqcx* K1427] came from the Harbor, where it grew in the mud {mmd 49} and was gathered during the months from July to September. Women would pull it out, wash it, clean it, and hang it in a shed to dry slowly. If left in the sun, the grass would break up [fracture] too quickly. Sweet grass was used as attractive trimming. At a marriage exchange between the inlaws, the half that was the bride's mother's gifts were trimmed baskets, some with beads inside.

Mountain grass ['ím' K115] was gathered at Skokomish in the old days, but, if they had the chance, it was best gathered in August on Mt Rainier, when mountain berries were also {mmd 50} ripe. People traded a dress, cloth, or skirt for it.

Cedar bark was dyed red with alder, or black by burying it in mud. Rusty cans, stove lids, and old rusty kettles were also used to dye cedar bark {mmd 50}. Mountain grass was dyed yellow by soaking it overnight in boiled Oregon grape bark {ph? 75}. Special dyes were gotten from Taholah (Quinault).

A twined market basket was made of white sweet grass by Mrs. Williams, who used cedar bark with mountain grass over a bottom of raffia on back {mpw 95}.

Basketry designs were passed down in families. Women did not dream or envision new ones {md 189}.

Baskets. [k'ʷá•łq K692, soft basket] = Woven basket of roots. roots on the bottom for basis. Grass on the outside, take to mountains to pick berries. Cowlitz hats for women made from willow bark twine for the basis, thin grass for the outside. Irregular [??] roots – mud coloring. {Mary Iley mi 7 Aug 1927}

[qʷasúqʷa' K1576, hard basket] = cooking basket [cf pəču'- K1265], add water, never put any trimming on these.

Trimming for berry baskets, just a <u>little</u>. When they "buy" a woman, the mother would pay back half with baskets having a lot of trimming. Put beads in the basket and give it back to the man's parents.

Pack basket, get little cedar limbs, split them, made an open weave. Used to pack wood.

By 1927, people used a store-bought coloring (Diamond brand name), but such commercial dye did not fix as well with sweet grass as it did with raffia. In 1927, baskets were made and traded for cloth, household goods, curtains, or maybe a chair. Chehalis made a modern basket of mountain grass, woven over ribs of cattails and covered with designs all over.

Horses

[verbatim]

Ponies. {ph 48} Indians here had ponies before the whites came. (No story of where they got them.) ?? *spastial/steqeo*[+u] = white man's horses, [stiqíw' K1956]because they were different from their own little ponies. (Heck does not know where the cb band bought their horses.)

Horses were a key motivation for the Taytnapam move across the mountains to settle on the coast side (Boxberger 1984).

Their saddles are made of dressed deer-skin stuffed with hair; the stirrups are wooden, with the bottom broad and flat, and covered over with raw skin, which when dry becomes hard, and lasts a long time. The bridles are merely ropes made out of the hair of the horses' tails, and are tied round their under jaw. The women ride like men: their saddled are high in front and rear, and formed something like the humps of a camel's back; and they must bring their horses to a rock or old tree to enable them to mount. The men are hard and unfeeling riders; the rope bridles cut the corners of the poor horses' mouths; and the saddles generally leave their back quite raw; yet in this state they ride them for several days successively without the least pity for the tortured animals. We got plenty of salmon while we remained there, and some lamprey eels, the latter of which are oily and very strong (Cox 1832: 54).

FOODS

Staple foods were: salmon, smelt, flounders, suckers, chub, sturgeon, eels, shellfish, meat, birds, and plants.

Salmon

At the First Salmon Ceremony for Upper Chehalis, a man, never a woman, cooked the first salmon as soup in a large kettle {ph 28}. For Lucy Youckton {ly117}, first salmon was cooked with dried camas and served in a small wooden dish set on a cedarbark mat. Everyone invited brought a spoon to eat some of this soup. Old women came, but not girls because first menstruants (M1) were excluded. Fresh salmon was propped open like a butterfly and roasted between split sticks used like tongs.

First Fish {ly 102}. Would invite several families to come to home. Cut it in small pieces and put it on a cedar bark mat. Long, and put in small wooden dish. Mix it with dry lackamas. Had small net like a sack, sink it. Pull it out. Tell he had the 1st salmon. Then calls the people *malak[+u]*, ate it with a wooden spoon. Old women eat but not growing girls. The *maisx* (M1) same with deer and elk. Not the first one. The *maisx* ate dried salmon.

Along certain sections of the river, the salmon had to be cut in specific ways. Sometimes, they cut along the backbone and spread the flesh to the sides. Sometimes, the flanks were cut up to the tail and hung on either side of a pole to dry. Once dry, the fins had to be cut off or the flesh would sour. Backbones were dried separately, often for soup or mashed flavoring. Salmon heads were cooked on sticks propped around a fire. In 1927, heads were dried on strings.

Women dried the fish over a slow fire, then packed it in cedarbark or cattail open-work baskets. Sometimes, the fish was packed carefully, layer by layer, at an end of the house. Dried salmon was soaked overnight before it was cooked. The tail piece was fed to children in hopes they would marry a chief and become well off. It was the poorest part of the fish and so acted as a reverse prayer. Peter Heck thought that it was also an excuse for the elders to be greedy and eat the best parts.

Salmon eggs were dried loose over a fine mesh rack or inside a fish bladder, sewn fish skin, or deer stomach {md 51}. Dried eggs were mostly eaten in the spring with mouthfuls of peeled salmonberry shoots. Only the blood, gills, and intestines were not used. Black and red salmon runs can be forced downriver by putting smashed blood and eggs into the water {md 186} [thereby delaying their arrival until gear was ready].

People at Grand Mound never fished in the Chehalis River, instead took good, fat silversides from Scatter Creek in December. Boys were sent up toward Tenino to watch for the high water that marked the run. These salmon stayed there until spring. This arrival was so sudden that a man, who lived with his grandmother and was in a hurry whittling a spear to get the first of the run, accidentally cut open his stomach and died {ph 31}. Since then people have prepared well in advance, taking care that the leader of the salmon got up safely, so all the others would follow {sh 148}.

?? k:'tLaqai&qł = at Grand Mound {ph 27-8}, a village and houses. These people never fished in the Chehalis River. They never fished, just looked on. They only caught a few fish when they wanted them to eat.

When scatter creek [sic] got salmon, then they got crazy about it because then there were good fat silversides = [saw- 'red, sockeye, blueback' K1716]. Heck thinks about December when Scatter Creek is going to have high water and snow fall. Those people know that *?? sxa:m n* (Why the snow fell, in Heck's language). Scatter Creek, the first month [it is] sick [slick], when that sign comes, they send young boys up toward Tenino to see where the water is coming from. It is coming from the head or so and so. They will know, for as soon as that water of Scatter Creek pours into the Chehalis River, then the fish go up Scatter Creek. They catch them. *sey lk^qe n xwaL al n* = when the water was roaring down from the head. Some of the old people always had 2 traps, one way up Scatter Creek and one way down to keep the salmon in Scatter Creek (both below and up [above]). The salmon stayed until spring. [qalawł 'stakes clear across river' K1489] = [weir] that kind of trap, little stakes going clear across the river. They always say – since there is just mud and no riffle, no gravel – that the eggs are getting long and the fish are inside the eggs already. They would dry all of the eggs that they could. Heck thinks they dried the last fish in December, when there were scarcely any fish in the Chehalis River. All of them were in Scatter Creek.

A crooked nose salmon had to be well treated because it was dangerous. In the towns where the salmon lived beyond the horizon, the smoke from this fish's house comes out crooked {ph 250}.

Fish trap. When salmon comes up the river, that is the time to put up the fish trap. Some people always have a trap for the spring salmon. The same way when the salmon come up in October when the river is dry. (Black salmon is the first in the fall, September perhaps, then red salmon, dog salmon, in the fall. black salmon = [k'ʷalé•' K691], red salmon = [čan- K428]. Spear them or any way. cooked, boiled, or roasted on k:yanap! Speared because they always dug on the riffle, spear at the dry back bone [sticking out of the water]. Dried, soaked over night on the river side, that is, *?? saqan* [spit] dried all the salmon that came up, were dried. [nunxʷ K1212] = dog salmon. Speared late in the fall, November perhaps. Steelhead came up both the Black and Chehalis Rivers. [qiw'x̲ K1473] = steelhead. Spring time did not have a net, the water was high, fish dig on the riffle then and are speared. [c'awł K324] = spring salmon. Come in from February until the last of June, perhaps. Use fish trap and with [cf pEttēcks K1340] *x: pakkł* = spear them.

First Spring or Chinook salmon was cooked and eaten by all the men on the Cowlitz River {mi 11}. All the bones were returned to the middle of the river and told to say "I got hurt" so all the other salmon would come to show concern, just like adults do when a child said this. To feed everyone, to stretch the first salmon, they were also served beef, sausages, cakes, and doughnuts. Cowlitz now [1927] gather together for first wild strawberries, blackberries, huckleberries, and spring greens.

Hoh <1-5> good spot for smelting – April – September [First try at drawing of dip net, shifted & enlarged to p4] Purse seine in surf for smelt.

Salmon eggs <1-85> put in spring salmon fish bladder or seal bladder – and dry them for winter use.

Fish eggs fresh = tdi•qəs

dried = s'bisuwa "stink eggs"

Smelt = t'o•piẋ large =   small =   night smelt = o'o•pac

dip net = a'a•yił

Lay eggs on gravel beach of smooth gravel, no sand Feb – August

Large silver smelt <1-87> April – September. Dip net – today used drag seine at half tide & incoming tide. Smelt were dried over fire – smoked, tied smelt to lines to lines at head. Hang on long pole near fire & dry for 3 or 4 days, then placed in basket (of split vine maple).

Smelt <2-24> are now sold to commercial buyers – the price ranges from 4-20¢ ? per pound. <2-25> Smelt fishing (dipping 6/20/49) – a watch is kept from hillside above village since one can see the whole beach, south to Ruby Beach. They watch for flocks of seagulls which sit on the beach or dive into surf after incoming smelt. Sometimes the smelt can be seen "flashing" as they are cast on the beach.

When the smelt are located the men get their dipnets and go down to the beach. The best times for smelt are at the half tides (going out ?). When the run is heavy, the men dip the smelt in, carry them up to the gravel area on beach, and dump them. The women put them in tubs, buckets, boxes, baskets, etc.

When dipping, the dipper places the lower cross bar (the one away from him) on the bottom in time to have the wave break and dump the fish in the dipnet. If only a few are caught, he constricts the net [drawing in at side], just above the fish in the bottom of it, with his hand & thus preventing these already caught from escaping while making subsequent dips. Thus it is not necessary to empty the net after each dip. As much as 100 lbs can be taken in a single dip during a heavy run. When the surf is rough, one often gets more rocks and bits of wood or kelp than smelt.

Hoh River <2-31> best place for smelt along coast. Sun-dried smelt – spread on smooth gravel beach – spread any way just so they <u>don't touch</u>.

When smelt <2-33> first start running, they are unsuitable for drying because they are too fat. Smelt are tied on cedar bark string about 1 inch apart on 12' strings, turned once a day, hung on racks inside the house [drawing of smelt on loop rotated hanging from pole]

Sun-dried <2-65> smelt = qa•li'tso – laid on rocks of beach, turned several times – too much rain will spoil them [about 5 days to dry].

Eat boiled smelt by dipping them in melted shortening (= pi'ts) <2-72>.

First <3-83> smelt – not boiled – roast on stick against fire.

If <3-89> a person wants to stop the smelt from running – u•qul to•piks "no more" + "smelt" – he will take a male & female smelt & bury them deep in the sand along the beach where the smelt run.

In order to get smelt to run again, these smelt must be dug up and dragged down the beach in front of the incoming tide. After this, lots of smelt will run because they are angry at what happened to smelt that were buried & come up on the beach to fight.

Bill Hudson said <3-89> One time at Hoh River some Indians from Queets (Quileute) were camped on beach at south side of river. There were lots of smelt running but some of these people (4) wanted to see the canoe races at Coupeville & didn't want the smelt to run while they were gone. Two ladies got a tub of smelt & buried them behind a drift log on the beach. They left for Coupeville, suddenly the smelt stopped running & didn't "hit" again for several days. Some children playing on the beach with sticks were digging around & found the pan of smelt. They took these <3-91> smelt down to the beach and through [threw] them in the water. The smelt began to run again on the next tide.

Smelt [qʷaləsti K1568] had to be eaten whole, but it was taboo to eat the tail. The fish got mad if you were a local and cleaned it {mi 5}. If you took off the head, guts, and bones, smelt would kill you. If you were a stranger, the fish were tolerant.

Smelt [qʷaləsti K1568] {mi 5} *xaxaa'* [xaxa'i K2288 'forbiddenly sacred, holy'] to eat the tail. You ate the whole fish, without taking off the head, bones, guts. The fish would get mad if you cleaned it. Cooked on sticks {*sawa`n*}, but you could eat it fresh if you cleaned it. Smelt would not care because they knew people who did this were strangers. In a story, smelt does not want to be cleaned. Smelt came together when everything was people. One said he would be eel, another would be smelt. Eel has something yellow inside – p'[eople] take it out and head off. No bones. Smelts said, "Eat me all, and not throw anything away but my back tail." "What would you do if they took your bones out?" "Kill them." "What will you do, if I clean you?" "It will be all right for strangers. They do not know my way. If the ?? *L'polmxq* clean me up, they know my ways, so I will clean them [out]." People used to die if they took something off smelt. Blood ran from mouth? and nose.

Smelt were caught in a net {ly 119}. If someone ate just smelts, they would die with something like puke coming out of their nose, ears, and mouth unless a doctor came to cure them. Smelt had to be mixed with berries or camas, maybe some Chinook salmon oil {ly 120}.

Fish

Suckers are here all year around. Speared, used small net to make a drive for them, to catch them. They always go [travel] in a bunch, go in a can[oe] on both sides of the river, in canoes, and hit the water with paddles toward where the canoe with the net was set. [sxʷuqʷtm's K2419.12] = [sucker], always next to the ground, kind of suck it up.

Chub is on the river all of the time. [łaq'ʷ- K833] = places where they always stay, in sloughs or slow, still water. In spring, they catch the large fat ones on a bit of fish hook made of bone. Sometimes use a little net set in places where the chub stay. net = [yúmt'i K2515]. Catch them at night when there is no light.

ts qł n ł = red mouth. Heck thinks they catch them in the spring time when they are good and fat. Plentiful all year around. Fished here all the time with net or fish pole. Dried.

Trout, here all year round. Don't fish much for trout. Just anytime they want, with a fish hook. [pak'ʷawš K1235] = trout. Follows after the salmon. Are around here all the time, those who come with the salmon have a different name. Salmon trout = [čám'cš K493]. Salmon come from the harbor. ?? *K'ikyalo* = to hunt for salmon eggs. White salmon with a small mouth.

?? *L!kalo* = white with no bones. similar to trout. Come at the same time in the fall as the salmon. Heck does not know how it is caught. Perhaps on traps, at times, they go on [in]. Perhaps with a hook, using salmon eggs as bait. Caught right below the riffle, where they stay waiting for the eggs. Cooked with *sqan* – sun (on roasting stick, crosswise on 2 split stakes) Pinch a little and tie at the ends when the stick is full. If catch lots, dry them. <p28> 2, 3, 5 different parties could make a fish trap, helping one another cut lots of little sticks to make it with. Cut [vine] maple = [p'áni- K1362]. Maybe 5 feet long, about an inch or more in diameter. Poles sharpened on bottom end. Tied together with willow bark about a yard apart, clear across the river. That is, make each section a yard wide. ?? *sKwvl wi w n* and then tie them together and put the sharp stick on the ground where the riffle is slanting, so it gets on [over] a hollow on the bottom, and one on top. The bottom one is perhaps a foot from the water. The other at the top perhaps 5 feet high, as high as the posts. Always have 3 ([cúpi- K272] = trap) or 4 [??] across the river. Make a hoop around about [yəxawt K2502], about 3/4 of a yard around, and make it from vine maple and always split it and tie it to the hoop with willow bark. Maybe 8 feet long, and when all round, they'll put a little pole around it, so it will bend until it gets to the tail, to keep the hoop over, just tie one on the end. Now, just tie it round. They'll make another about a yard wide, make it the same way, but half the size, 1/2 a circle. String put across the bottom, like a bow and arrows to hold it in the round shape. Tie the ends, tied here, bowed, bark put around it. Salmon got in here, then turn around and go back into the [basketry] cylinder and stay there where they are caught. ?? *t'sa t* = (no, small one) name of the 1/2 circle part. ?? *yasal k n* = big one.

Flounders were also taken from Mud Bay by searching the bottom with the feet. In the old days, a sharp stick was kept between the toes to hook [impale] the fish. They were good in June {ph 107 ThA}.

Sturgeon were bad luck to see {mi 11}, but its flesh was eaten near the mouth of the Cowlitz. They come up as far as Kelso naturally, where they used a bait of smelt and salmon, but they can be seen as a bad omen anywhere.

Dried sturgeon was traded from Bay Center or Grays Harbor. [Famous sturgeon hunters there were Putsenay, a Hoquiam shaman, and Cosmopolis Pete.]

Sturgeon = [cf. spánw'əł K1244] L'vq[+c]xq[+u] {mi 11}. Bad luck to see it. A little girl was fishing. A sturgeon came close. She and her uncle died right then, her 2 brothers later. She did not know what it was. One was described to Mrs. Iley that they got in the fall. They gave it to a grandson to show to the grandfather, but he urged them, "Put it back. It is a Boogey." That spring, the grandson died. Sturgeon is bad luck whenever it is seen.

Way down toward the mouth of the Cowlitz, it was eaten. It comes up as far as Kelso, but they never see them above Kelso. Unless it was bad luck, then they would show themselves anywhere. At Kelso, smelt was used as sturgeon bait, or, 2-3 on a hook, to catch salmon.

Lamprey "Eels"

Pacific Lamprey (*Lampetra tridentata*, locally called "eels"), so important to the Chehalis and other tribes, including Cowlitz and the Yakamas, have been largely ignored in print. Lamprey ( ) pass along the Columbia and Cowlitz Rivers, and through Grays Harbor on their way up the Chehalis River, where they are taken at certain narrow riffles associated with families and at Rainbow Falls. They also spawn in the Skookumchuck. People know to look for them when big carpenter ants appear. They usually swam toward Rainbow Falls on the first day in May to reach 80 degrees of temperature.

Two kinds are distinguished by Chehalis: day eels and night eels. Those swimming at night ($ʔaq^w s$) are bluish silver, bigger, and are taken at Rainbow Falls, especially while

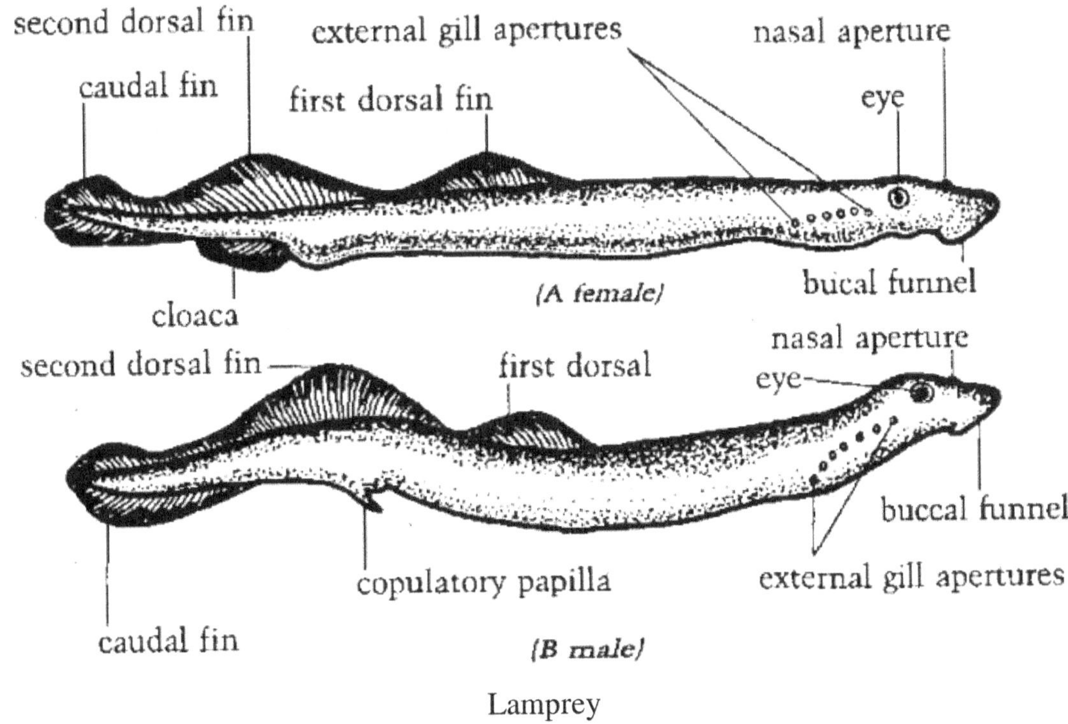

Lamprey

resting in two deep holes in the rocks left there in mythic time by Coyote (Speelyai). The day eels ($k^w uṗa$, meaning "old man") are dark brown, taken at riffles (Kinkade 1991a: 215). Wayne Barr, a noted Chehalis "eeler," only uses a gaff hook for eels to give them a fair chance to escape (just like giving a fish a chance "to spit the hook"). Other native fishers use dip nets on long handles to take dozens at a time.

According to Peter Heck in 1927, eels (lampreys) go upriver at night. Any lampreys that traveled by day were no good. They were caught below Dryad at the dark of the moon using a

105

pitch torch, mostly in April when the new leaves came {ph 102 ThA}. They were caught by hand, with five fern roots across each palm for traction, and bitten below the eyes to snap the backbone. The use of knives was forbidden. Eels were sometime caught from a platform built across the river. Franz Boas (notebook 10: 606) recorded the word for such an eel platform as *kwa•xuntEn* [cf. kʷaxʷntn K618].

Franz Boas (notebook 1, p1′; notebook 4: 199) learned, in 1927, "*agᵘs* = eel (he is younger brother of spring salmon)", while *kupa* are black or daytime eels, which were caught and wrapped up for good luck and medicine after being dried. In 1942, Emma Lucier told JP Harrington (reel 17, frame 0720) "where the bridge just this side (s.) of piyell [Pe Ell] it was full of Indians [unreadable word] in shovelnose canoes. They have to catch those eels at night time & put moss in hand to grasp, & the next day they have to smoke them."

Mary Iley added that eels wanted to be cooked with their head off. The cut-off heads were roasted on sticks. If you throw a head far off, it will live for a long time. If you throw it close, it dies quickly {mi 5 ThA}. From Oakville up the Chehalis River, the stick was put through the eel's mouth; maybe from Oakville downriver, the stick was put through the neck {ph 38 ThA}. Eels were dried on sticks, up to 10 eels on each. Mary Iley's father never ate eels because they were like his power.

The actual wording from notebooks of ThA for this summary is as follows:

Eel said {mi 5}, "When I am cooked, leave my head off. Throw the head on the stick. If you throw it far off, it will live for a long time. If throw it close by, it will live only a short time. If they eat me well, not mash me before eating, they will live."

If Taytnapam throw me up, can't [go] through head or mouth. Go [through] any excrement?? No eels on the Cowlitz. Eels up in Taytnapam country in the Fall. Father said, "Do not eat eels." My aunty said, "Never mind, it is food. That is his spirit power ['əxt-kʷliš K93]. Just he did not eat it. It wasn't really eel, but so nearly like it that he couldn't eat it because this power was a person when he found it. One person could not eat another, so my aunty explained. It was [cf ʼuqʷa K156] *sik'vlxaiyo* = snake.

Eels {ph 34, 39}. From Oakville up the Chehalis River. The *saqan*? [stick] was put from the mouth straight through the body, back to the tail. Perhaps, although this is not certain, from below Oakville, the *saqan* was put from his neck back through the whole body. There were at least 2 rules on the Chehalis river. Heck does not know from where the 2d one [of these rules] begins.

Eels {md 139 27 July}, cont from No 20. When they stretched the net, Robert, Clarence, Sam Smith, Mrs Y[ouchton], and Bertha, nobody lucky to get salmon, only Sam Smith. 1 or 2 every night, the only one. Bertha said, "Well, Sam Smith, he is awful poor and nearly dead *sa sa* [*xaaxa* ?], clean, no intercourse with his wife."

Eels. Same way with hunting salmon or for anything. Some doctors are celebate [celibate]. Must not have intercourse.

Women had their own designs for slicing and hanging eels to make them look pretty. In August, eels were big and spotted. Eel oil was used to soften and water-proof moccasins. [Today, as noted, both day and night eels are caught by gaff or net.]

Eel Life Stages

These fish are parasites, without stomachs or bones, using suction-cup-like mouths to attach onto fish or sea mammal to feed after the tongue has filed a hole through the skin. Once full, the eel drops off and the wound heals. Lamprey have a fossil record of 500,000,000 years (Clemens and others 2010).

The Columbia Basin hosts three species: Pacific, western brook, and river lamprey. Each has two large eyes, one nostril atop the head, seven gills, and two dorsal fins. A lamprey goes through several life stages. It hatches from the egg as an ammocoete (blind larvae) living in freshwater silt and gravel for four to seven years by filter feeding. During these years, it metamorphoses into a macropthalmia (smolt-like with eyes and toothed mouth disk) to emerge from the river bed, migrate into saltwater, and become a lamprey over two to three years. Once mature, they return to freshwater streams (July to September) to spawn, moving upriver by swimming and resting by sucking onto rocks. Like salmon, they do not feed during this migration, and die after spawning. A mated female lays 10,000 to 200,000 eggs in a shallow nest made by the pair whisking their tails and moving small rocks with their mouths. Pacific lamprey are dark bluish-grey when they arrive in freshwater, then turn reddish brown when spawning. These color changes are basis for their Tsamosan names.

Like salmon, lamprey populations have declined due to urban development, habitat destruction, water pollution, forestry practices, and dam blockage. Commercial uses of lampreys included raw-ground hatchery food, vitamin oil for livestock and poultry, and scientific research into medical anticoagulants. This commercial fishery for lampreys began in 1941 by harvesting at Willamette Falls, which later became the first TCP in Oregon because of its ongoing cultural associations with native Pacific lampreys.

Shellfish

Chehalis got clams from Mud Bay, dug by both men and women, dried over a fire on a stick, then strung on cedarbark for transport and storage. Oysters and mussels were eaten fresh, not dried {ph 107}. Freshwater clams in the Skookumchuck River were not eaten by natives because they were transformed villagers who capsized while going across.

Meat

A hunter sang his spirit song before starting out. He had to have proper power and respect for it by taking sweat baths and rubbing his body with cedar or fir boughs {gs 114}. He could not eat fresh meat before hunting. In August, all the hunters in a place might agree to go on an elk hunt for several days. A boy went along to serve as messenger. They got enough for a whole winter supply on one trip, killing up to 20 elk.

Pits were dug into trails to catch [trap] deer or elk. Fences were built for deer drives {ph 78}. Elks were hunted in the fall along the North River. Many small hunting canoes were left there for men to use {ph? 79}. They were also hunted along the Satsop, the Skookumchuck, and in the mountains near Boisfort {ph 335}. Elk tallow from the foreleg was like candy {ph 335}, but Silas Heck preferred that from the thigh. It was also used to keep the face from chapping and for greasing guns.

Deer were butchered by removing the skin, cutting off the legs, taking out the insides, saving the blood, and slicing up the flesh to eat fresh or to dry. Liver, heart, lungs were saved {md 51, 166}. A piece of the deer was burned in a fire for the hunter's spirit help before the rest was eaten. Mary Heck's husband would burn the ears {sh 151}. Bones were cracked with stone maul for their marrow. Blood and fat was used for soup, along with backbone segments. Meat from the head was eaten only by men or old ladies. Brains were saved and used for tanning.

Bears were butchered in the same way. Their blood was made into a soup. Hides and grease were valued, but the meat was rarely eaten except as a strictly personal preference because consuming this animal might pass on some of its traits.

Before a woman healer recited dicta [power words] during a cure, she rubbed bear oil on her hands and touched the afflicted body part [of the patient] she wanted to relieve {md 183}.

Bear skulls could be placed as a path by someone with power so a stream or river would then make a shortcut {md 183}.

If a wounded bear attacked a hunter and he squealed like a woman, high and shrill, the bear would not harm him. If he screamed like a man, he would be maimed ("chawed") or killed. It was best to shoot a bear through the heart {md 190}.

Skunk grease was used to treat a boil or headache. This meat was sometimes roasted and eaten.

Mountain rat intestines were cooked and eaten in the fall when they ate grass.

Chipmunks were eaten by Taytnapam, but Chehalis children only used them for hunting practice {ph 252}.

Beaver meat was a favorite boiled {ph 23}.

Seal meat and oil-filled stomachs were traded from Grays Harbor and eaten with dried sturgeon {ph 284}. Seal oil was drunk only by Taholah Quinault, Lower Chehalis, and Bay Center Chinook {ly 130}.

Not eaten in the old days were dog, rabbit, muskrat, fox, wolf, mole, or mice {ph 254}.

Birds

Eggs of duck, pheasant, and grouse were eaten {ph 107}.

Mallards were hunted at Chehalis with bow and arrow, later guns, and then roasted or boiled. Black ducks came only to Mud Bay [and Grass Creek].

A net, over 10 feet high, was hung across a riffle for ducks and geese. People ate the meat and saved the feathers for pillows and blankets. The five duck feathers worn by women with a certain spirit were selected at that time. Duck-wing feathers were good for arrows {md 191}.

Pheasants [actually native grouse] were snared while drumming on a log (mating), lured by a decoy made of moss. The bird became jealous of a rival and choked in the noose {ph 108}.

Crows, bluejays, or smaller birds were never eaten.

Thrush brought the rain so if one was killed and thrown in the river, it would storm.

Hummingbird nests brought luck. If a hummingbird hovered around a girl, the old people said it was measuring her for a dowry. The buzzing meant "one string, two strings, and so on."

Yellowhammer (a flicker woodpecker) feathers were used on boys' arrows {ph 292}.

Cranes or storks [these are introduced species, but this may be a local term, perhaps for geese] used to nest at Grand Mound and the Nisqually Delta {md 189}. They flew in a V led by a captain. Children ran underneath them praying, "Leave me a big salmon backbone," so their families would not starve that winter.

Larks were avoided because if a child struck one, he or she would never stop quarreling. A quarrelsome woman was called a "lark" {ph 251}.

Pigeon, called "crying bird," was eaten but not preferred. The very first one had been a person who lost all his children and cried and cried until he became this bird.

Eagles were killed for feathers. A big doctor always had on [wore] a fine wing feather from an eagle. Eagle spirit was good for hunting, gambling, curing, and war.

Hawk was the leader of all the birds so people left it alone.

Plants

Berry patches were burned over every two or three years to get a continuing good crop {ph 73, 79; ly 124}.

Berries were picked into baskets lined inside with leaves {mpw 96}. Each fall, everyone went to pick in the mountains. Old women picked the first ones and held a feast. After everyone brought their dried berries back home, more feasts were held, served out of wooden troughs {js 132}.

Red elderberries were "canned" in soft baskets shingled with layers of maple leaves {ph 270} and kept fresh by being submerged in a slough, where thieves sometimes poked for them.

Raspberries and blackberries were made into a dried cake that was sliced up during the winter for meals.

A girl at first menstruation (M1) held a "bridle" stick, loosely tied behind her neck, in her mouth, while picking berries so she could not eat any. Old women later inspected the stick for stains, just to be sure {sh 140}.

Strawberries were so abundant at Grand Mound that you could smell them drying on a hot day.

Only women dug and prepared roots, while the men gambled or held foot or horse races {ph 69}.

Sword [probably bracken] fern roots were used for medicine, and ground up for flour. Fronds were used to spread out berries to dry or for wrapping camas to roast. The roots were charred, scraped, pounded up, and sometimes mixed with salmon eggs, or baked overnight in a pit {ly 127}.

Wild rhubarb, carrots, camas, and sunflower roots were baked for storage. Wild sunflowers, growing at Rochester and Grand Mound, were sometimes used to make a sort of root beer. Tiger lily roots were gathered from prairies in the fall and boiled {md 56}.

Acorns were gathered, baked in a pit, and eaten with salmon eggs. Some were buried in the mud over the winter. They were bitter if the tannin was not leached out.

Nuts were collected in the fall, but people had to be careful to say, "There is just one nut" in front of a treeful or the crop would disappear.

Camas (*lackamas* in Chinuk) were dug from marshes, steam baked in a pit, and dried or ground up for storage {ph 72}. Often camas was baked overnight, mashed into a loaf, and dried to be sliced up during the winter. Blackberry cakes were used the same way {ph 69}. A M1 gave her next dug camas to an old woman for luck, otherwise she would be eating up [shortening] her own life.

Spruce roots were dug up for making baskets.

Willow roots were ground up fine to make tinder for starting fires {ly 124}, and the inner bark began to be used for basket trim, dyed black, instead of using rope or a quick, convenient twine.

Wild cherry bark was used for a tough binding, especially on salmon spears {md 190}.

Alder bark was chewed to make an orange-red dye. In 1927, though, people did not want to chew it, so they pounded it with a hammer and soaked it in water {md 183}.

Moss was gathered and cleaned to use as diaper stuffing {ly 125}. Catnip leaves were put on a baby's head to make it sleepy.

Blossoms and flowers were to be avoided by children because they were said to belong to the ghosts {js 132} since they bloomed in the spring when ghosts were leaving and so could take a soul away {sh 140}. [The worlds of the living and the dead were reversed, so winter here was summer there, an active time for them. Spring flowers came as ghosts were leaving and so could relay "hand off" a soul, particularly that of a vulnerable child as ghosts went off to their winter.] New cedar saplings were the same way. If berries had a second crop or lasted into the winter, these too belonged to the ghosts.

Lilies and wild cherry blossoms were people long ago who transformed in a graveyard {mi 325}. Early white lilies were the worst [most dangerous] {mi 325}.

Though not mentioned in the notes by ThA, the importance of cattails was brought out by Mary Kiona (1953: 24, 30) in her land claims testimony. "they used to trade salmon, camas, berries, meat … and various things. They used to trade like woven rugs they used to make out of barks of trees and cat tails from these swamps and different places … they used to use those cat tails that grows in the swamp. They used to use that for food."

Seasonal Labor Parties

In the spring, everyone fished the runs and dried salmon for the winter. They used weirs, traps, nets, gaffs, spears, and arrows.   The nets were made from nettle fiber and were dyed to match the water color of a stream. During the summer, they harvested roots, berries, and nuts. Men went hunting in the fall, particularly for elk, then for deer and bear. During the winter, families holed up in plank house towns.

Families owned weir sites. A shaman blessed the finished construction. The Sanders built theirs at Klaber below Ceres {gs 115}. One man could put it up alone after they had axes and saws. In the old days, they needed a work party, treated to a big feast, and all could thereafter share in the catch. The weir was built with many small poles of maple or fir tied with cedar or hazel. A 25-foot cottonwood log braced the back. Builders used it beneficially in turn, but others had to return some of their catch to the group.

Houses were also built by work parties. The ground was dug out and leveled before the bunks and walls were built inside the depression. Racks were constructed along the sides to hold mats, foods, and goods. Planks were made from cedar using elk-horn wedges, yew wood mauls, and stone hammers, preferably by someone with Carpenter power. Then the planks were adzed and planed, before being floated down the river to the construction site. Sometimes, the wood was gathered in the spring, seasoned all summer, and used in the fall.

The chief looked over the building to make sure it did not impose on others. The house should reflect the status, position, and class of the owner. At Grand Mound, the town went across the prairie to the present state [reform] school. Sanders had a "living room" house there, and another for cures "like a church." White homesteaders later destroyed these house remains.

In February, everyone had to be very still; all loud activities were forbidden and taboo {mh? 206} because the earth was sleeping. The best food providers remained celibate (chaste) during a fish run or hunt {md 166}.

Burnings and Warnings

Prairies and berry patches maintained their productivity due to regular burning over by Tsamosans. Ritually prepared by sham battles, boys set these fires in August and during winter under the direction of the chief. Presumably this activity gave warning to resident species before their home range was set ablaze.

In this tribe here {mi 325}, the chiefs in month of August compel the Indians to burn the prairies, to make the grass grow well, the strawberries plentiful, and blackberries.

Sham Battle. August, before burn it. Boys compelled to have sham battle. Used to get bunch grass 2 or 3 feet high. Used to make a bow from bunch grass. Cut the stem, which is hard, fix sharp point, then the boys will advance upon each other, naked, going to sting each other with the straws, the weakest side will retreat, or the one who is hurt most will loose [lose]. Might last 1/2 day or day. Might do this several times before burn the prairie. Warriors, boys, and whole tribe of boys compel the commons. And again in the winter, when bunch grass is gone. 3 or 4 times in winter time. Use clam shells, little necks, plenty on each side. Advance to firing line, throwing clam shells which curve. Don't go straight. Hurts when hit. Boys were compelled to do it, were made to do it. Throw shells when get close. After retreat, will chase each other until clam shells are all gone and their [there] (before his grandfather's time) were many boys, several divisions of tribes. Tribe became small. Sometimes the boys will be here too because were friendly, and other divisions that were quite friendly.

Elsewhere tribes used games and competitions as a way to transfer youthful vitality into the soil to boost the sprouting of plants.

POTLATCHING

Reasons for hosting a potlatch included a) raising in social position, b) giving names, c) saving face (removing disgrace), such as after being thrown in a wrestling match, d) piercing the ears of a girl, and e) returning a favor {sh 147}.

People with spirit power hold small potlatches every winter when they sing in public. At big gatherings, 4 men and 4 women were appointed to help, and a special repeater (song catcher) made sure that the words and tunes of each song were correct. At a big winter spirit dance, communities would come in groups with a leader who came in backwards when he danced them in. The best kind of leader was painted in stripes and acted funny like a clown. The women who followed him each had a painted face, wore 5 white duck feathers stuck on top of her head, was wrapped in a shawl, and shook bunches of deer dew claws hung from a stout cane. Everyone there helped a person sing his or her own song, like at gospel hymn sings.

The dancing paused at midnight so everyone could be fed, often salmon skins stuffed with salmon eggs. Some were boiled and some baked nice and crispy. Hosts passed out spoons, with important people getting bigger ones traded from the Chinooks; others brought their own. After several nights of dancing, gifts were given out before all left.

Important or royal families held small potlatches when their first child was born and a daughter became M1.

John Heyden, Jim Walker gave last potlatch {ds 263}. Pierce was agent then, just one gave it, Heyden. Walker helped him, they gave money away, perhaps $1500, gave [to] them to have just a good time, and "Nat[urally] believed in the family." Does not think a man would need to "borrow" money from his friends. When call a whole lot of different tribes and anyone in his tribe will help, that is anyone who can afford to.

In old times, a chief who gives a potlatch will always be called, and they'll always make up for what [he] gave, and he'll never be out anything at all. A great man always gives a big potlatch, and he'll always be known as a man who has given and will be called the 1st thing when visits another tribe, a visiting chief would take his whole tribe, exactly as return baseball games.

The maker of the house {ph 71}, carpenter = [putəs potlatch K1290, sa'a make, do sa'aax^w make house K1690.10, sa'pa'tsn' potlatch house maker 1690.14b]. taixit n = Potlatch Heyden. Last potlatch house, Heck was a little boy, perhaps 50 years ago. Later used "shakes" boards, 2 or 3 feet wide, split it. Spliced boards, long time ago to make so long. Perhaps 200 feet long, lots of tribes came. All joined in, put it up together. "Others" costs lots to give away, never thought they'd go broke, never feel that they were going broke, just the same as ever. Celebration took perhaps 5 days. Just pierced her ears, that is all. Heyden kinda a chief. Came from "just the same as those people in England." Each boy and girl out of chief, got to be a chief. Same as royal people in England, queen and all that. Heyden had just one wife, law forbid others. One man s k' mm n had 4 wives, most Heck remembers of any one in Chehalis. Common man, this fellow. Chief Cinitiya died before I was born.

Gifts were always given at a funeral. The more important the deceased, the more elaborate the potlatch. These were also held at reburials (renewing graves) and for memorials. The person, known for this special power and strong lungs [to hold his breath], who moved the bones, was paid with many gifts {ds 368}.

A person could advance their social position by saving and hosting a potlatch. A Lower Chehalis woman, "of no known family and a long ways from being pretty," gave a potlatch to earn more respect than most people of royal blood.

If a royal boy or man had a baby with a slave, the family hosted a potlatch to make the infant into a "person." Even so, that individual was always regarded as tainted and at least half slave {mi 14}.

Upper Chehalis had different words for giving things away, with or without spirit powers involved ['ax̱ʷa throw K61, kʷəɬ divide K624, 'umal give K149, aɬč given K426, čis come K524]. Intertribal potlatches were held rarely because they were so expensive. A special large house had to be built and people fed for 5 to 10 days.

The most famous historic potlatch, about 1870, was hosted by Chief John Heyden, half Oakville and half Tenino, helped by Jim Walker, a second chief of Oakville, by Charley Walker of Oakville, and by *Ulipanx"*, half Quinault and half Upper Chehalis. It was held in the oak grove about 70 yards from Secena's house {mi 14}. People were invited from Grays Harbor, Cowlitz, Skokomish, Puget Sound, and all over. It was held to have a good time, but the formal reason was to mark Heyden's daughter as M1. Jim Walker took the name *swtwpc*, from a Puget Sound [Swinomish, swdabsh] ancestor.

Potlatch. {ph 74-5} Some fellows, 2, 3, 4 of them, not just one, to give the things away to some other tribe or some other people. Davis {md 56} does not seem to know much about the exchange. He seems to think they gave a number of potlatches here in the old days.

John Heyden was head of the potlatch. He was 1/2 Oakville and 1/2 Lemicilos. 2d chiefs were Jim Walker = Oakville, a little below Olympia, just this side of Johnson's Point; Charley Walker = same; and U lipanx[+u] = 1/2 Quinault, 1/2 Upper Chehalis.

I {md 57} was a small boy at that time, it must have been 57 or 8 years ago. All gave it together, about 70 yards from Secena's house in the Oak Grove. (Reason - just to have a big time, so they could be called big men.) As people from Billow [Below ?], Gray's Harbor, Cowlitz, Puget Sound, all over that way. Those people who came from way off, would have to give a return present. Chehalis people were also present, not much information forthcoming here.

Jim Walker {ph 74-5} when named, he wanted to be named a dead man's name, joined with John Heyden. Save lots of presents when they called him who he was going to be. Was middle aged. Named him a Sound name. Sw-twp[c] feels that just one name was common, if took mother's name, other would be cancelled. Just big man gave away presents when named, common people "just got names, that is all". Common people just give away little things to buy a girl, that is all.

Messengers were sent out ahead with sticks to invite important guests, who used the sticks to count the days until they were due to arrive. Invitations were serious business because someone might be left out, offended, and take revenge through sorcery or hostility.

At a Nisqually 4th of July gathering, Marion Davis was once denied food and took his revenge by killing his biggest Durham steer and feeding everyone. John Smith, an Upper Chehalis Shaker leader, reminded everyone never to get Davis mad at them {md 193}.

At Taholah potlatches, everyone was fed blueback salmon until they could eat no more. A chief with eat-all power could do this without ill effects. Sometimes, they fed guests whale grease or poured it into a fire. This grease was very valuable. Such conspicuousness was important at a potlatch.

At Centralia, women were given shiny tin plates that they waved around to attract light {202 mh?}. This potlatch was held to pierce the ears of a young girl. It was held in a potlatch house built by 2 men. Mary Heck's father held the girl's head, singing a spirit song twice, while 4 holes were put in each of her ears.

Another big potlatch was held at Westport, just this side of Damon's Point, so everyone could meet the dying son of the host. The family was royal and wanted everyone to remember this boy. So many people came that they overflowed the house. People, especially children, who performed got clothing as gifts which had been piled around the boy. The Westports were rich in silk and cloth because so many ships and steamers went aground there. Old Secena got a bolt of ribbon, pinned one end to his hat, and let the rest stream behind him as he rode horseback. The ribbon flew far behind him very pretty. The boy died after everyone left.

At public feasts men ate first, then the women. At a potlatch, people ate by community, both men and women together. The host ate last of all, along with everyone in his family who helped serve {ph 294}.

Lower Cowlitz?? {ly 111} Heyden brought bones of Kemol&mx kʷəntal'uc'ɬn Queen Susan, *yawnvs* Lizzie Johnson's sister, buried other side of Chehalis. And he brought them here to Grand Mound, hired 2 or 3 men to dig them 4 out, brought it to Grand Mound. He put it all in one coffin, and then gave away lots of things and money. Was related to Queen Susan, an aunt, and uncle to Yawonis. Tsnitia was not alive when Yawonis was made chief. My father's grandpa related to Yawonis. Cati, son of Tsimtin. Cati was alive when Yawonis became chief. All the people related to Yawonis made him chief so to protest against whites, so would not be moved from their territory.

John Heyden. was kind of a chief, daughter probably 9 or 10 when ears pierced. Some people pierce ears when 6 months old, Sometimes at 3, would give-away lots of presents away at the time. Cowlitz did it both for boys and girls. Old Mr. Youckton had pierced ears, would give name at same time as ear piercing. give presents and food. Usually give names at same time that ears pierced. Some had *tahmanawas* names, my father gave my sister a *tahmanawas* name, not many *tahmanawas* names. If someone can sing *tahmanawas* then would give his children *tahmanawas* names, but if not *tahmanawas*, would not call *tahmanawas* name.

Silas Heck's *tahmanawas* name was ts'ɑmmi•ps 'old wolf with hair only on his sides' [K: 336 A7], probably from his father.

TSAMOSAN

Tsamosan (from its names for the numbers 2 and 4, formerly called Olympic Salish) is a subgroup of the Central Coast Salish branch within the larger Coast Salishan language family. Its four languages have coastal and inland subgroups. Coastal includes Quinault-Queets and Lower Chehalis; inland includes Upper Chehalis and Cowlitz. Upper Chehalis included three dialects – Satsop, as well as Downriver and Upriver splitting at Grand Mound. Upriver used back of the mouth sounds (k k̓ x), where downriver used front of the mouth ones (č č̓ š) in the same words. For example, the word root for "slender" is *čema* for speakers downriver and *k̓ema* for speakers upriver, producing variants for a 'narrow trail' such as *čemašuɬ* and *k̓emašuɬ* (Kinkade 1991a, 40 #502).

Upper Chehalis call themselves *q̓ʷay̓ayiɬq*, based on *sq̓ʷay̓ayiɬ* as the name of Mud Bay at the head of Eld Inlet near Olympia, and the suffix -q indicating 'language.' Further, the familiar Kamilche is a place name that is only analyzable in Upper Chehalis as *k̓e•m-* 'narrow, slender' + *-či* 'water' with an *-iɬ-* connective to accurately describe this slim arm of Puget Sound. Another place name near Shelton on Oakland Bay is the Chehalis (and Proto-Salishan) word for red cedar (*catawi*), distinct from the name for this tree in Puget Sound Lushootseed (*xpay̓əc*) or in Hood Canal Twana (*q̓ʷili*). In this way, place names and other grammatical forms provide a linguistic window on the ancient history of this region. Place names, unlike excavations, say softly what is locally inherent in the Earth.

Over time, some sounds from proto-Salish (the ancestral or parent language) have changed in Tsamosan. For example, Quinault and Coastal Lower Chehalis (Copalis) shifted from protolanguage word-initial sounds of *y to ǰ and of *w to gʷ. The most distinctive feature of Tsamosan among the whole Salishan family is a contrast between long and short vowels, which carry grammatical information (like choose/chose indicate verb tense in English).

Tsamosan Consonants

p	t	c		č	k	k̓ʷ	q	qʷ		stops, afficates
p̓	t'	c̓	λ̓	č̓	k̓'	k̓̓ʷ	q̓	q̓ʷ		glottalized
		s	ɬ	š	x	xʷ	x̣	x̣ʷ	h	continuants vl
m	n		l	y		w			ʔ	resonants
m'	n'		l̓	y̓		w̓				glottalized

Tsamosan Vowels

Upper Chehalis has 9 vowels, plus consonants x and g.

i	e	a	o	u	ə	short
	ee	aa	oo			long

Quinault has 7 vowels, plus consonants ǰ and gʷ.

i		a		u	ə	short
ii		aa		uu		long

Lower Chehalis uses Upper Chehalis consonants and Quinault vowels

Tsamosan vowel locations within the mouth cavity

front [i] to back [u]
high to low [a]

i   u

ə

a

Pronunciation of these sounds follows that of these same English letters. The rule for linguistic or technical writing is that each distinct sound have a single distinguishing letter.

č = ch

š = sh

ə = is a neutral or midrange vowel like that in the middle of the word "but".

ʔ = glottal stop is the pause in the word uh-oh. It is more of a catch or space than a sound.

' = glottalization adds the constriction of the flap at the back of the throat (glottis) to make hard sounding versions of plain letters t' instead of t.

ʷ = Raised W means the lips are rounded when the sound is said, Kʷ rather than plain K, with Q said farther back in the throat than K.

More complicated sounds for English speakers are back X, barred L /ɬ/, and glottalized barred Lambda /ƛ̓/.

The barred L /ɬ/ is said with the tongue tip at the ridge behind the upper teeth making air flow around to the sides of the mouth. The sound is like that in the middle of Catholic [kaɬək] or athlete.

Appendix B

Place Names

Gray's Harbor
Rivers, Creeks, Streams, and Features

North Side

  North Bay

   James Rock aka Neds Rock, Lone Rock, Point New, Brackenridge Bluff; shoreline there is
     named = ɬəmiṁ jm 86 44

    Humptulips = xʷəmtulapš < /apš/ 'stream' B04 175

    Chenois = čənus, name of a Lower Chehalis leader B04 93 ; qi'əsqal'ʔux jm 86 44

    Grass Typso Creek

Hoquiam = x̣ʷəqʷyamc < x̣ʷəqʷ- 'hungry' + yamc Douglas fir, wood = driftwood 'hungry for
     wood' B04 173

Fry Creek chominim jm 86 42

Wishkah = xʷəšqaɬ̓ < xʷəš- stink + qaɬ̓ water = 'stinking water' B04 572 . Its epic legend is
     treated at the start.

Wynoochee = xʷənuɬč B04 576

Camp

Sylvia Creek

Satsop = sacapš < /sa'a/ 'make, do' + /capš/ stream = 'made stream'   B04 422

Newman crk

Mox Chehalis < Chinuk Wawa 'two, twin, double' + Lower Chehalis 'sand' B04 299

Porter

Gibson

Shelton

Cedar

Black

  South Side

   South Bay

    Andrews R

Elk River Nushiatska jm 86 40

117

John's < "Uncle" John Hale land claim, Wilkes called it Dinsmas River. H85 138 ; two cabins, burials, prairie above high tides jm 86 39

Beaver Creek camas beds jm 86 40

Stearns Bluff aka Roundtree Point, Judsons Point, Crabappale Point, Jones Point, South Arbor jm 86 39

O'Leary plankhouse and weir jm 86 39

Stafford < a settler. Wilkes called it Typha Creek H85 267

Indian

Chapin

Newskah = "good water", with tidal weir nearby

Charley

Blue Slough

Preachers Slough < 1859 transit of Rev JS Douglass, a Methodist Episcopal. H86 240

Stevens

Elizabeth

Workman < settler, aka Mason's Creek

Delezine

Eaton

Gaddis

Riverine

Chehalis River mouth from Cow Point to Cosmopolis = nsulapš

Cosmopolis = qaysalməs

Elliott Slough

Coastal

Quinault < k̓ʷinayɬ B04 405

Wreck

Moclips = nəẃmuɬapš shortened B04 292

Joe

Elk

Boone

Copalis = k̓ʷpils < /-ils/ 'rock' B04 121

Connor

Oyhut

"p'αstαn [Bostons, whites] gave the name ʻoˑyhαt, which is jarg [Chinuk jargon] for trail, mg [meaning] in appl [application] to this place [is] trail to go down to the beach. Mr. Daman gave this name.

At Oyhat was one long house, like a row [inside], in which the Sampson John family lived. There were a large fam. [family] of them, & all lived in 1 smokehouse. Mrs Mary Sampson, wife (widow), died in the hospital at Hoquiam three months ago. Tony (my son) took me in the car to the funeral at Hoquiam, internment in Hoquiam graveyard up the hill in Hoquiam. She talked Squally – her mother was Oakville and her father was a whm [whiteman]." R017 f622

Wishkah The name is a distortion of the Indian word Woosh-kla, meaning "stinking water" or "stink river." Indian legend relates that a whale swam some distance up this river and died. Hitchman 85, 335

Lit. stinking-water, name of the Whishkah River of the map.

Acc to a story Thunder (s.ḥαnαs) got a whale in the ocean & dropt it when flying with it & the whale traversed the river & after a while the whale got rotten & made the water stink. Ams [Americans] call it Hoshka ca.

The water of that river stank so that nobody drank it. Later on when I [JPH] asked the name of Aberdeen, she [Emma Millet Lucier] gave me the name of this river.

There was just Thunder, thunder along that river all the time, many trees struck by lightning, & it was that Thunder tensing [??] to fly & catch a whale, & once the Thunder went & got a whale & dropt it & it landed by mistake right across the river & Thunder tried to get it out of there, the whale rotted there & the water dstr [downstream] of there tasted from the whale, & the Inds had to move away from there. This was <u>long</u> ago. R017 f624,

That is where Thunder dropt the whale f565, 590.

Appendix

Legends of the Wiskah and Hoquiam Rivers
Seattle PI Sunday 10/15/1905

The name Wishkah, although musical to the ear, has a repulsive translation, meaning "stinking water." The name is accounted as follows: Many, many moons ago, long before the white man first appeared before the startled gaze of the Indiens , a tribe of Chinook Indiens , under the paternal care of the great chief Yac-a-la-da, flourished at the headwaters of the Wishkah river. Their location was a choice one, being a little savannah, sloping gently to the water's edge, behind which the heavily timbered hills rolled back towards the unknown eastern country.

Its slopes doted with the lodges of the tribe, and the children played among its meadows.

Yac-a-la-da was a great chief, and a good one; a father to his people; wise in counsel and great in battle. Under his fostering care the tribe grew and prospered.

The young braves were mighty in the chase, bringing in much game for the squaws to dress; the rivers teemed with fish, which supplied their daily needs; and luscious wild fruits and berries grew in abundance during the lovely summer season, which the squaws picked and of which they prepared and put aside a store for winter use.

All was going well with the tribe and there was not a thought or premonition of the evil soon to befall them.

But one fatal day a small peck was discerned coming towards them, through the clear, blue sky, and as it gradually became clearer and clearer, it was discovered by its eager watchers to be an immense bird, bearing in its talons a great fish, which it was carrying to its aerie to feed its young.

The fish, which was still alive, was writhing, and squirming in the talons of its captor, who suddenly lost hold upon it, and it fell across the narrow stream that formed the headwaters of the river.

There it lay until the fish became putrid and poisonous, so contaminating [B] the clear waters that all who partook of them became ill. So a dreadful pestilence fell upon the people; there was no lodge which did not contain the sick and the dead; and the tribe became almost extinct. The small remnant left, sorrowfully pulled down their lodges, loaded their canoes, and sadly sought another dwelling place. As they passed down the beautiful river, winding among its curving banks, they kept time with their paddles to the plaintive measure of the "death song," sung by the squaws in melancholy tones.

The noisome smell of the infected stream so impressed the savage mind that the name of "Stinking Water" was given to it; and it was shunned as a thing abhorred. To this day no Indian will dare paddle his canoe on its surface, though they are frequently seen on the Hoquiam river, only a few miles away. History relates that a great many years ago there was a fearful scourge of smallpox among the Indians on the Wishkah river, and the legend probably had foundation in fact.

120

Appendix B

Native Tsamosan Place Names*
In Upper Chehalis Region

Places names appear in Appendix A of the <u>Upper Chehalis Dictionary</u> (Kinkade 1991a, 329-355), with those relevant to the Study Area extracted below and retaining their number in that sequence.

#

1 nsúlpaš [1763] Chehalis River

39 ƛaqáyqɬ [951] Mound Prairie

40 ƛaqá•yqɬ [951] west end of Mound Prairie

41 ʔiɬtáĺs [110] north part of prairie on edge of Rochester called wəxe•uws #44, Little Rochester Prairie

42 sxwá•qw [2257] rock at 'Star'

43 ɬačís [818] 'star' at Grand Mound

44 wəxé•uws [2154] prairie around Grand Mound

45 n os [1227] creek dividing Grand Mound Prairie

46 siyǽt'k'o [374] "stick Indian", sasquatch, prior name of Bucoda

47 niné•naẏɬ [1195] Hanaford Swamp

48 sxasáʔɬmaqʷm [2318, 1054] Wauch Prairie

49 náčalɬ [1155] Lincoln Creek

50 máqʷmaqʷm [1054] "prairies" Galvin, on Lincoln Creek, west of Chehalis

51 tá•ɬṅčšṅ [1881] Ford's Prairie "resting place"

52 té•ẇtṅ [1960] Skookumchuck River "fording place"

53 aL'aqauus [186] Centralia

54 mə́qa [1089] China Creek, Centralia

55 Pawak'um staleon [1349] little prairie on railroad south of Centralia 'pawakm station'

56 nəwé•k̓ʷĺšn [1185] Salzer Creek "medicine creek"

57 laik ! ut [809] prairie south of Centralia

58 nsšəʔúmš [1820] prairie north of Centralia "weeping prairie"

59 suq̓ʷə́h [1771] prairie across the river from Centralia, where the ʔilawiqs band lived

60 kwɑlɑ́xwàṅ [680] Chehalis town "where the trail came down"

61 Poisał [1322] "bent lake" lake below Chehalis []

62 náwaqʷm [1168] Newaukum River "big prairie" for wild carrots & camas

63 nɑwq'u [1232] south of Newaukum

64 la tc' t [736] prairie north of Napavine Cowlitz lák't

65 napawən [1230] Napavine

66 nə́xʷċaɬx̣ [1187, 310] Newaukum River, south fork "crawfish river" {Quinze Sous R}

67 x̣wɑ´t̓ [2425] Newaukum River, North Fork

68 xwɑxwɑtʊ´xwɑxwɑtʊ [2425] Little North Fork

69 xatxato [2342] swampy prairie near Newaukum

70 łak̓ʷítu [821] Claquato, prairie south of Chehalis

71 malɛ [1147] person-looking rock near Claquato

72 kᶜtoicʋn [583] two or three miles above Claquato

73 mítiɬxʷ [1110] Bunker Creek

74 qʷasúqʷaʔ [1576] hill north of Klaber

75 łačáyqs [817] Thunder Mountain, towards Klaber

76 tsamatx [303] Lake Creek

77 ċax̣ʷápn [332] near Klaber

78 ná•wmaqʷm [1168, 1054] prairie at Klaber "big prairie"

79 pʊhpʊh [1351] north end of Klaber hop field, fishing place

80 t̓á•lalɑn [2024] Boisfort, upper Willapa

81 wápu [2121] < French pronunciation of Boisfort

82 Slōsĭid [?] Rainbow Falls

83 tɬ'ɑx̣x̣à [1031] Doty Prairie

84 swa•l [2189] Klaber, Pe Ell tribe ethnonym <swaal>

85 q̓ʷaláwc [1643] Pe Ell

86 ts'ɑx̣wa•'sɑṅ [333] Pe Ell "roasting place"

87 ʔípxʷáṅmcxṅ ʔaɬ x̣ʷən [2389] hole in Chehalis River 1-2 miles from Pe Ell "hiding place
    of xʷani"

88 ła•ts'q̓ɑnɑyʊ [934] Willapa

89 q̓ápnɬ [1510] Winlock "blueberry plant"

90 káwlicq̓ [559] Cowlitz River

91 našḱwa•naxt [683] Lackamas Prairie

122 nsúlapalucn [1763] mouth of the Chehalis River

* key to this list

= number on place name list in <u>Upper Chehalis Dictionary</u> (Kinkade 1991a: 329-355)

[K] = Kinkade (1991a) dictionary entry number

[K:] = Kinkade (1991a) dictionary : page number, column A or B, number down

" " = literal translation ' '

Place name sources: Kinkade 1991a, 329-335; Hitchman 1985; Bright 2004.

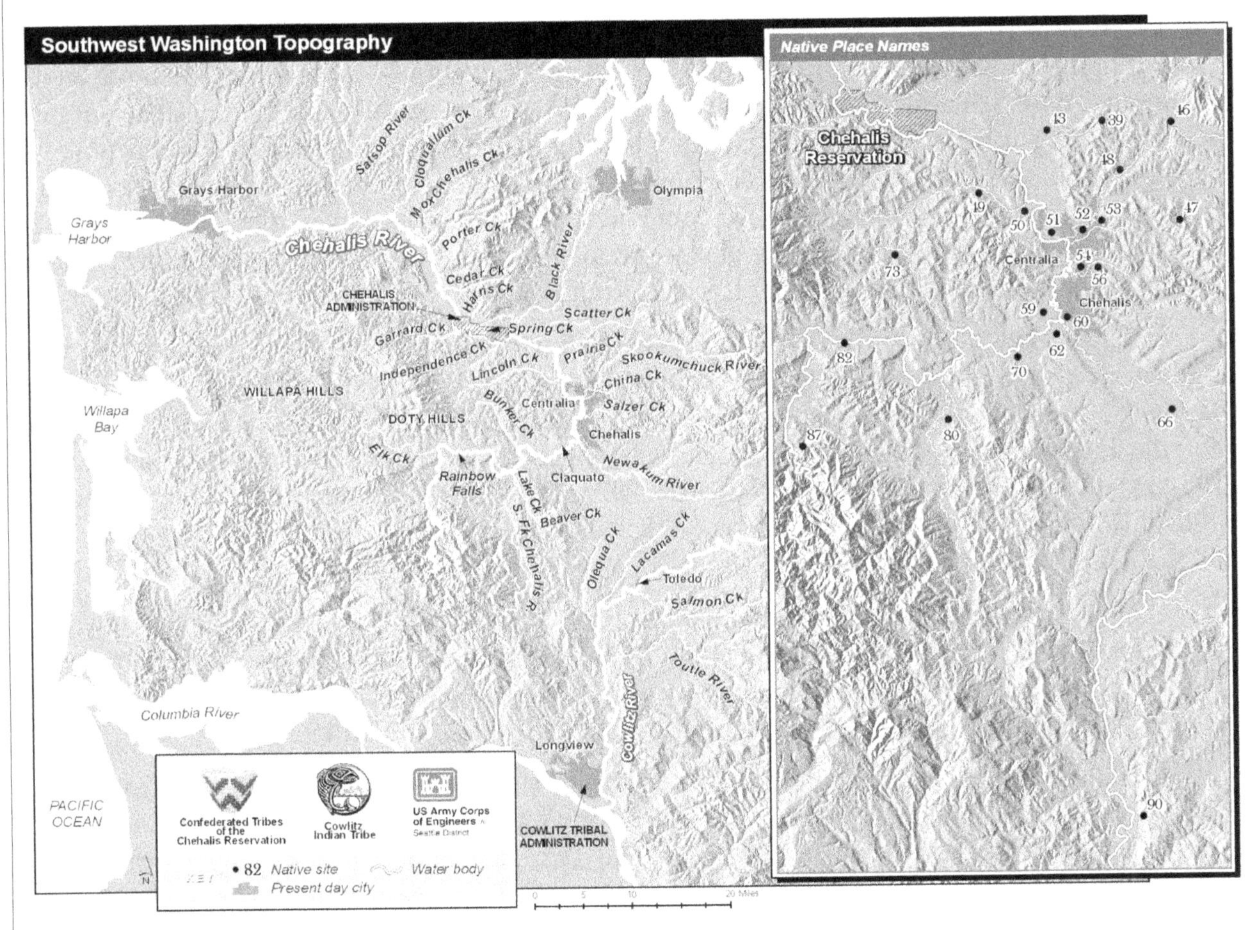

Appendix C

Missing Misp[h]:
Restor(y)ing the Transformer of Tsamosans of coastal Washington

Abstract

Virtually unknown among Northwest Changer ~ Transformers is Misp[h] of the Tsamosans in southwest Washington. As twins born miraculously to a murderous mother, they destroy her ogress sisters, save nebulously-formed children, and decree skills, foods, and customs at specific places and times. Their living embodiment is a duck – once call old squaw (old swawk), now longtail – with appropriately complex changes in bright plumage by season and gender.

Introduction

The major loss, academically, from the life-long institutionalization of Thelma Adamson after her fieldwork among Tsamosan Salishan speakers of Southwestern Washington has been the continuing failure to recognize Misp[h] as a major transformer in the oral literature of the Tsamosan Coast Salish of Southwestern Washington. As a graduate student, Adamson spent 1926 collecting folklore among the Upper Chehalis at Oakville, followed by a concern with ethnography in 1927, when her mentor Franz Boas joined her to conduct linguistic research at the same community. Her dissertation, completed, approved, but never filed in May of 1929, was a study of transformers and tricksters among Coast Salish. Her supporting folklore collection was published, through the efforts of Ruth Benedict, in 1934 and reissued in 2009.

Salish oral literature is particularly well known because of the sustained efforts of linguists and storytellers concerned with recording in these natives languages, as well as the interest of internationally known scholars and folklorists (Walls 1987), such as Franz Boas, Melville Jacobs (1959, 1960), Dell Hymes, Dale Kinkade, Arthur Ballard (see all), June Collins (1952b), and Vi Hilbert (Miller and Hilbert 1993, 1996, 2004), as well as popular collections (Matson 1968, 1972), culminating in a recent Salish compendium (Thompson and Egesdal 2008) and the Adamson reprinting.

This reissue makes more available the epic of Misp[h] and his brother Kumol told by Lucy Heck (pp. 329-432), a noblewoman from the Lower Chehalis of Grays Harbor. Earlier, among Quinault, Livingston Farrand heard versions of Misp[h] from Bob Pope in 1902. Ronald Olson learned it from Billy Mason, Bob Pope, John Dixon, and Jonah Cole in 1926.

The earliest reference found so far appears in a letter, dated 20 July 1855, from James Swan at Shoalwater to George Gibbs, who asked for word lists of various native languages of the Northwest. Swan's source seems to have been Old Toke, a Chinook leader living at Tokeland on Willapa Bay, now the location of the tiny Shoalwater Bay reservation. The six page letter includes stories of Thunderbird, the Smisspee (duck), the winds, and customs and religious beliefs of Indians from Columbia River to Nisqually. Smisspee is obviously Misp[h], as explained in this extracted quote from page 2:

> The Smisspee is a small duck of the Sheldrake species and the only tradition about it that I have heard is that it was formerly a man or as the Indians express it they were "ankartz Tillikums" [*ahnkutty tilakums*, past people]. This bird came to the ?ema? [Nemah] River in this bay when a great many Indians lived and seeing the river full of salmon asked why they did not catch them. The Indians replied they did not know

what salmon were, and were afraid of them. The Smisspee then showed them how to make nets and spears and they took immense quantities of fish. And from this bird all Indians learned to catch fish.

Quinault creation, according to a cultural and economic overview by Justine James and Leilani Chubby (2002, 99), involved three distinct epochs, each with its own reformer. At the beginning was Xwani Xwani [X^wani X^wani], then came the protean Animal People, and third, setting the stage for the time of human people, was Misp^h – the culture hero ~ transformer ~ reformer.

Misp^h and his twin, in particular, did much to form present Grays Harbor, and coastal Washington state. He was a key ancestral figure for Tsamosans. While other regional reformers are well known, such as K'^{w}ati of the Quileute and Makah, Misp^h is not. In part this is a consequence of the fate of Thelma Adamson. Thus, Misp^h has remained unheralded for seventy-five years.

Such great epics of Native American can easily be misunderstood by mainstream readers because they teach by negative examples, rather than extolling the rewards of virtue or financial success. Presenting these stories in English voids many of their nuances. The idioms used in the native language explicitly indicate what is real and what is not, what is worthwhile and what is greedy, or what is good for everyone and what is selfish. By the end of these epics morality, decency, and community values are instituted, not always in the easiest or safest manner.

Only at the end of each epic are Misp^h and his brother identified with their duck avatar – the immature male in winter plumage most like a "long-tailed", once also known (among 20 local names) as "old squaw," though "old squawk" is more appropriate since its species Latin name *Clangula hyemalis* refers to its noisy clanging in winter. Though attributed to the female, it is the male which is the most noisy. This species is remarkably apt for a transformer since it is so changeable, going through two complete annual bright plumage changes, unlike the bright and dull ones of most birds, as well as gestational ones. It can also dive to 200 feet deep. Its diet is also human like, relying on mollusks, crustaceans, insects, and aquatic plants.

To aid in following the epic versions, a generalized condensation of versions follows:

An industrious young man (Wildcat) camps alone, either drying fish or making a canoe. He soon becomes backlogged, while continuing to gain more materials. One day, while he is away, his work is done for him. After several days of this unknown help, he hides to see who is doing it. A young woman appears who then marries him. They live together until the fishing season or canoe is done and then go back to his home town. Before they get there, she lets down her hair to hide her face and, once inside, sits backward looking at the wall. She lives quietly in the house, tormented by Bluejay who wants to see her face and hear her laugh. When she can endure no more, she hides her husband, pulls back her hair to reveal a frightful face and laughs five times, killing more people each time until everyone is dead, even her disobedient husband. She eats all of them, but saves her husband's genitals in a basket above her bed. She becomes pregnant and has twins. The oldest one is Misp^h, the other Kəmol

The twins grow quickly and precociously. When their mother leaves for the day, they do everything she had forbidden them to do, finding their father's parts in the basket and his former town littered with gnawed bones. Alarmed, they go home to burn down their own house and flee. The mother sees the smoke and ash, including a bit retaining the design on the side of her cherished basket. Angry, she rushes home, finds the smoldering ruins, and chases after her sons.

They trick and kill her, then move on. Along the way they meet and kill her four sisters, each of whom kills children (unformed souls/spirits) in a special way before eating them. Each aunt is gutted and the more recently dead children are revived and given professions that are thereafter passed down family lines. They go from town to town around the Olympic Peninsula, decreeing livelihoods and abilities specific to each community. Near the end, the brother is killed and revived as a duck, while Misp[h] becomes a stone at the mouth of the Columbia River. Their spirits return as ducks in the late Summer.

Since the motivation of Misp[h] and his twin is to make the world ready for today, the epic by Lucy Heyden Heck is summarized next because it is the most detailed one known and would have been the basis for Adamson to properly highlight the importance of Misp[h]'s role among the Coast Salish.

The Reformer Twins

paraphrase of Lucy Heck to Thelma Adamson (1934: 329-342)

Chief Woodpecker lived in a town of twelve houses at present Humptulips City. He was a skilled carpenter who built all the houses and many of the canoes. His son worked with him, so as to master woodworking. When it came time, the son was sent alone into the forest to make his first canoe, and his father insisted that no one was to help the boy. He had to succeed on his own.

The boy selected a cedar tree, felled it, and began shaping it until dusk when he returned to his camp for the night. The next day he shaped the inside. When he came back on the third day, he found a big camas bulb inside the canoe form. It was tied with a long black hair. Surprised and suspicious, he hid the bulb in nearby brush. The fourth day, two bulbs were in the canoe, each tied with a long hair. On the fifth day, there were three bulbs, and on the sixth, four camas and elk marrow used for a protective greasing (sun block) of the face. When he returned the seventh day to rough out the canoe, nothing was there. Instead, he worked for a while until he became sleepy and took a nap inside the canoe.

He dreamed a pretty girl with very long hair was sitting beside him, asking why he did not eat the camas she brought to him. She pledged her love to this boy of royal blood. When he awoke, she was actually sitting there and they agreed to marry. She said she lived upriver, but would move to his town as long as it was after dark because she was very bashful.

Just outside the town, the girl unbraided her hair so it hung over her face. Inside the house, she sat with her face to the wall. At bed time, she slept beside her husband in the chief's section. The next morning, she again sat facing the wall with her hair down, weaving a basket. She ate her meal of camas in the same position. Ever nosey, Bluejay began to mutter about this overly modest behavior. When he got no response, he kept insisting to see her face and hear her laughter. He kept this up for five long days.

The fifth morning, the wife asked her husband to go with her far beyond the prairie while she dug camas. Instead, when they got there, she dug a very deep hole and told her husband to hide inside it. She stuffed his ears and nose with fine cedar bark, covered him with a box, and left him in supposed safety. Too curious, the husband raised the edge of the box, waiting to hear her laugh.

Back at the house, the girl began to dress up, braid her hair, and grease and paint her face. Then she went to Bluejay and said they would now laugh. She clapped her hands together and shouted. Bluejay fell over dead. As she continued laughing out loud, everyone in the house died, their eyes bulging out and tongues lolling. She went house to house in the town, shouting and killing. Then she started at one end and ate everyone up.

When she went to find her husband, he was dead. She wept. Then she took his torso, put it in a basket, and hung it over their bed at home. During the night, the basket shook. The next morning, the girl was pregnant with twins, who were born five days later. The elder was Misp^h and the younger was Kmol. Two days after birth, they were walking and using bows and arrows. She favored Misp^h and always threatened to eat Kmol if he cried. After five days, they were men. Each day their mother left to dig camas, warning them not to look in her basket nor go downriver.

They became suspicious and looked in the basket, identifying their father's remains. They went downriver and found his village, littered with skeletons. They knew the worse and decided to flee from home. They burned their house and walked away, with Misp^h behind his brother in front. Their mother sensed something was wrong, then saw ashes in the air. One cinder showed the design pattern of her basket, and then she realized her home had burned up. She raced after her sons, singing a song to weaken them. They prepared for her attack by climbing to the top of a tree covered in loose bark, praying to the tree to hold on tightly to its own bark. The tree gave them special words (dicta) to grip onto its trunk. When their mother saw them in the tree, she spoke softly and nicely to lure them down. Instead they suggested she climb up, telling her the special words. She did not always remember them so she only got up slowly. Near the top, Misp^h pushed the bark with his foot and it fell off and crushed their mother.

They climbed down and went on, knowing they had four aunts who were cannibals like their mother. A prairie, named Seated Children, near Humptulip City had a stepped slope filled with children, who were known as "Always Tears" because they were crying, dirty, and fearful. At the bottom were two trees leaning together with a swing between them. Further out was a huge bloody rock. Those children warned the twins that the woman who lived on the prairie would eat them.

They greeted their aunt, and she asked after their mother. They said she was slowed by a heavy pack and would be along soon. Their aunt tried to get Kmol to swing, but Misp^h took his place, teaching the children instead to chorus "Go and Come Back". Misp^h jumped off the swing beyond the rock and survived. He told his aunt it was her turn to swing, urging the children to sing "Go and Never Come

Back". She hit the rock and died as her belly burst open. The twins revived the most recently dead children, but those longest dead stayed dead. The uneaten children were washed, dressed, and painted. They were told they would live there to become very old. Those who revived would live to middle age, while those (pre-souls) who stayed dead became stillborns.

The twins went on until they came to a prairie where they saw a pile of dirt covered in clam shells, shaped like a seated child. Five wide seats behind this figure were filled with children. The men greeted their aunt, and she asked after their mother. They said she would be along. The children explained that each was sent to fetch a stick standing near the figure without laughing, but he or she always failed, was dashed against the rock, and eaten. Misp^h fetched the stick soberly, then said it was the aunt's turn. She laughed, so he grabbed her by the heels and dashed her against the rock so that she burst open and children's bodies tumbled out. The most recent victims revived fully after they were washed and cleaned, but those longer dead were slower to recover. Some never did. These children founded royal-blooded families.

At the next prairie, children were speared as each came to sit on a large fungus. Misp^h sat but was not harmed, so it was the third aunt's turn. He speared her heart and threw her against a rock so her belly burst open. Again, the most recent meals were revived, but those longer dead were less lucky. These children became spirit helpers for hunting (Hunt power).

The twins went on to the prairie at Carlyle, where they met the fifth aunt, who killed children with a boy's game of see-saw that had a flat rock at either end. The aunt and Misp^h got on the teeter-tauter. He jumped off when she was on the high end and she burst on the rock below. Victims were cleaned up and revived, founding a community of hunters, both men and skilled women.

At the mouth of the Humptulips, where they decreed the building of fish traps, the twins resolved to right the wrongs of the world. They went westward, coming to a house where people were shooting arrows inside. It was raining and no one there knew how to fix leaks in the roof. Instead, they shot arrows at the drips to try to stop them. Bluejay spoke for the household, explaining their tactic. The twins went up on the roof and saw that the shingles were placed the wrong way, so they set them right and the leaking stopped. All subsequent roofs were built this way.

They went toward the shore and came upon a house where Bluejay and his wife were cohabitating on the roof, so the Twins decreed modesty in the future. Further up the beach, clams were stuck on sticks to cook in the sunlight. Instead, the twins taught people there to cut out the clams from the shell and cook them on sticks over an open fire.

They went on and, at the surf, met a man walking upside-down carrying firewood between his legs. They set him upright and instructed everyone to carry firewood on the right shoulder. Farther up the coast they came to a house where they heard groaning, "Ouch, my head; Ouch, my hand." A man was splitting wood by driving the wedge into the log with his head. Instead, Misp^h made him a stone mallet and gave instructions still followed to split wood. People there tried to cook their food by dancing on it. The brothers told them to get their nets to catch salmon, but the people instead got digging sticks for clamming.

At Corner Creek, they met a man sharpening the edges of three big clam shells and singing about how he would deal with the reformers. Instead, Misp^h stuck the shells in his head and butt, turning him into a deer to be hunted to feed people. At Copalis, they met a man being dragged into the sea by his own head lice. The twins washed his hair in urine and rinsed it in fresh water, killing the lice. Then they carved him a comb that was made of wood, and taught him to comb, oil, and braid his hair. Finally, they called for people to bring out their salmon nets, but instead they got their clamming sticks. Ever after, they have clammed there.

At the Rocks, Wolves were eating raw crabs. Misp^h tried to reform them into proper people who cooked their food, but they asked to remain as they were and so became five brothers consisting of four Wolves and a Dog. At Moclips, they taught proper sex technique to the people (especially modesty and respect by girls). At Rock Creek, they found a deeply sleeping man and attached clam shells to his front teeth. He became X^{w}ani X^{w}ani [active in a later age]. At Taholah, they called for people to bring out their fish gear and they did. As a reward, the twins taught them to make tight basket traps. Farther on they found empty houses, and following the stream [Raft Creek] there came to a suspicious whirlpool. They heated rocks in a fire and dropped them into the water until it began to boil. A huge black being with an enormous mouth floated up and they cut it open, finding whole families, canoes, and houses. Those most recently killed could be revived. Among them were Bluejay and X^{w}ani X^{w}ani, who decided to repopulate that locale using skin rubbed off Misp^h and himself. They blew on the exfoliate pellets and they became people, gifted with a special fish trap.

They went on and shouted for people to build fish traps because they already had fire, good houses, and tools. But they were dirty, so the twins taught them to bathe and groom. At Quileute, they shouted for fish traps but instead people launched canoes and ran out trolling lines, as they still do. Feeling threatened, the twins ran away and decreed the Quileutes would be mean. At Ozette, they also called for fishtraps, but some went into the hills to hunt and others went out to troll. They did everything properly.

They went on, calling for fish traps at each town, but some just went out to sea, others embraced warfare, and some developed other skills. At one town, they cleared away rocks creating a whirlpool and so killed a monster.

When they got along the Columbia River, at Clatsop, they called for fish traps but instead people caught crabs. Clatsops were confirmed in their royal blood. At Astoria, people came out with their nets and received runs of huge Chinook salmon. Across the river, people were drying sturgeon heads on warm rocks, but the twins instead taught them to smoke sturgeon. Further on they met people who did not know how to eat, putting food into every body orifice but the mouth. They were taught to chew and swallow, as well as drink. They then had to teach them how to sleep and to use a net.

At the next town, people packed everything they had and then went to sleep, thinking that was how things could be moved. Instead, the twins taught them to pack things up and move them by canoe. At Fort Columbia, everyone had a huge snake as a pet. If they did not feed these serpents enough, they ate children. Misp[h], instead, arranged to kill all the snakes and burn them up on a high hill, where the place where he sat to rest is now marked by a rock shaped like a duck.

At Chinook City, the town was infested with woodrats, who ate people alive. The twins set fire to the area, killing all the rats and enabling people to set out their nets. At Ilwako, people had their nets and used them well. At Nasell, they called for nets, but instead people went out to hunt or to hook sturgeon. They had no fires and had to be taught to use firesticks and to cook. At Nemah, people went out to hunt or built small salmon traps. At Bay Center, people brought out herring traps. Then the twins went across the bay and met people spearing salmon.

At Westport, people got crabs and clams, and the twins decreed "A whale will always wash ashore here; you are good people [and deserve it]". Further on, people at Ts'e'tc hunted elk and were decreed to have royal blood to establish the chiefly families of the Harbor people. At Mulla, people hooked sturgeon. At Hoquiam, people hooked sturgeon and set out herring traps. At James Rock, people had herring traps and boxy canoes. Instead they were taught to make proper canoes. At Owl, people ate gophers and changed into these night birds. At Chinoose Creek, people kept their herring traps and sturgeon hooks. At Cold Water, people caught only silver salmon.

Finally, they returned to the Humptulips, where they started and decided that they would finish by becoming a kind of duck that arrived in the middle of the fishing season. Before they came, salmon had to be prepared in a very strict manner, using a sharpened clam shell to gut the fish and separate head and tails from the body. After these ducks arrived, people could prepare fish in whatever manner was convenient. These are river ducks that are always in pairs, like the twins, that go north in the spring and arrive back in the fall.

Conclusions

Restored to the scholarly record, Misp[h] and his twin transformed the Tsamosan world to be as it is today. Their living embodiment is the longtailed [old swawk] duck, which breeds in the high arctic, and visits coastal waters. Its very changeability makes it an apt representative of Transformers ~ Changers who prepared the world for the humans were "coming soon".

Clangula hyemalis   Clangula clang, noise   Hyemalis of Winter

Appendix A: Roster of Old Squawk Duck Names (Terres 1980:197)

Calloo	John Connelly	Old Wife	Scoldenore	Swallow-tailed duck
Cockawee	Long-tailed	Old Molly	Scolder	Uncle Huldy
Coween	Old Billy	Old Injun*	South Southerly	Winter Duck
Hound*	Old Granny	Quandy	Squeaking Duck	

*Hound references its baying cry
*Old Injun for its travel single file

BOB POPE

The place where I first came to myself was at the village of *nokedja'kt*.   There were three houses there at that time.   In one lived the village chief *sa'utonux*; the second was owned by *tci'tamin*; and in the third lived my father.   These men were heads of their houses, but there were several families in each.

In those days people wore only robes for clothes.   It was customary to bathe each morning the year round.   Almost every night there was singing and dancing in one of the houses. Usually the only food was salmon, salmon eggs, and potatoes.

From that village the people of all three houses moved downriver to *t'o'nans*.   Soon afterward there came an epidemic (smallpox?) and most of the people of the village died, and only a few of their descendants are alive today.   We used to come frequently to the village of *kwi'naił* to gamble at slaha'l.   Here we would meet people from Queets and Grays harbor. Sometimes a game would last for several days.   Gilbert Sodomic's father once lost everything he owned — even his dried salmon, even to the last kettle of salmon that was cooking at the time, and the kettle as well.   When the Queets and Chehalis had lost all they had they would send back to their relatives for more.   The women would also gamble with beaver teeth dice.   Doc Hays Otuk's mother usually won at this.

The war between the Queets and Quinault was before my time; they were living in peace ever since I can remember.

When I first started to hunt I was just old enough to handle a gun.   At first I hunted only ducks with a flintlock.   Later on I killed a deer; then a bear.   The first big game I killed was two elk.   After that I often went to the mountains with other hunters and we killed all kinds of game. I also trapped for furs.   At that time there was a trading post at Wynooche and we went there to trade furs and hides for whatever we needed.   We would come down the river by canoe, then go by horse down the coast to Oyhut, then by canoe to Wynooche.

In those days the old people of my village were able to get a young man a wife when he was about fifteen.   They bought me a wife and soon I moved downriver to *no'skałan*.   There I lived for a long time, hunting and fishing for a living.   When I had collected enough property I began to think, about giving a big potlatch.   This was the beginning of my potlatching.   But the idea was not from my own mind, but my "property guardian spirit" told me to give it.   To my first potlatch I invited the Queets tribe.

About that time many of the Quinault were invited to a potlatch given by the *djołodjol* (a Nootka tribe).   The Queets, Hoh, and Quilleute were also invited.   On the way we passed one village where there were only women and children.   All the men had been drowned while hunting seal.   At the potlatch only blankets were given away.   The white trader had a large store full of blankets.   He had been there so long he could speak the Nootka language.   Most of us were given nothing, even after coming so far.   Chiefs were given two or three blankets each.   We were fed only rice, with dried halibut and herring eggs.   The next year eight of us went to the same place again to invite them to a potlatch that Chief *Taxo'la* was giving at *kwi'naił*.   It took us two and a half days.   The first day we got as far as Neah bay.   There was a southwest wind and we used a sail.   Near that village is a dangerous place.   One can go between the island and the mainland only at high tide.   Outside the island is a great monster that sinks all canoes and ships.

I have heard that the whites have tried every means of killing it but never can. [This is Devil's pass?]

Across the strait from Neah bay we stopped at a village where a potlatch was being held. Ten tribes (villages) had been invited. When they danced they used two houses, for not everyone could get into the one. A middle-aged man was the host, but he did not give many presents. It was mainly a feast. He had a whole house filled with pilot bread. Chief *Taxo'la*'s younger brother (who was married to a Makah woman) was given nothing, and his wife received only a tin pan.

At Neah bay there was a canoe of *xosit* (another Nootka group) who had come from the north to invite the Makah to a potlatch. But as the Makah were at this other potlatch they were waiting for them. The *xosit* appeared to us to be real savages. They wore only fur robes and their [183] bodies were covered with grease. *Taxola*'s brother asked us if he should give them some food. Finally he gave each of them a blanket. We were wearing red shirts and we took these off and gave them as presents. They looked clean then, for the time being. Then they stood up and danced for us. Their spokesman made a speech, saying they had never before met such good people.

The potlatch which *Taxo'la* gave was the greatest ever given. They built a roof over the space between two big houses and thus made a single house so large one could hardly see from one end to the other (perhaps 200 feet). All the Hoh, Quilleute, Makah, and Queets were there. At that time I saw a Quilleute man with a strange guardian spirit. He came dancing into the house, a curious bird resting on his hand. When he extended his arm it would disappear. When he closed his hand it disappeared into his hand. It was the most real thing of its kind I have ever seen. He was a short man and was naked except for a belt of cedar bark. H e led the Quilleute dancers into the house. It was one of the few times that I have seen a really great medicine man — most supposedly-good ones never did much.

At the same potlatch I saw two shamans challenge each other to a contest. One was a Queets, named *Xwåtå'm*, the other a man from Grays harbor. We liked to see such contests. They went down to the river and dove in. When they came up each had a piece of ice several feet long on his shoulder. They started ashore with it. But the Grays harbor shaman was beaten, for his ice melted before he got ashore. *Xwåtå'm* carried his ashore and up the bank. Then he threw it down and it turned to water and ran into the river. It was not hard ice but was soft and quivered like jelly. Then the Grays harbor man planned to kill *Xwåtå'm* with his power, in revenge for the beating. *Xwåtå'm* was lying across an ocean canoe in the river. The Grays harbor man shot his power at him but missed because *Xwåtå'm*'s power warded it off. But I heard it hit the canoe, and it was so strong it split the canoe from end to end. *Xwåtå'm* jumped up and said, "He missed me!" Later *Xwåtå'm* told his friends, "Now I will try to get even with him for that." Soon he got a chance and shot the other from behind with his power. The Grays harbor man told his friends that the other had "got" him. He no sooner reached home than he was taken ill and soon died. (When *Xwåtå'm* first got his power it was in him so strong that he could walk up to a green tree, seize a limb and tear it out, together with the knot to the heart of the tree.)

It was customary in those days to carry a nearly dead person out of the house and lay him near the grave. Once they had taken out a dying woman. I went over to her to test my spirit power. I saw that there was nothing really wrong with her except a "pain" (disease object). I told her she must not tell anyone if I cured her.

She said, "I am sure not to tell if you do me a favor and cure me." I told her she would not die if I took that "pain" out. Then I took it out and showed it to her and said, "This is the only thing wrong with you; now you will be all right." I asked her to give me a little camas root when she was well. She walked back to the village, bathed, and went into her house.

(That is the secret of some medicine men — they never tell that they have power until they have had a chance to test it. If they find that they can really cure people then they tell what spirit it is they have. But they do not talk about it except when they are curing. If a man talked frequently about his spirit power he would not live long.)

That was the beginning of my career as a medicine man. I knew then that I had power to cure people. It was one of the most real things in my life. Most shamanism is mere playing and contesting at potlatch time.

During my life I never traveled a great deal, only when I was invited to go somewhere to a potlatch.

When it was rumored that some new shaman had a powerful helper, then I used to like to see if he had the real thing. In my time not many men had great power. I know this because I went to see many. Perhaps long before my time there may have been many great shamans. That is all.

Appendix E

DOCUMENTS

Research materials on the SWWA corner are available at the University of Washington Special Collections, Seattle Public Library, Washington State Library, Washington State Historical Society, Seattle USACE, Bureau of Indian Affairs (BIA) Hoquiam office, and Washington State Department of Fisheries. Early references include: The surveys of Robert Gray, George Vancouver, John Work, David Douglas, Charles Wilkes, and the U.S. Coast and Geodetic Survey; the personal research of George Gibbs (1855, 1877, 1970), James Swan (1857, 1971, also McDonald 1972a, 1972b), Ronald Olson (1925-27, 1936), William Elmendorf (1960), Jacob Fried 1974; Verne Ray (1937, 1938), William Rule (1945), Camilla Summers (1978), Herbert Taylor (1974a, 1974b), Thelma Adamson (1926-1927 fieldnotes, also Miller 1999a, book of 1934 and reprint of 2009); and local histories by William Welsh (1942), Edwin Van Syckle (1980, 1982), and settlers Andrew Levitt, Patterson and Michael Luark, Mary Ann Francis Foxwell James Shepard, and John Rogers James (Shepard 1910). Native authorities included Charles and Henry Cultee, John Heyden, Peter and Silas Heck, and others who shared stories with Thelma Adamson, Franz Boas, and Dale Kinkade (Gerdts and Mathewson 2004).

Archaeological work in the area (Ames and Maschner 1999, Roll 1974, Sobel 2004, Thrush and Ludwin 2007, Wesson 2000) includes the important surveys of Jeanne Welch (1973, 1983). At the mouth of the Newaukum River, where there was once a joint community of Cowlitz and Chehalis, monitoring is on-going. Other TCP studies were consulted, along with scholarly assessments (Smythe and York 2009). Local contract work has been done by Cascadia Archaeology (Herbel and Schalk 2002; Schalk, Breidenthal, Stenholm, and Wolverton 2005), AMEC (Rooke, Cooper, and Chatters 2011), and, as damage assessment, at the Opus site by Archaeological Investigations Northwest, Inc. (Punke and others 2009). Of note, AMEC reported the mouth of the Skookumchuck shifted to the south, burying older deposits (Rooke, Cooper, and Chatters 2011, 21, 135, 241).

Early linguistic materials were assembled by George Gibbs (Beckham 1969; Gibbs 1855, 1877, 1970; Stuckley and Gibbs 1860). Later research was conducted by James Teit (1916), Franz Boas (1894, 1901), John Donovan (1963ab, 1964abc, 1966, 1967abc), Isadore Dyen and David Aberle 1974; John Peabody Harrington (1942a, 1942b, 1981, also Laird 1975), Eric Hamp (1966, 1967, 1968, 1971, 1973, 1976), James Hoard and Thom Hess 1971; Robert Jackson (1906), Joseph Jorgensen 1969, Leon Metcalf (1951, 1952a, 1952b, 1955), Wayne Suttles and William Elmendorf (1963), Sarah Thomason (1981, 1983), and Dale Kinkade (*vide*, see all). The unsorted archive at Gonzaga of Verne Ray (1937, 1938) – expert witness in many of the tribal land claims trials of the mid-twentieth century – includes maps, testimony, excerpts, and supporting evidence.

To plot the names and locations of aboriginal groups living in what became Washington State, Leslie Spier (1936) analyzed explorer, settler, and academic sources. For the Chehalis River, he located Lower Chehalis continuously along the southern shores of Grays Harbor, but divided the northern section into "tribelets" associated with its tributaries. From west to east, these were Copalis, Humptulips, and Wynoochee. Linguistically, however, they were all Lower Chehalis speakers, while upriver were the Satsop and Upper Chehalis. Cowlitz and Swaal-Willapa shared the upriver resources.

The Upper Chehalis area, especially around the modern Twin Cities, was a dynamic linguistic and cultural area. People from as far away as Yakama came to Rainbow Falls for eels. Sometime before 1800, some Swaal (sometimes Su'wal) vacated the Skookumchuck for Oregon. "According to a tradition recorded by [George] Gibbs, [Edward] Curtis, and [James] Teit, the Clatskanie ['little oak-ers' in true Chinook] once lived on the Skookumchuck River but migrated across the Columbia where the hunting was better" (Kraus 1990, 530). Their most likely route was down the Cowlitz corridor. These migrants effectively left a gap that drew in Sahaptin speakers from east of the Cascade Mountains who became known as the Taytnapams.

The earlier visual record begins during the period 1845 to 1848, when the Canadian artist Paul Kane (1925) drew images of people, places, and possessions along the lower Columbia River, the Cowlitz River, and Puget Sound (Eaton and Urbanek 1995: 92; Harper 1971: 245). James Swan's drawings (Miles 2007), now at Yale University, include scenes from the 1850s, of the Cosmopolis treaty council and Sidney Ford homestead. Weinstein (1978) provided an array of historical photographs.

Comparative information (Ruby and Brown 1992; Suttles 1987, 1989, 1990, 1991; Suttles and Jonaitis 1990; and Sicade 1940) is cited from Shoalwater Bay (Shoalwater Bay Tribal Community 1998), Quinault (Farrand 1902, Olson 1936), Coastal Oregon (Beckham 1977, 2006; Boyd 1996, 1999a, 1999b), and Tidal Columbia (Ray 1937, 1938; Rubin 1999; Ross 1986; Spier and Sapir 1930), as well as the closely related Lushootseed of Puget Sound (Amoss 1975, 1978, 1981, 1987; Asher 1995, 1999; Ballard 1927, 1929, 1999; Castile 1985; Christy 2008; Collins 1952, 1974, 1979, 1994; Curtis 1913; Duwamish and others 1920s, 1933; Eells 1886, 1887, 1889, 1985; Elmendorf 1946, 1960, 1961a, 1961b, 1970, 1993; Gunther ms, 1925, 1928, 1973; Haeberlin 1916-1917, 1918, 1924, 1974; Haeberlin and Gunther 1930; Harmon 1995, 1999; Hilbert and others 2001; Hunn 1990, 1994; Jacobs 1934, 1959, 1960; Kowrach 1978; Miller 1999b; Miller and Hilbert 1993, 1996, 2004; Norton [vide, see all], Smith 1940a, 1940b, 1941, 1946, 1949; Swindell 1942; Walls 1987; Waterman 1920, 1922, 1973; Wickersham 1898; Work 1912; Wyeth 1899).

Plants receive keen consideration (Gunther 1973; Turner 1975, 1979), as noted by James Swan (1857, 87-91). Important foods were and are evergreen huckleberries, red huckleberries, blue huckleberries, blackberries, black raspberry, salal berries, salmon berries, gooseberries, red elderberries, blue elderberries, cranberries, and strawberries. Nutritious roots include wapato and camas, while "tideland greens" featured Pacific silverweed and springbank clover.

The Tsamosans (Hajda 1990; Wray 2002; see Appendix A) shared with the Puget Salish concern with rank and class, salmon and cedar, and the complex Soul Recovery or Redeeming Rite (Haeberlin 1918; Elmendorf 1935; Miller 1988, 1999b; Waterman 1930), as well as knowledge of the specialized Growler initiations (Elmendorf 1948; Suttles and Lane 1990) and the Indian Shaker Church, founded at Squaxin Island (Amoss 1982, 1990; Barnett 1955, 1957; Castile 1982, 1985, 1990; Collins 1950; Fitzpatrick 1968; Gunther 1949; Richen 1974; Ruby and Brown 1996; Waterman 1924).

More recently, research on Tsamosan was the life work of Dale Kinkade (see all). His fieldwork focused on three Salish languages: Columbian (in the Interior branch), Cowlitz, and Upper Chehalis (both in the Tsamosan branch). In fact, we are indebted to him for almost all we know about Tsamosan (named by him from the words for "two" and "four"). In addition to dictionaries of these three languages, he published over 100 papers, touching on every aspect of

Salish languages, phonetics, phonology, morphology, syntax, semantics, discourse, ethnobiology, and place names. Kinkade (1991a, 155 #2189) also rescued the proper linguistic spelling of the Swaal tribal name from the fieldnotes of John Peabody Harrington, a master linguist. A link with the word Thelma Adamson and Franz Boas cited as the Satsop word for "arrowhead" = .swāāls (Kinkade (1991a, 155 #2174) seems likely because of the strong ties of this group to hunting.

Today, among the most important concerns for native people are the protection of fish (American Friends Service Committee 1970; Boxberger 1989) and of sweetgrass (Blukis Onat and others 2007, 62; Jones 1977). The CTCR are particularly concerned with both kinds of eels (day and night), taken along the Chehalis and at Rainbow Falls, as they swim upriver to spawn. Sweetgrass, according to Katherine Barr, harvested in July is greener than that taken in August, which is more golden. Weavers regard sweetgrass as a special gift, and some object to its sale, preferring that it be shared freely.

Missing in all prior work is any consideration of the lamprey ("eels") that are so important to the Chehalis and other tribes (Robinson 2009; Appendices G, H), including Cowlitz and the Yakamas. Lamprey (eels) pass through Grays Harbor on their way upriver, where they are taken at certain narrow riffles and at Rainbow Falls. People know to look for them when big carpenter ants appear. The eels use their teeth to attach to spawning salmon to feed on oils. Two kinds are distinguished: night eels and day eels. The night eels ($\check{?}aq^w s$) were silvery bluish, bigger, and taken at Rainbow Falls, especially while resting in two deep holes in the rocks left there in mythic time by Coyote. Those swimming in the day ($k^w u\dot{p}a$, meaning "old man") were dark brownish and taken at riffles (Kinkade 1991a: 215, #46, # 653). Wayne Barr, a noted Chehalis "eeler," currently uses only a gaff hook for eels to give them a fair chance to escape (just like giving a fish a chance "to spit the hook" [out]), while other natives use dip nets on long handles to take dozens at a time.

Today, eelers can safely fish only at night because their fishery is in a public park, heavily used during the day. Fresh eels are filleted, breaded, and fried. Others are hung up to dry for trade or later meals. Eel oil has many uses as lubricant, tonic, and medicine, especially for chapped hands, sores, and scabs.

Euro-Americans entered the Upper Chehalis from many directions, by ship, canoe, wagon, and on foot. This area is accessible from the Pacific through its estuary on Grays Harbor, from Puget Sound through the Black River, and from the Columbia River through the Cowlitz Corridor.

George Vancouver, 1792

Captain Joseph Whidbey of the *Daedalus* surveyed Grays Harbor between December 20 and December 26, 1792, during the George Vancouver expedition (Anderson 1939, 1960). He named the northern entrance point for Captain (later Rear Admiral) Brown, the south point for Lieutenant Hanson in command of the *Daedalus*, and Point New after the master of the store ship. His reference to locals speaking "Nootka" implies their use of an earlier trade jargon developed at Nootka Sound on Vancouver Island, indicating Chehalis involvement in the extensive prehistoric trade network throughout the Northwest.

Mr. Whidbey estimated the number of Indians inhabiting this place at about one hundred; they spoke the Nootka language, but it did not appear to be their native tongue …

They seemed to have three subdivisions among them, were not "jealous" of their women, and had war canoes with "a piece of wood rudely carved, perforated, and laced at each end, three feet above the gunwale; through these holes they are able to discharge their arrows, without exposing their persons to their adversaries, either in advancing or retreating. Each canoe held twenty people or upwards … (Vancouver 1798, 82-84).

John Work, 1824

Eventually a mobile, ship-based fur trade moved into land-based forts. The Hudson Bay Company (HBC) bastion in the Northwest was Fort Vancouver, founded on the lower Columbia River (in 1824) to replace nearby Forts Astoria (in 1811) and George (in 1813). Fort Langley was built on the Fraser River (in 1827) and Fort Nisqually in the south Sound (in 1833). These were intended to fortify the British claim to the region staked by the HBC, chartered in 1670. Much of Canada remained under HBC control until 1870 when Rupert's Land was transferred to that nation. The joint claim to Oregon ended in 1846, with Americans crowding into the region over the Oregon Trail.

During the last two months of 1824, in a "weighty rain," forty Hudson Bay Company men (including Iroquois, French, and Hawaiians) went from the Columbia to the Fraser River by a series of miserable portages into Grays Harbor and through the Chehalis and Black Rivers into Puget Sound. Among the group was an Irish clerk named John Wark, better known as Work, who kept a journal. Once in the Sound, on Tuesday, December 7, they went to Steilacoom (later Chambers Creek) to hire native guides to scout the region for likely trading post locations. They hired Sinoughton and his wife, who was far more useful along the way (Elliott 1912).

As they entered the upper Chehalis, Work mentioned the Holloweena or Halloweena, as though this were a different group. However, this is simply the Chinuk jargon word for "different, strange, other", and probably only designated a slightly distinct band (Kinkade 1991a: v).

David Douglas, 1825-1827

Botanizing for the English Horticultural Society, David Douglas lived from 1825 to 1827 at Fort Vancouver, trekking to collect seeds and seedlings for British gardens once these plants were made known to the world by Lewis and Clark (Munger 2003). He first came to Grays Harbor in October 1825, suffering from a swollen leg caused by stepping on a rusty nail, and returned to Fort Vancouver down the Cowlitz.

Morwood (1973, 103-115) has surmised from Douglas's journal that he was cared for by chief Cockqua's daughter, who took him collecting basketry plants. They had a child, but both mother and child died before Douglas returned to London. Van Syckle (1982, 37) gave the name of this chief at Westport as Tha-a-muxi. Trying to reach Siberia by ship, Douglas was trampled to death after he fell into a bull pit in Hawaii (Morwood 1973; also Davis 1980, Capoeman and others 1990: 96-97).

Charles Wilkes, Henry Eld, 1841

While their command ship was anchored off Fort Nisqually (Joyce 2001), Midshipmen Eld and Colvocoresses were sent to survey Grays Harbor (July 19 to August 24), following the Black River route shaped by glacial outflow from Puget Sound. In the harbor, invaluable aid was provided by a noblewoman, Kai-kai-sume-lute, according to Delmar McBride (1972), a descendant and museum anthropologist. She was known for her fine horses and cargo canoes, which she rented to local whites. With pomp and wealth, like others of her family, she was buried on a hill along Mounts Road on Cowlitz Prairie. Though often identified as Chehalis, her parents were Cowlitz and Nisqually, in keeping with the intertribal marriages so characteristic of high-born families. Her high rank made her an effective leader throughout the region.

Luarks, 1850s

The Luarks were a pioneer family from Tennessee. Patterson Fletcher Luark (December 16, 1814 to April 3, 1901, at 87 years) kept a diary (ms.) that mentions the transfer of cattle to Chehalis City, the above-ground burial of a local chief (*tyee* in Chinuk Wawa) named Tehalie ~ Roberts, as well as Lincoln's assassination and Lee's surrender.

11 March 1865 Saturday "last night the tyee here: Tehalie or Roberts died of consumtion [consumption]: acute haveing [sic] dwindled to a skeleton in the space of three months: the remains was duly intered [interred] this morning early in a large box; <u>above terrafirma</u> [emphasis added]: containing four mats, eleven or twelve blankets with various other trinkets. Conner, Joe Hill and I attended with only a few of the tribe: the mourning was limited."

19 April 1865 Wednesday had news of the assassination of Abraham Lincoln and of "Rebel General Lee" surrendering.

22 April 1867 Drove 100 head of cattle to Chehalis (City).

More significant than the Luarks for long-term local history are the James family.

Jameses, 1850s

Emigrating from Cornwall on the southern English coast, Samuel and Anna Maria James were the parents of Samuel, William, Thomas, John R., Richard Oregon, Ann Eliza, and Mary Ann Foxwell. After homesteading upriver at Grand Mound along the upper Chehalis River, two James children settled on Grays Harbor on the east side of North Bay near a landmark they called Lone Rock, but nautical charts named Ned's Rock. It has subsequently become known locally, if unofficially, as James Rock.

John R. James (born in Cornwall in 1840 and died in Grand Mound in 1929 at age 89) recorded his memories of settling on North Bay in 1857. He later moved to a cabin that established the town of Hoquiam.

In Spring 1857, James built a flatboat scow (14 by 45 feet) to take livestock downriver.

Walter King … an old time Mississippi flatboat operator … navigate[d] the craft to tide water 30 miles below [Montesano]. Lines cast off; away we drifted; the first craft to navigate Grays Harbor for carrying livestock.

Mary Ann Foxwell James Shepard (1910) recorded her own memoirs of those times, including fascinating interactions with the native community. Good relations with local natives included visits, gifts, and observations on women's skills.

> ... we made a treaty with the Indians for our land – Father always recognized that they were the rightful owners of this county. ... Father took flour, sugar, salt, calicoes, and lots of beads as a present. [p7]

> women [were] weaving mats and baskets; some were spinning yarn from wool of mountain sheep and goats and this is the way they spun: they held the wool in one hand and with the other hand rolling it into coarse yarn, upon their bare knees and thighs. You would be surprised to see how evenly they made the threads. These were woven into small blankets on a rude wooden frame. Much of the wool was gathered in the fall from mountain thickets, torn from the sheep as they broused [browsed] among them. [p8]

> The old Chief replies through his son that the tract of land we had located upon was ours forever, and he was our friend. Then he spoke to the girls, who went to one of the numerous [p9] trunks and took out some very pretty blue plates and wooden spoons, giving each of us a plate and spoon; then from a clean-looking basket one of the girls emptied into our plates a lot of fine salmon berries, and then Oh dear! From a blue and white jug she poured over them whale oil. We simply had to eat some of them so we picked and nibbled away.

> The old Chief was greatly pleased with Father's presents and told us to come again.

She mentions various types of canoes, ranging from smaller "ducking" [duck hunting] canoes to huge Chinook ocean canoes. When only the James women were home, three canoes of Makahs came to their beach selling sea otter pelts ...

Regard for the James family at Grand Mound figured in a major event in the life of Marion Davis (told to Thelma Adamson, see next section explaining the citation style {md 161 ThA}), when an unusual dream came when he was coming from Centralia and took refuge in the James family barn. It was late and he was wet and cold. He went to sleep but was awakened by a song. He went to find out who was singing and saw a rooster jumping on the ground and singing. He learned the song and went back to bed. Another night, he listened to a pig speaking in the Grays Harbor or Lower Chehalis language about Davis being a carpenter.

Claquato

According to Adamson notes, Claquato was a training and contest goal for young nobles. Upper Chehalis were from Cedarville to Lequito {ph 296 ThA}. Boys and men practiced weight lifting with boulders. Some, as at Lequito, were specially prepared. Towns or tribes would challenge each other at weight lifting, foot racing, or wrestling. Boys ran far as part of their training. Before dawn, a royal boy should swim and then run from Rochester to Lequito and back {ph 111, md 188 ThA}.

In 1852, Lewis Hawkins Davis left Indiana and homesteaded Claquato (said by locals to mean "high prairie" in the Chehalis Indian language, though "across finally" is more accurate and probably refers to the Moon epic). He built a sawmill and insisted all early buildings benefit the community. Among the first was a Methodist church (45LE236), the first Protestant one north of the Columbia River, in the late 1850s. A court house was finished in 1862. Davis died in 1864 after a fall at his mill, and the town dwindled after it was bypassed by the Railroad and Chehalis absorbed its political and social roles. It was removed from county records in 1902 (Johnson n.d.; Pearson 1955, 20-21).

Esq. Davis called his prairie Claquato, an Indian name for high land. A road was cut through the heavy timber by the settlers, from the prairie to the mouth of the Skookumchuck, and other roads radiating from this point made Claquato a very pretty little town – nature having been lavish in her adornments, the scene was of picturesque beauty. For a number of years Claquato was the county seat of Lewis county. A half mile of heavy timber separated us from this little town. An overflow from the river caused the road, for a time, to become impassable (Judson 1984 [1925], 143).

The Claquato church cemetery continues in use, grown from a small parcel donated by Davis. The first burial was a girl in 1856, followed by periodic expansions. In 1893, the International Order of Odd Fellows platted a five-acre cemetery tract nearby. In 1927, local women formed a Women's Auxiliary to beautify the site, and a water system was installed, bringing irrigation water up from the nearby Chehalis River. Also in the 1920s, a "Baby Rose Garden" was established to offer a quiet spot where infants could be laid to rest, and parents could fine solace and comfort. In 2006, the Cemetery Association generously supported the installation of an Oregon Trail marker on the grounds of the old Claquato church, thus demonstrating the Association's ongoing interest in area history.

Centralia

According to Peter Heck, native activities continued at Centralia after it was founded, and people learned boxing and horse racing. Horse Races were held after these animals were traded from east of the mountains {ph 110 ThA}. Both horse and rider fasted and thirsted for a few days before a race. Heavy bets were made, including slaves and clothes. There was a race track near Centralia {ph 297}.

At a potlatch at Centralia, women were given shiny tin plates that they waved around to attract light {mh? 202}. This potlatch was held to pierce the ears of a young girl. It was held in a potlatch house built by 2 men. Mary Heck's father held the girl's head, singing a spirit song twice, while 4 holes were put in each of her ears.

In her land claims testimony, Mary Heck provides context for her remarks to Thelma Adamson: "where the city of Centralia is located now was a large village, composed of 10 houses, and in that village was located what they call now a potlatch house – what you might call a community hall, where people get together and entertain other tribes" (Duwamish and others 1933: 535).

Located halfway between the Columbia River and Puget Sound, Centralia has the advantage of location, as well as being at the confluence of the Skookumchuck and Chehalis Rivers. Its abundant resources include timber, fish, fertile land, coal, and a level plain amidst rolling hills (Campbell 1986, Ott 2008a).

Colonel Michael Simmons (1814-1867) led a group of Americans north of the Columbia River in 1845, into lands jointly claimed with England. Traveling from the Columbia River and up the Cowlitz Trail, they reached the confluence of the Skookumchuck and Chehalis rivers, then went overland along what had been the outlet of the Puget glacier. Later, George Waunch

(1812-1882) returned to the confluence to settle on land now known as Waunch Prairie, just north of today's downtown Centralia. Joseph Borst (b. 1801) settled on the north bank of the Chehalis River, just downstream of the confluence, and Sidney (1801-1866) and Nancy (1806-1898) Ford settled north of Borst on what is now Fords Prairie with their children. Contacts with local natives were so frequent that these children learned to speak native languages as well as the trade jargon (Chinuk).

Until 1846 Britain and the United States shared the Oregon territory jointly under the Convention of 1818. But no treaties were signed to legally transfer ownership from natives to settler governments. Therefore, even after the Donation Land Act of 1850 made provisions for claiming tracts of land, the settlers in Oregon Territory were squatters until treaties were reached with each tribe and ratified by Congress.

In 1851, George Washington (1817-1905), the founder of Centralia, claimed squatter's rights to a tract east of the Skookumchuck and north of the Chehalis on what was known as Skookumchuck Prairie. Oregon Territory law prevented black men from owning land, and threatened by Lash Law periodic floggings until he left the state. Worried about losing his land to white settlers, Washington's former guardians, James (d. 1859) and Anna (d. 1867) Cochrane, filed on his land and later sold it back to him once Washington Territory's laws made an exception to allow for his ownership in 1853. Throughout his long life, he was ever generous to those in need, though some were racists.

Originally called Skookumchuck, this community included a mixture of Upper Chehalis and other native peoples, as well as settlers from all over the United States, Europe, and China. These interactions were not always beneficial. An 1852 smallpox epidemic decimated the Upper Chehalis population, when at least 275 Indians died in the vicinity of Skookumchuck. As a deterrent to further contamination, Americans burned the Upper Chehalis village named [ƛ]'aqáygt at what is now Grand Mound (Ott 2008a).

During the 1840s, settlers retrieved their mail on annual trips to Fort Vancouver. After 1854 Henry Windsor carried the mail up the Cowlitz Corridor on a mule. In 1857, the Military Road linked Fort Vancouver on the Columbia to Fort Steilacoom on the Sound, passing through Claquato and Skookumchuck just west of today's Interstate 5. This road became the route of regular mail service to a post office which opened on Fords Prairie.

In February 1855, Territorial Governor Isaac Stevens sought to make such a treaty with several tribes, including the Chehalis, Quinault, Chinook, and Cowlitz. The Upper and Lower Chehalis, though separate tribes, were treated by Stevens as one. Gathered at Cosmopolis, this council ended in disarray. At the start of 1856, Stevens signed a separate treaty with Quinault and Quileute.

During the 1855-6 Treaty War, local men formed Company F of the First Regiment of Washington Territorial Volunteers, led by Captain Benjamin Henness, whose name was attached to Fort Henness, a stockade fort (100 by 130 feet) that sheltered 224 people for 18 months. (The site is across the road from the pioneer Grand Mound Cemetery.) Many of the original settlers, however, never left their homes to keep trust with local natives.

Although the Judson family had little difficulty fording across the mouth of the Skookumchuck, "shortly after [they settled] the nephew of Governor Stevens, a very promising young man, lost his life while attempting to cross this same ford on horseback". After the Treaty War, the betrayers of Chief Leschi turned him over to pioneer official Sidney Ford, who took him to Gov. Isaac Stevens. Stevens was intent on convicting Leschi for murder (despite being a combatant in war) and finally railroaded a second trial that sent the chief to the gallows (Judson 1984: 82, 167). (In December 2004, Chief Leschi was retried and exonerated in the annals of history.)

The momentous change in 1872 was the arrival of the Northern Pacific Railroad between Kalama and Olympia, which opened the Cowlitz Corridor to the outside world. The line crossed George Washington's property east of the rivers, where George, his wife Mary Jane (1841-1888), and his stepson Stacey Coonness (b. 1863) platted a town named Centerville on 8 January 1875. The town grew to 50 residents in the first year.

A store owned by Isaac Wingard existed at the townsite and, in 1867, the post office had moved to James and Mary Tullis' home (1st Street and Euclid Way). Joseph Young built the Pioneer House Hotel (Main Street and Tower Avenue) and Clem Crosby (kin of Bing) built another store to the south of Wingard's. The railroad brought both access to outside markets for farm produce and timber, and employment providing cordwood to the locomotives.

In 1869, a public school opened at George Washington's old log cabin. Anna Stevens, the first teacher, came west as a "Mercer Girl", one of the young women brought west by Seattle resident Asa Mercer (1839-1917). In 1875, the town built a one-room schoolhouse (Rock Street between Cherry and Chestnut).

In 1883, the name changed to Centralia, becoming incorporated by an act of the legislature in 1886. The town had hotels, shops, flourmills, shingle mills, a door factory, and sawmills. Late in the 1880s and into the 1890s the population grew from just over 300 to about 5,000. It prospered by extracting from nearby coal and gold mines and huge old growth forests.

After the national depression of 1893, Centralia's economy began a boom in 1898. It grew to 1,600 in 1900 and to 7,311 in 1910. Railroad branch lines linked outlying areas, with nearly 60 trains passing through town daily. This web of rails, rivers, and roads gave the town its nickname of "Hub City". Railroad cars carried goods from Centralia Shingle Mills, Wooden Eave Gutter Factory, and American Iron and Brass Foundry, as well as millwork, bottled drinks, work gloves, ice, cigars, pottery, milk, and marble products. Mining operations extracted coal, iron, and gold.

Logging remained important, but led to disaster and massacre. After the 1919 Armistice Day parade, marchers from the American Legion confronted local Industrial Workers of the World (IWW) at their union hall. Four Legionnaires were killed and Wobblies (I.W.W. members) were arrested and taken to the city jail. Later, vigilantes hanged Wesley Everett, himself a veteran, from a bridge over the Skookumchuck.

In 1951, the White Pass Highway crossed the Cascades, opening markets on both sides of the mountains (timber went east and crops west). Tourists took this route for skiing, hiking, camping, hunting, and fishing.

In 1955, Interstate 5 bypassed downtown Centralia, shifting development to the freeway corridor as a shopping destination. Logging industry continued a steady decline, hastened by restrictions placed on logging in the 1980s to protect spotted owl habitat. When the TransAlta coal mine closed in 2006, 600 people lost their jobs. Today, I-5 has shortened the time spent between homes and jobs, expanding the range of employment.

Chehalis City

Several spirits lived around Chehalis City. A whale lived in a crooked-shaped lake near the town of Chehalis {ph 258 ThA}. Other powerful spirits looked like a tall man or like a woman with huge breasts who raped men and covered them with slime {ph 256}. She lived in the dark timber near the town of Chehalis.

The Chehalis town site at the confluence of the Chehalis River and Newaukum was claimed in 1850 by Schuyler (1810-1860) and Eliza (1826-1900) Saunders, from New York and Ireland respectively, and became known as Saunders' Bottom because of its marshy ground. They divorced in 1859, but Eliza kept control of the land and the growth of the town through three more marriages (*Chehalis Bee-Nugget* 1915, Ott 2008b).

One family, Obadiah B. McFadden (1814-1875), chief justice of the territorial Supreme Court, and his wife Margaret (b. 1819), bought the southern half of the Saunders' claim in 1859. Their house is the oldest standing structure in Lewis County (Ott 2008b).

Notably, in 1863, he raised a subscription to clear and corduroy (laying logs like the cloth) a road through the bog. In 1870, he took over the post office from Saunders, changed its name to Chehalis, and had it confirmed by the state in 1879.

Today's State Highway 12 follows an ancient native trading route that went eastward through the Cascade Mountains to the Yakama Indians in the plateau, but Americans traded north at New Market, which became Olympia, the state capitol.

The river assisted in transporting goods by canoe only as far as Fords Prairie, at which point it turned west and farmers loaded their produce into wagons for the overland trip to New Market. In 1866, JT Browning started a steamer service along the Chehalis River. He followed the river down to the Black River where he turned upstream to Shotwell's Landing. From there freight went by wagon overland for 10 miles to Olympia. The trip, extensive either by canoe and wagon or steamer and wagon, limited the settlers' involvement in the cash economy, which in turn limited the area's development (Ott 2008b).

Chehalis blossomed under the efforts of William West (1839-1915), who arrived with his wife Elizabeth (b. 1830), his oldest son Robert, and his brother-in-law John Dobson (1841-1907) in 1864. After his farm was established, he maneuvered for a Northern Pacific Railroad (NPRR) station at the site of Chehalis, invested in the joint stock company formed to build the first warehouse in town, helped organize the school district, served as county auditor, county treasurer, and deputy sheriff, served on the Chehalis City Council, steered the effort to have the county seat moved from Claquato to town, and helped found the town's Episcopal church.

When he needed a plow, a very scarce object, he tried to trade for it with his farm produce but struck out. Instead, West negotiated with Captain Percival, who kept a local store and offered to take his eggs, bacon and other produce to get the plow. He also agreed to pay cash for any extra produce over and above the amount of purchases.

The NPRR initially set up a depot on high ground at Newaukum, but Chehalis residents began setting out a red flag to force the train to stop and eventually the railroad gave in and moved its station downtown.

With this bamboozling of a NPRR depot in 1873, Chehalis City became a hub for logging, mining, farming, small industry, and retail. Most of its population moved across the river from Claquato, which was on the Military Road and the first county seat. George Hogue, a storeowner in Claquato, opened a branch next to the new warehouse, precipitating the 1874 move of the county seat from Claquato to Chehalis, which paid $2,000 of the $3,000 cost of building a courthouse.

Incorporated in 1883, Chehalis added a sash and door factory, the *Chehalis Nugget* newspaper, the Superior Coal Mine, a tin shop, sawmills, shingle mills, and a brickyard. Refinements included Tynan Opera House, a Catholic school for girls, the courthouse, a few churches, and a school. The entire downtown down twice in 1891, then suffered the 1893 financial panic. A rebound after 1900 saw additions of Pacific Coast Condensed Milk Company, Palmer Lumber and Manufacturing, Shaw's Cigar Factory, Simmons Glove Factory, and the Pacific Tank and Silo Company. "I.P. Callison and Sons, founded in 1903, paid local independent harvesters for cascara bark, which was used as a laxative. Once synthetic ingredients replaced cascara bark in medicines, the company shifted production to peppermint and spearmint oils," as well as the sale of ferns, salal, and digitalis (Ott 2008b).

During WW II, Boeing opened a plant in Chehalis, where "workers, many of them women, built pilot and copilot seats, wings, lower turret mounting assemblies, and interspar ribs for B-17 and B-29 bombers" (Ott 2008b). Afterward, national highways like 99 and I-5 fostered the Chehalis-Centralia area as a distribution center, particularly for Fred Meyer.

Hops

Both Chehalis and Cowlitz members worked in the hop years, and the reservation school was scheduled accordingly. Since a quarter of Chehalis members lived off the reservation, they found outside employment.

Hop-picking was seasonal employment for men, women and children at the fields near Oakville and Klaber. People living at Copalis and elsewhere along the coast traveled to the hopfields and met their relatives there (Marr, Hicks, and Francis 1980: 31).

Heyday of Chehalis hops was 1912-20, though some fields continued into the 1950s (Lingreen and Tiller 1981). Two thousand pickers were hired during September, many of them natives. The aptly named Plant Yard was at Chehalis, as was Pincus. Other yards were named Garbe, Matter Home, Dodson, Regan, McCarthy, Long, Betty, McLaughlin-Goff, Ditmar, Senn, and Chase. The hop yards between Alexander Bridge and Claquato were Bush, Dobson, Christina, Clinton, Forster, Goff, Hazzard, Lowries, Purcell, Whitaker, and Young. Herman Klaber established the largest hop fields in the world (140 acres) at the place named for him.

Indians camped on the opposite side of the Chehalis southfork, crossing the river on a swinging bridge that yard owners built (Lingreen and Tiller 1981: 16).

The first Northwest crop was planted in 1866 at Puyallup by Jacob and Ezra Meeker and they made a profit of .75/lb. Ezra, who eventually became known as the "Hop King", wrote the manual that encouraged the rapid growth of the industry. The six-inch starts came from England in 1863, but needed rich soil to prosper. At the beginning, starts were put in using all-purpose digging sticks, a native mainstay of harvesting roots and clams. But the end began in 1892 when black aphids (hop lice, *phorodon humuli*) attacked the fields and damaged the yields, aggravated by black mold. Various costly strategies were tried, including a mixture of whale oil and tropical quassia wood chips, but none were successful and hop farming died on the coast but survives in the arid interior of Washington (Raibmon 2005: 74-97; Lutz 2008). Vegetable and berry, especially strawberry, farms replaced the yards, relying on local canneries and railroad transport.

In 1914 a public market was established in downtown Centralia. Waiting rooms, rest rooms, and hitching posts for the convenience of customers were advertised. Natives and others sold their produce there.

A Cowlitz elder recalled having the duty as a small child in the 1950s to stomp down hops piled in a huge basket. Since she had to be lifted in and out of the basket, she had to be sure to do a good job to win release.

Federal Schools

Schooling was integral to US plans to "civilize" natives, with boarding schools preferred because the children were removed from their families and under complete school control (Chalcraft 2004).

An Industrial Boarding School was set up on the reservation in 1879, after having been requested for over seven years. There were forty-five students attending the school in 1883. They went to school ten months of the year, their vacation being in August and September when most children went either to pick hops or berries (Marr, Hicks, and Francis 1980: 29).

In addition to local reservation schools, children were also sent to boarding schools at Puyallup or Tulalip in Washington, and to Chemawa in Oregon.

Labor & Fun

Until paved roads and cars made driving easier, native people went to Centralia and Chehalis for special reasons, not routine trips, particularly to earn money and to celebrate at fairs, picnics, and movies. They usually shopped near home for grocery staples, and raised much of their own food. Barter was important, with baskets and handiwork often exchanged for used clothing and food. At Centralia and Chehalis, some families sold firewood, furs, knit woolens (socks, vests, hat, gloves), or baskets.

Sources of money from wages were limited to four options: log booms, woods, trains, and farms. The booms, provided by logging in the woods, fed the sawmills. Track crews and watchmen were hired by the railroad, with the nearest station to the Chehalis at Gate City, a long walk to work for some native men. Farm or stoop labor was seasonal, but included spring plowing and planting, training hops to poles, and some weeding. The fall harvest was the busiest time. Just in case, particularly if money was in short supply, families also set nets in the rivers and kept them clean from dugout canoes until recently.

Many more worked as harvesters, picking hops before and after 1900. After hops died out locally, trucks would gather up men and women, with all of their camping gear, and take them to Yakima for the hop harvest. Farm crops replaced local hop yards, and families earned wages picking strawberries, potatoes, and cherries. At the end of the harvest, women canned berries and vegetables for family use.

By season, locals harvested from nature. Families caught salmon, eels, and smelt at favorite locations. Until a few decades ago, boys would camp along the Chehalis and Black River, tending a weir they made of chicken wire to catch and eat fresh fish. Men would gather on the Chehalis at the eastern edge of the reservation to harvest the first eels as they arrived. Families went to gather cattails for drying, making mats and baskets of them during the winter. While picking huckleberries in the mountains, families also gathered bear grass for basketry. Today, illegal brush pickers have endangered these plants.

Every tribe and community had a baseball team, playing against each other all summer long. Secenas were famous ball players, insisting on the use of only wooden bats. They still host an Old Man Tournament in September, where they serve salmon. Local race tracks for horses also brought people together. Will Sanders of CTCR had over a hundred race horses.

County Fairs and Heritage celebrations drew crowds. Native families camped for several days at the Southwest Washington Fair grounds between Centralia and Chehalis, with food provided. For Pioneer days at Chehalis, most recently at Borst Park, Silas Heck had charge of local arrangements and took families there in a large truck owned by Adams. Again, free food was provided to campers. Silas was also the official interpreter for the reservation and in court. As noted, he was the primary speaker for the linguistic work of Dale Kinkade.

Flooding was an ever present danger, in the mythic past and the present day. Marion Davis lost a team of horses during one flood, and many families suffered property damage. Today, Chehalis families along the Black River use stakes to mark the advance of flood waters onto their yards. The owners of the store on Moon Road marked the highwater of every flood on their back wall, providing a local reference.

Appendix F

Dale Kinkade UW Special Collections
lch = Lower Chehalis / upch = Upper Chehalis
5108-005 28 March 05

Box 1

F 3x5 cards, 1 per Indien name x̣əytn = Hayden of Tenino band, xaiitn = John Hayden ?, Peter
Heck lch name = yanm   Queen Susan of Gate City = k̓ʷəntaɫuc̓ɬn z of yawnis   Lucy
Heck = k̓ʷoʔɬpača   George Heck lch name = ɫaamaq   Silas had Klallam name =
mətx̣ʷtn"muscular body" old dr from Hoquian nawekwəlicw   James F = k̓alaẇaks
crooked nose @ Jamestown at Grand Mound Joe Pete lch name = šaʔalucn   Lillian
Young Cowlitz name = wəɫx̣ən yawnis = Liz's pat aunt 1ˢᵗ hus (JPH) cinitiya = Upch
chief under Yawnis, also sqanawm ~ sininaxan (Dan Secena) Silas = ts'ɑmmɪps "old
wolf with hair only on its sides" (JPH) skʊhmɑ = F of old man Youckton (JPH) Silas's
F = k̓ʷuqʷɫa L!aq!mamix = Santos, last person to live at Cedarville stketxu "eldest bro
who gave the potlatch at Centralia" < Mrs Heck A1 Yb = swvtap

F1 in pen notes on Boas (lexicon 1935 497.3), red pencil corrections, 85 small pages, both sides;
Thelma, APS notes bear & bee loose sall nb pages IJAL 21, 121-137 reprint of Bear &
Bee IJAL 8, 2, 103-110 Dec 34. Reading notes in brown medium notebooks

F2 Boas xx Freeman 590 sheets by morpheme? No page #s, few examples per page, some full
s to k' checked against dictionary 4-2-79 by MDK

F3 upch clause types

F4 pencil grammatical notes

F5 Tsamosan Erna words Diary of James Douglas 4/22 – 10/2/1840 of S Sound prairies Gibbs
cf voc , Dawson & Tolmie , cf pages of lo satsop ch2 , envelope backs , HKH, Thelma
list from Thelma mss

F6 phoneme count

F7 morphology

F8 upch topical lists

F9 upch diminutives

F10 upch word formation notes

F11 texts in Eng Bjay to Land of Dead, Sun& Moon, Xwan & chief's daughter, hunter & baby
boy, flood, 5 Cougar brs, Wren GM & Otter, Wren GM & Elk , Wren GM & Snipe

F12 slow redup

F13 empty morpheme

F14 upch articles

F15 upch thematic roles

F16 irrealis

F17 upch quantifiers

F18 Flood interlinear Spicik washes his face, Muskrat gets dirt / printed on back of draft of
discourse, with Mattina

F19 grammar notes

F20 upch quantifiers

F21 grammar categories examples

F22 negatives

F23 questions
F24 auxiliaries
F25 prefixes
F26 rejection from Language
F27 computer printouts
F28 dict draft ċeles = Silas Heck FFF at mouth of gray's harbor
F29 morpheme sheets
F30 upch phonemes
F31 draft PhD
F32 Dale/Voegelin A in Az replies summer 1960, 61 Finds Leon Metcalf at home 22 July 1961
      Report #4 p3
F33 sample stories for Terry
F34 Pentlatch texts / Comox
F35 Pentlatch texts /
F36 Pentlatch texts /
F37 Pentlatch APS
F38 Pentlatch draft dictionary
F38 Pentlatch / English word finder
F40 Pentlatch possessives
F41 Pentlatch negatives
F42 Pentlatch colors
F43 Pentlatch by Boas draft
F44 Pentlatch texts interlinear
F45 Pentlatch particles

Box 2

F1 Cowlitz personal names, other dictionary addenda: Possible Cowlitz names 4 Cowlitz at
      Cosmopolis treaty = ʔəmtəč / wəhəwə / ċix̣ʷuł / k̓ʷənəsapm
      Place & tribal names from Meany, Tolmie, Warre & Vavasour, Nisq journal
F2 Cowlitz notebook Lucy Northover James / Emma Northover Mesplie June 1967 129pp
F3 place names < Curtis, Jacobs, JPH, yellow 3x5 sheets
F4 cz = Cowlitz voc, Catholic records, short texts   Hale Voc, loan words, genealogy
F5 3 xerox pages, 3 Jerome Miller 10 Aug 1978 fish names & locations
F6 Short List lwcz sheets of notes
F7 classified word list
F8 tissue paper map, Katherine Tate MA on Skilloots
F9 Cowlitz geog & ethnography thick!! Teit mss, Marilyn Graff on 4 T Adamson collections at
      Indiana / Treaty records
P30 Tu-h
P33 Chah-lat = subchief N side Gray's Harbor
      Treaty journal legal size pages
      Herb Taylor Cowlitz report 1811-55 90pp William Fraser Tolmie History of Puget
      Sound and the NWC BC Archives 27pp M-567
F10 dozen cz place names < Herb Taylor, Fried, work, Gibbs/Warbass 14Feb 1858 Photo of
      John Slocum & Louis Yowaluch
F11 3rd Person Possessives in Cowlitz ISL 6 Aug 1971

F12 cz lists deictics, cz plurals, 3rd person possessives, imperatives, relationals, causatives,
       applicatives, detransitives, reflexives, reciprocals, imperfective middles, passives,
       reduplications, diminutives, compounds, lexical, automomous, inchoatives, interrogatives
F13 cz dictionary draft
F14 time, day, dollar, rows 1 sheet
F15 Adjective examples in text lines
F16 Feb 67 ~ June 68 journal typed I page 26 May 70
F17 cz ch ł = lusootseed ʔə
F18 binder cz texts Simcoe 22pp, winter basket 44pp, cure 8pp
F19 Southern Paiute text, analysis
F20 Blackfeet Roy Old Person 16 Feb 1966
F21 Korean 4/20/66 U Kansas
F22 Ponca 4 May 70 Lloyd Deere Xerox
F23 Yapese 16 May
F24 birthdates of Moses speakers by name   dialect geography
F25 voc cards Gibbs 63, Gill 09, Lower Chehalis ? typed slips from published sources
F26 Swadesh list, Yakama 24 Nov 1964 Nov 10, 12,
F27 cf Interior Salish (Flathead?) AL 9, 2, Feb 67
F28 Alex Sherwood, Chewelah, recorded 16 july Coulee Dam,
F29 spiral notebook Columbian Salish Summer 70 Isabel
F30 spiral notebook 2 Columbian Salish Summer 70 Emily Peone, Auburn 199pp
F31 spiral notebook 3 Columbian Salish Summer 70 200pp
F32 Twana loose sheets 6/26/72
F33 spiral notebook 4 Columbian Salish Summer 70 Jerome Miller 92pp
F34 Twana Irene Teo Baptist Toppenish 72 121pp
F35 Cowlitz notebook 2 Emma Mesplie 131-259
F35 Cowlitz notebook 3 Emma Mesplie 261-559
F35 Cowlitz notebook 4 Emma Mesplie 563-829

Box 3

F1 Upch sheets of words
  Nb Upch notebook July-Aug 1960
F2 Upch Lillian Young 27 july 1987
  Nb Lillian Young 18 June 1970 23 July 1974   satsop < Leon Metcalf of Alice Johns 12 Feb
       1955
F3 Irene Shale 6 Sept 1978 kin terms
  Nb1 lch Irene Shale 6 Sept 1978 12 Sept 1978 Irene Shale & Nina Baumgarner
        x̣iʔc̓us razor clam   Irene Shale FF young = telx̣əq old = mutut
  Nb 2 lch 1978-9 28 Nov   soul sPis Irene Shale pp Lo 2-1-9
  Nb Nina (Charley) Baumgarner 5 April 1967 born 1898 Bay Center genealogy chart
        Nicola> Ives Goddard, with his own tumor report

Tu-hah-uk / Tu-leh-uk LCh

F = folder + #

Accession No. 5108-005
     Cowlitz

2	Names	undated
2	Geography Terms	undated
2	Vocabularies	1967
2	Dictionary Printouts	undated
2	Geography & Ethnography	1983
2	Cowlitz Stuff - Including Texts	1984
2	Cowlitz Stuff	undated
2	3rd Person Possessives	1971
2	Word List	undated
2	Lists of Examples	undated
2	Cowlitz Place Names	undated
2	Correspondence with Tate on Cowlitz Place Names	1980
2	Geography & Ethnography	1953
2	L. Cowlitz Data	undated
2	Journal of Work	1967-1970
2	Cowlitz Texts	undated
2	Grammar Data	undated
2	Upper Chehalis & Cowlitz	undated

Appendix G

Indian Claims Revive Ancient Memories
Tribal Origins, Customs of Misty Past
Figure in Federal Hearings

By Harold F Osborne
Seattle Times Sunday 13 June 1954

GHOSTS of long-dead Indians will be stalking through the United States Courthouse here Wednesday, Thurday, and Friday as witnesses speakbeneath symbols of Anglo-Saxon and Roman justice, of the stone age customs of the Puyallup, Nisqually, Stellacoom and Squaxin Indian tribes.

These four tribal units, sometimes called the Medicine Creek Tribes, are among 12 Western Washington tribes seeking to recover what they consider is their due for lands taken from them by the white man.

This month's hearings are part of a prolonged legal process by which the Indians are attempting, to prove to the Indian Claims Commission that Federal government owes them substantial sums of money, plus interest for 100 or more years.

Government attorneys estimate the total of the 400-plus claims filed by the tribes in all parts of the nation, including those in Washington; In the neighborhood of $50,000,000,000.

Even the Western Washington suits, made possible by the Indian Claims Act of 1946, represent very substantial amounts, possibly, $150,000,000 or more.

Lands claimed as Puyallup holdings include parts of the present city of Tacoma. The Snohomish seek recompense for the site of Everett and nearby areas. The Duwamish formerly occupied Seattle, their claim notes. All claims are based on original values, not present real-estate prices.

The Chinook and Snohomish Tribes, for example, each seek $30,000,000 as a "reasonable valuation" of their holdings when the white man arrived. The Chehalis Tribe asks $8,000,000.

Most of the claims also seek payment of interest from the time the Indians parted with the lands. The Chinooks, for example, ask "interest from September 27, 1850" on $30,000,000 to 'the time of settlement, perhaps a year or more from now.

On the basis of past settlements with Indian tribes under special legislation; the government estimates interest for 105 or 106 years well might be more than three times the basic claims.

From a practical standpoint, the totals asked are not of primary importance, since the amounts to be paid will be determined later by the. United States Court of Claims.

There is little doubt that the Supreme Court also will be asked to review at least the first award under the 1946 legislation which permitted any tribe to seek recompense. .

THIS week's hearings, as did previous ones here last year, will give the tribes a chance to prove their identity as separate and autonomous units, it they can, and to set forth what the boundaries of their land holdings were.

Neither of these is easy to do, since the origins of a primitive people with no written language often are clouded by confusion between the tribe's oral .history and its mythology.

How do you show on a present-day map, for example, just where several hundred nomadic Indians had their home a century or two before the first maps were drawn?

Or if Tribe A lived on one river and Tribe B on the next river and both hunted in some of the hills between, can you prove who actually owned the high country?

Or it several bands of Indians .had the same myths, as a basic part of their culture, does that prove they were of the same tribe, or were the myths universally known to all Indians and shared by them?

Were the Puyallups, the Nisqually, the Squaxins and the Steilacooms really separate tribes, or was each group just part of an indefinite larger body of fish-eating Indians which was mislabeled by early white settlers as a "tribe".

Donald R Marshall, the Department of Justice attorney who has defended the government against the Western Washington tribal claims at past hearings, explained, "In general the government can rely on only three main defenses in contesting he claims."

These, he said, involve efforts to prove:

1. That the Indians making the claim do not constitute really a separate and autonomous tribe.

2. That the tribe making the claim did not have' exclusive occupancy of the land it claims;' or

3. That the tribe cannot show definite boundaries of the area claimed.

Attorneys representing the various tribes have tried to prove the converse.

In so doing, many accounts of the Indians' traditional ways of life — the potlatch, the spirit dance, the pursuit

Venerable Indians whose memories reach back almost to the prewhite period have been among witnesses in the past. Batteries of anthropologists explaining tribal folkways and customs also have testified at length.

Journals of early-day trading posts, records of explorers and the original treaties, where they exist, also have been called upon for basic Information.

It has been a toss-up, in some of the previous hearings, as to who listened more intently — the Indian spectators to the scholarly anthropologists, or the anthropologists to the wrinkled oldsters brought in from their reservation homes or tideland cabins.

Color was supplied in these proceedings by such notable witnesses as Emma Millet Luscier, 93, a Chinook from Bay Center, Pacific County; by Mary Shelton, 96, from the Tulalip Reservation; Andrew Joe, about 70, of La Conner, and Roland Charlie, a Chinook of about 65.

They testified about tribal customs, gave the Indian and English names of their villages and told of life in the days when the white men were trickling into this area.

The government's position in the various claims cases will be heard later at Washington, when the Indian Claims Commission again will sit as a court of evidence.

The Indians' claims basically are all the same.

Malcolm Stewart McLeod, young Seattle attorney who has worked since 1949 on preparation of Cases for many of the tribes, noted that the transfer of land to the whites, deprived the Indians of valuable forest, fishing and mineral rights, their means of livelihood and the source of their food, clothing, and shelter.

The Chinook claim, a typical example, is based on the tribe's asserted occupancy of some

rewhite period, have been among .ample, is based on the tribe's asserted occupancy of some 2,000,000 acres by 1,000 to 1,500 tribesmen in 1850.

The $30,000,000 claim is based on a "fair and reasonable estimate" of the value of the Chinooks lands, their their petition states. It figures out to $15 an acre, which would go to the 500 Chinooks still alive.

What the Chinooks obtained in exchange for these lands, their petition sets forth, was "grossly inadequate and unconscionable consideration." It adds that the white roan acted "unfairly and dishonorably in his dealings.

Early treaties with the Chinook never were ratified by the United States Senate. (The independent Chinooks, incidentally, walked out of the parley with Gov. Isaac Stevens in 1855, at which many other tribes ceded their lands.)

The Snohomish claim, also typical, is based on cession of 224,000 acres of land. Under the 1855 Treaty of Point Elliott, the United States paid $150,000 to several tribes for all the land from the Duwamish River to Canada, between the crest of the Cascades and the west side of Whidby Island.

The Snohomish share of this sum was $13,636.

Aged Chinook Tells of Indian Culture

By Harold F Osborne
Seattle Writer
Sunday Oregonian Magazine 27 September 1953

WORD-PICTURES of the culture of Oregon's Chinook Indians, aristocratic anid independent master-traders of a century and more ago, were painted in bold colors and careful detail in a Seattle courtroom last month.

The color was supplied, for the most part, by Mrs Emma Millet Luscier, Bay Center, Wash, 93-year-old Chinook whose quick intellect provided several highlights in nine days of hearings before Louis J O'Marr, one of three members of the U.S. Indians claims commission of Washington, DC.

Mrs. Luscier told, among other things, of Smallpox epidemics that decimated her people, of tribal specialists, in fashioning the famed high-powered Chinook canoes, and of her own purchase, as a maiden, to be the bride of a French trader.

The detailed sketching, by contrast, was provided by a battery of anthropologists.

It was a toss-up who listened with more fascination — the Indian spectators to the scholarly accounts of their ancestors' home life as presented by the anthropologists, or the scientists themselves to Mrs. Luscier's reconstruction of aboriginal tribal folk-ways.

The hearings were held to hear new evidence in support of claims by the Chinook and 11 other tribes seeking to recover what they consider is their due in return for lands taken by the white man. The 12 are among more than 400 tribes which have filed petitions under the Indian Claims act of 1946.

The claim of the Chinook, only Oregon tribe heard at the sessions last month, is for $30,000,000, plus — and this is a big plus — "interest from September 27, 1850" to the time of settlement, probably a year or more hence.

On the basis of the few settlements with Indian tribes which already have been made, under special legislation, government attorneys estimate the interest, if allowed for 103 or 104 years, might amount to more than three times the basic claim.

Two and one half years ago, the Alsea tribe of Oregon, for example, won a $3,000,000 award, on which the interest amounted to an additional $14,000,000. The interest awarded the Alseas by the U.S. court of claims, however, was nullified by a later supreme court of the United States ruling.

The Alseas' settlement was obtained under special congressional legislation enabling the tribe to sue the government. So, too, was the $33,000,000 settlement secured by the Utes of eastern Utah, and several others. There have been no awards yet under the 1946 law, which was drawn up to permit any Indian tribe to file a claim for lands.

• • •

The Chinook claim was filed by John Grant Elliott, chairman of the general council of the Chinook tribe and its subordinate Waukikum, Willopah and Clatsop bands. It sets forth that the Chinook occupied some 2,000,000 acres of land in Oregon and Washington — the entire seacoast from Tillamook head to Grays Harbor and inland as far as the vicinity of Longview, Wash.

In 1850 there were between 1000 and 1500 members of the tribe; today they number some 500. The petition bases the $30,000.000 claim on a "fair and reasonable" estimate of "the lands, timber, fish, and minerals, and the Indians' dwellings and farmlands on September 27, 1850. That was the date of the Oregon Donation act which encouraged the white settlement of Oregon Territory.

And this, says Malcolm Stewart McLeod, young Seattle attorney who has worked on preparation of claims cases for many of the Northwest tribes since 1949, deprived the Chinook not only of their possessions but their means of livelihood. The right to hunt and fish and the right to gather materials for food, shelter and clothing were lost with I he land itself.

Mrs. Luscier put it another way in her testimony. "We used to roam everywhere and be able to hunt," she said. "Now it you hunt or fish in many places you can be arrested."

What the Chinook obtained in exchange for their lands and way of life, their petition states, was "grossly inadequate and unconscionable consideration." And the white man, in general, acted "unfairly and dishonorably" in his dealings, the Chinook insist.

The Chinook claim, it also should be mentioned, is in general accord with those of other Northwest tribes. The Snohomish tribe of western Washington, for one example, also asks $30,000,000, plus interest, for loss of their 224,000 acres of land.

Donald R Marshall, justice department attorney from Washington, DC, handled the government's defense against the claims of the 12 tribes. He explained that the government can rely, in general, on only three main defenses in contesting the claims.

These involve efforts to prove:

1. That the Indians making each claim do not really constitute a separate and autonomous tribe;

2. That the tribe making the claim did not have exclusive occupancy of the land it chums; or

3. That the tribe cannot show definite boundaries of the area claimed.

Attorneys representing the various tribes sought, of course, to prove the converse of each of these points. In so doing, accounts of the Indians' way of life necessarily were set forth in detail.

Into the record, also, went historical accounts, records of early explorers and traders as well as anthropological and ethnographic treaties to support first-person accounts like Mrs. Luscier's.

• • •

That striking old lady, slightly hard-of-hearing and dependent upon two crutches when she walks, proved that her mind is still alert and active.

At one point, she delighted all in the courtroom by declaring from the witness stand:

"I'm having lots of fun here."

Another time, she turned her piercing black eyes on O'Marr, and assured him soberly:

"I have had no education, Your Honor. But what my mother and my grandmother have told me I know is true. And what I have seen with my own eyes I know is true."

She told how survivors of epidemics piled the bodies of smallpox victims in a single house, then burned the dwelling and the bodies to prevent spread of the disease. French traders, she said, advised this policy rather than the more typical practice, in deaths of high-class tribesmen at least, of placing the dead in canoes raised on poles.

Later, one of the anthropologists, Dr Herbert Taylor of Western Washington College of Education, told the commissioner that nine of every ten Chinook fell victims to white men's diseases between 1810 and 1850. This circumstance, he said, wiped out almost all vestiges of the original tribal organization.

"To say that the rather pathetic remnants of a people that once numbered 12,000, and was reduced by disease to a mere 1100, had no tribal organization or autonomy in 1850 ... [3] is to ignore everything we know," he declared.

The fact that the Chinook numbers were reduced apparently did not shackle their independent spirit entirely. Although other tribes met with Governor Isaac Stevens of Washington Territory in 1855, the Chinook walked out on the parley.

(Earlier treaties with the Chinook and its subordinate bands, negotiated by the superintendent of Indian affairs for Oregon in 1851, never were ratified by the U. S. senate.)

Mrs. Luscier's account of canoe-making had a note of the old tribal pride in it. "Our canoes were the finest made,'" she said. "We had experts, like carpenters, who made them for all.

"A man's wealth was measured by the number of canoes he owned. Canoe makers were highly regarded in each village."

• • •

She told how four-foot-thick trees were felled by burning, rather than axes, in order to make the deep-draft vessels. The logs were hollowed out and filled with water, which then was heated with hot stones, she explained. When the hot water had softened the wood fibers, the sides of the center hollow were forced apart with wooden spreaders to shape the craft.

"I saw them made when I was a little girl," Mrs. Luscier said. "They would carry 10 or 20 people. They would go up the rough water of the Columbia or out into the ocean."

Mrs. Luscier also told of catching beaver and otter by placing traps at the bottom of the mud-slides on which the animals entered the rivers. The furs, she said, then would be traded at Hudson Bay company posts for sugar or calico.

She also described the location of each Chinook village and named its chief. Her people roamed the Columbia banks upstream as far as The Dalles, although they felt actual ownership for territory only up to Longview, she said.

Roland Charlie, a Chinook of 65, was another Indian witness. He testified principally about the villages, chiefs [b] and territory of the Chinook. Concomly, he said, was the Chinook nation's greatest leader.

Establishing the legal proof of any event a century old necessarily is a difficult task. But the problem of establishing tribal identity and political organization among people who had no written records, or determining ancient boundaries in an unmapped area obviously is even more complex.

For that reason, additional hearings are expected in almost all the tribes' cases. The Indian claims commission, incidentally, serves only as a court of evidence, and the final awards, if any, will be made by the US court of claims. The supreme court review may follow before any cases finally are settled.

Marshall, who is charged with defense of the government's position in all the cases involving western Washington tribes, noted that those filed by Indians of the Pacific Northwest are only a drop in the overall bucket.

"Some lawyers estimate that the total claims against the government may run as high as $50,000,000,000 under this one piece of legislation," he declared.

Since each case is similar in some degree to many others, it is important, for the sake of precedent, that each be defended conscientiously.

McLeod, in turn, set forth the Indians' position this way:

"In 1850 Indians occupied the whole [c] area of the present states of Oregon and Washington. They were Stone Age people, living in Stone Age ways.

"The United States, through its agents, took the land, and dispossessed the aboriginal inhabitants by encouraging settlers to occupy the territory under the Oregon Donation act. It is for this that the Indians seek compensation.

• • •

"Although treaties were negotiated with certain of the tribes, in general, the United States has failed to give adequate consideration for the lands taken. In every case where consideration was given it was grossly inadequate.

"Actually, the payments, made to Oregon and Washington Indians make the purchase of Manhattan island for $24 look like a reasonable and profitable transaction for the Indians there." McLeod, whose work on the Indian cases since 1949 has made him something of an expert on Indian lore, declared.

"Sometimes the government provided for barrels of rum to be paid in exchange for lands. Sometimes clothing was given. Sometimes the Indians were granted all dead whales which might wash up on their beaches in the future — but not the live whales off shore which the white man might want for himself," McLeod said.

"It is to right this sort of inequity that these cases were brought."

ATTORNEYS for the Indian claimants and the government discuss a point before a map on which claims of various tribes are indicated. At left is Malcolm Stewart McLeod, representing the Indians, and at right is Donald Marshall, Department of Justice

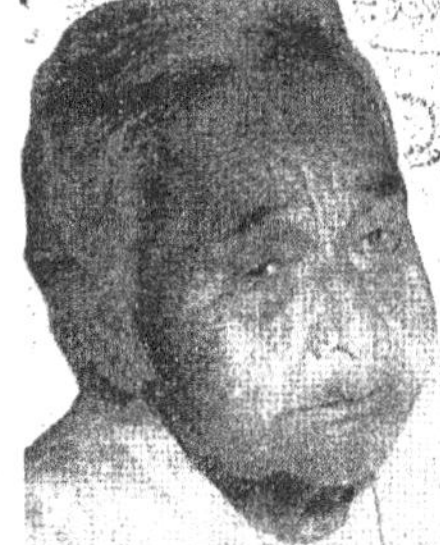

SPECTATORS at Seattle hearings included Capt. Forrest N. Elwell, Marysville, Wash., retired steamboat captain, and Mrs. Elwell. He is descendant of Chief Seattle. Emma Millet Luscier

157

BIBLIOGRAPHY

Adamson, Thelma

1927   Unarranged Sources of Chehalis Ethnography. Seattle: University of Washington, Special Collections, Melville Jacobs Collection.

1934   <u>Folk-Tales of the Coast Salish</u>. New York: Memoir of the American Folk-lore Society, Volume XXVII.

1999   Chehalis Area Traditions, a Summary of Thelma Adamson's 1927 Ethnographic Notes. Jay Miller, ed. <u>Northwest Anthropological Research Notes</u> 33 (1): 1-72. [same as Miller 1999a]

2009   <u>Folk-Tales of the Coast Salish</u>. William Seaburg and Laurel Sercombe, eds. Lincoln: University of Nebraska Press. [reprint, with new introduction]

American Friends Service Committee

1970   <u>Uncommon Controversy</u>. Fishing Rights of the Muckleshoot, Puyallup, and Nisqually Indians. Seattle: University of Washington Press.

Ames, Kenneth, and Herbert Maschner

1999   <u>Peoples of the Northwest Coast</u>. <u>Their Archaeology and Prehistory</u>. London: Thames and Hudson.

Amoss, Pamela

1975   Catalogue of the Marian Smith Collection of Fieldnotes, Manuscripts, and Photographs in the Library of the Royal Anthropological Institute of Great Britain and Ireland.

1978   <u>Coast Salish Spirit Dancing</u>. The Survival of an Ancestral Religion. Seattle: University of Washington Press.

1981   Coast Salish Elders. <u>Other Ways of Growing Old</u>: 227-261. Pamela Amoss and Steven Harrell, eds. Stanford University Press.

1982   Resurrection, Healing, and "the Shake": The Story of John and Mary Slocum. <u>Charisma and Sacred Biography</u>. Michael Williams, ed. Journal of the American Academy of Religion, Thematic Studies XLVIII (3/4): 87-109.

1987   "The Fish God Gave Us": The First Salmon Ceremony Revived. <u>Arctic Anthropology</u> 24 (1): 56-66.

1990   The Indian Shaker Church. <u>Northwest Coast</u>. Wayne Suttles, ed. Handbook of North American Indians, Volume 7: 633-39. Smithsonian Institution Press.

Anderson, Bern, ed.

1939   The Vancouver Expedition: Peter Puget's Journal of the Exploration of the Puget Sound, May 7–June 11, 1792. <u>Pacific Northwest Quarterly</u> 30 (2) April.

Anderson, Bern

1960   <u>The Life and Voyages of Captain George Vancouver</u>. Seattle: University of Washington Press.

Andrade, Manuel

1931 Quileute Texts. Columbia University Contributions to Anthropology XII.

Asher, Brad

1995 A Shaman-killing Case on Puget Sound, 1873-1874. American Law and Salish Culture. Pacific Northwest Quarterly 86 (1): 17-24 Winter 1994/95.

1999 Beyond the Reservation. Indians, Settlers, and the Law in Washington Territory, 1853-1889. Norman: University of Oklahoma Press.

Ballard, Arthur C.

1927 Some Tales of the Southern Puget Sound Salish. University of Washington Publications in Anthropology 2 (3): 57-81.

1929 Mythology of Southern Puget Sound. University of Washington Publications in Anthropology 3 (2): 31-150.

1999 Mythology of Southern Puget Sound. Kenneth (Greg) Watson, ed. North Bend, WA: Snoqualmie Valley Historical Museum.

Barnett, Homer

1955 The Coast Salish of British Columbia. Studies in Anthropology 4. Eugene: University of Oregon Press.

1957 Indian Shakers, A Messianic Cult of the Pacific Northwest. Carbondale: Southern Illinois University Press.

Beckham, Stephen Dow

1969 George Gibbs, 1815-1873: Historian and Anthropologist. Ph.D. dissertation, University of California at Los Angeles.

1977 The Indians of Western Oregon. This Land Was Theirs. Coos Bay: Arago Books.

2006 Oregon Indians. Voices from Two Centuries. Corvallis: Oregon State University Press.

Bent, AC

1919 Life Histories of Diving Birds. US Nat Mus 107

1925 Life Histories of North American Wild Fowl. USNM 130, part 2.

Blukis Onat, Astrida, James Phipps, Karen James, Kathryn Bernick, Timothy Cowan, and Lacosta Browning Lykowski

2007 Cultural Resource Study Report of the Port of Grays Harbor Industrial Development District Parcel Number 1, Hoquiam Washington. BOAS, Inc: Report No 200511.03.

Boas, Franz.

1894 Chinook Texts. DC: Smithsonian Institution, Bureau of American Ethnology, Bulletin 20.

1901 Kathlamet Texts. DC: Smithsonian Institution, Bureau of American Ethnology, Bulletin 26.

1905 The Jesup North Pacific Expedition. <u>International Congress of Americanists</u> 13: 90-100.

1920 The Classification of American Languages. <u>American Anthropologist</u> 22: 367-376.

1924 Vocabulary of an Athapascan Tribe of Nicola Valley, British Columbia. <u>International Journal of American Linguistics</u> 3 (1): 36-38.

1925 Comparative Salishan Vocabularies. MS, Boas Collection, American Philosophical Society Library, Philadelphia, Pennsylvania. 1628 strips of paper.

1927 Chehalis Field Notes. MS, Boas Collection, American Philosophical Society Library, Philadelphia, Pennsylvania. 14 notebooks.

1927-1935 Chehalis Lexical File. MS, Boas Collection, American Philosophical Society Library, Philadelphia, Pennsylvania. 8,000 slips.

1929 Classification of American Indian Languages. <u>Language</u> 5: 1-7.

1934a Chehalis Vocabulary. MS, American Philosophical Society Library, Philadelphia, Pennsylvania. 79 pp.

1934b A Chehalis Text. <u>International Journal of American Linguistics</u> 8: 103-110.

c1935 Chehalis Lexicon. MS, American Philosophical Society Library, Philadelphia, Pennsylvania. 845 pp. [c = *circa*]

Boas, Franz, ed.

1911 <u>Handbook of American Indian Languages</u> I. Bureau of American Ethnology, Bulletin 40. Washington, D.C.: Government Printing Office.

1917 <u>Folk-Tales of Salishan and Sahaptin Tribes</u>. Memoirs of the American Folklore Society 11. Lancaster, Pennsylvania: American Folk-Lore Society.

1930 Bureau of American Anthropology, 45th Annual Report, 1927–28. Washington, D.C.: Smithsonian Institution. [Reprinted, Shorey Book Store, 1973.]

1938 <u>Handbook of American Indian Languages</u> III. Glückstadt, Germany: J. J. Augustin Inc., and New York: Columbia University Press.

Boas, Franz

2002 Indian Myths and Legends of the North Pacific Coast. Victoria: Talonbooks. Randy Bouchard and Dorothy Kennedy, eds. Dietrich Bertz, translator. Originally Indianishe Sagen von der Nord-Padifischen Küste Amerikas. Sonder-Abdruck aus den Verlandlungen der Berliner Gesellschaft fur Anthropologie, Ethnologie und Urgeschichte. Berlin: Verlag von A Asher. 1895.

Boas, Franz, and Ethel G. Aginsky

1927 Chehalis Notebooks. MS, American Philosophical Society Library, Philadelphia, Pennsylvania.

1934-1936 Chehalis Materials. MS, American Philosophical Society Library, Philadelphia, Pennsylvania. 440 pp., 5 slips.

Boas, Franz, and Pliny Goddard

1924   Vocabulary of an Athapascan Dialect of the State of Washington. International Journal of American Linguistics 3 (1): 39-45.

Boas, Franz, and Hermann K. Haeberlin 1927 Sound Shifts in Salishan Dialects. International Journal of American Linguistics 4: 117-136.

Boas, Franz, Herman K Haeberlin, and James A Teit

1920   Salishan Dialects.   MS, American Philosophical Society Library, Philadelphia, Pennsylvania. 12 pp.

Bowers, Nora , Nick Bowers, and Kenn Kaufman

2004 *Mammals of North America*. NY: Houghton Mifflin Co.

Boxberger, Daniel

1984   The Introduction of Horses to the Southern Puget Sound Salish: 103-119. Western Washington Indian Socio-Economics ~ Papers in Honor of Angelo Anastasio. Herbert Taylor and Garland Grabert, eds. Bellingham: Western Washington University.

1989 To Fish In Common: The Ethnohistory of Lummi Indian Salmon Fishing. Lincoln: University of Nebraska Press.

Boyd, Robert

1996 People of the Dalles. The Indians of Wascopam Mission. Lincoln: University of Nebraska Press.

1999a The Coming of the Spirit of Pestilence: Introduced Infectious Diseases and Population Decline among Northwest Coast Indians, 1774-1874. Seattle: University of Washington Press.

Boyd, Robert, ed.

1999b   Indians, Fire, and the Land in the Pacific Northwest. Corvallis: Oregon State University Press.

Bright, William, ed.

2004 Native American Placenames of the United States. Norman: University of Oklahoma Press.

Campbell, Kathleen

1986 Glimpses of Historic Centralia. Centennial Edition.

Capoeman, Pauline, ed., Jacqueline Storm, David Chance, Jim Harp, Karen Harp, Lawrence Lestelle, Sarah Colleen Sotomish, Larry Workman

1990 Land of the Quinault. Taholah: Quinault Indian Nation.

Carlson, Barry, and Thom Hess

1971 Canoe Names in the Northwest, An Areal Study. Anthropological Linguistics 12 (1): 17-24.

Castile, George

1982 The 'Half-Catholic' Movement: Edwin and Myron Eells and the Rise of the Indian Shaker Church. Pacific Northwest Quarterly 73: 165-174.

1990 The Indian Connection: Judge James Wickersham and the Indian Shakers. Pacific Northwest Quarterly 81 (Oct): 122-129.

Castile, George, ed.

1985 The Indians of Puget Sound. The Notebooks of Myron Eells. Walla Walla: University of Washington Press for Whitman College.

Chalcraft, Edwin

2004 Assimilation's Agent: My Life as a Superintendent in the Indian Boarding School System. Cary Collins, ed. Lincoln: University of Nebraska Press.

The Chehalis Bee-Nugget

1915 Historical Souvenir Edition. Illustrated. 14 May 1915.

Christy, Melissa, ed.

2008 Wisdom of the Elders. Traditional Food Ways of Five Tribes in Western Washington. Phoenix: The National Society of American Indian Elderly (NSAIE).

Chronicle

2008 The Flood of 2007. Disaster and Survival on the Chehalis River. As Reported by the Chronicle, Lewis County, Washington.

Clemens, Benjamin, Thomas Binder, Margaret Docker, Mary Moser, and Stacia Sower

2010 Similarities, Differences, and Unknowns in Biology and Management of Three Parasitic Lampreys of North America, Fisheries 35 (12): 580 – 594. December. Online 15 February 2011.

Collins, June

1950 The Indian Shaker Church: A Study in Continuity and Change in Religion. Southwest Journal of Anthropology 6 (4): 399-411.

1952 The Mythological Basis For Attitudes Toward Animals Among Salish-Speaking Indians. Journal of American Folklore 65 (258): 353-359.

1974 Valley of the Spirits: The Upper Skagit Indians of Western Washington. Seattle: University of Washington Press.

1979 Multineal Descent: A Coast Salish Strategy. Current Anthropology: Essays in Honor of Sol Tax: 243-254. Robert Hinshaw, ed. New York: Mouton Publishers.

1994 Kinship, Social Class, and Religion of Northwest Coast Peoples. North American Indian Anthropology: Essays on Society and Culture: 82-107. Raymond DeMallie and Alfonso Ortiz, eds. Norman: University of Oklahoma Press.

Cox, Ross

1832   Adventures on the Columbia River. Six Years on the Western shore of the Rocky Mountains. Reprinted Narrative Press, Santa Barbara, 2004.

Curtis, Edward

1913   The North American Indian, being a series of volumes picturing and describing the Indians of the United States, the Dominion of Canada, and Alaska. Written, Illustrated, and Published By Edward S. Curtis. Frederick Webb Hodge, ed. Volume 9 of 20. New York.

Daehnke, Jon

2017   Chinook Resilience ~ Heritage and Cultural Revitalization on the Lower Columbia River. Seattle: UW Press.

Davis, John

1980   Douglas of the Forests. The North American Journals of David Douglas. Seattle: University of Washington Press.

Donald, Leland

1997   Aboriginal Slavery on the Northwest Coast of North America. Berkeley: University of California Press.

Donovan, John

1963a Chehalis Warfare. Cowlitz County Historical Quarterly 13. September.

1963b Kleeshws and Sulachulwultchs, Cowlitz County Historical Quarterly 11. November.

1964a Chestowi. Cowlitz County Historical Quarterly 1. November.

1964b The Clambake. Cowlitz County Historical Quarterly 2. September.

1964c Spoop: Cowlitz County Historical Quarterly 5. February.

1966   The Witch Woman of the Upper Chehalis. Cowlitz County Historical Quarterly 20. May.

1967a Hyutuum by Frank Pete. Cowlitz County Historical Quarterly 2. May.

1967b Legend: The Bright Shining Star. Cowlitz County Historical Quarterly 10. February.

1967c Legend: Why There Are Crippled Children. Cowlitz County Historical Quarterly 29. November.

Duwamish and Others

1920s National Archives, Record Group (RG) 123, F275, Duwamish and Others, Boxes 3687-3693.

1933   Consolidated Petition in the US Court of Claims. DC: Government Printing Office, 2 volumes.

Dyen, Isidore, and David Aberle

1974   Lexical Reconstruction. The Case of the Proto-Athapaskan Kinship System. Cambridge University Press.

Eaton, Diane, and Sheila Urbanek

1995 <u>Paul Kane's Great Nor-West</u>. Vancouver: UBC Press.

Eells, Myron

1886 <u>Ten Years of Missionary Work among the Indians at Skokomish, Washington Territory</u>. Boston: Congregational Sunday-School and Publishing Society. [Shorey reprint 1972].

1887 The Indians of Puget Sound (nine parts). <u>American Antiquarian</u> 9.

1889 The Twana, Chemakum, and Klallam Indians of Washington Territory. Smithsonian Annual Report for 1887: 605-681.

1985 <u>The Indians of Puget Sound. The Notebooks of Myron Eells</u>. George Pierre Castille, ed. Seattle: University of Washington Press.

Elliott, TC, ed.

1912 Journal of John Work, November to December, 1824. <u>Washington Historical Quarterly</u> 3 (3): 198-228.

Elmendorf, William

1935 The Soul-Recovery Ceremony Among The Indians of the Northwest Coast. Master of Arts Thesis. University of Washington.

1946 Twana Kinship Terminology. <u>Southwestern Journal of Anthropology</u> 2: 420-432.

1948 The Cultural Setting of the Twana Secret Society. <u>American Anthropologist</u> 50: 625-633.

1960 <u>The Structure of Twana Culture</u>. Pullman: Washington State Research Studies, Monographic Supplement 2. (with Comparative Notes on the Structure of Yurok by Alfred Kroeber).

1961a Skokomish and Other Coast Salish Tales. <u>Washington State University Research Studies</u> 29 (1): 1-37; (2): 84-117; (3): 119-150.

1961b System Change in Salish Kinship Terminologies. <u>Southwestern Journal of Anthropology</u> 17 (4): 365-382.

1970 Skokomish Sorcery, Ethics, and Society. Chapter VI: 147-182, <u>Systems of North American Witchcraft And Sorcery</u>. Deward Walker, ed. Anthropological Monographs of the University of Idaho 1.

1971 Coast Salish Status Ranking and Intergroup Ties. <u>Southwestern Journal of Anthropology</u> 27: 353-381.

1993 <u>Twana Narratives</u>. Native Historical Accounts of a Coast Salish People. Seattle: University of Washington Press.

Farrand, Livingston

1902 <u>Traditions of the Quinault Indians</u>. With assistance by WS Kahnweiler. NY: Memoirs of the American Museum of Natural History IV, Publications of the Jesup North Pacific Expedition III: 77-132.

Fitzpatrick, Darlene

1968   The 'Shake': The Indian Shaker Curing Ritual among the Yakima. University of Washington: MA Thesis.

Frachtenberg, Leo

1920 Eschatology of the Quileute Indians

1921 The Ceremonial Societies of the Quileute Indians

Fried, Jacob

1974   The Territorial Distribution of Some of the Aboriginal Population of Western Washington State and the Economic and Political Aspects of Their Culture. <u>Coast Salish and Western Washington Indians III</u>: 193-243. American Indian Ethnohistory. Indians of the Northwest. David Agee Horr, ed. New York: Garland Publishing.

Gerdts, Donna, and Lisa Mathewson

2004 Studies in Salish Linguistics in Honor of M. Dale Kinkade. Missoula: University of Montana Occasional Papers in Linguistics 17.

Gibbs, George

1855 Report on the Indian Tribes of Washington Territory. Pacific Railroad Report 1: 402-36.

1877 Tribes of Western Washington and Northwestern Oregon. Washington: Department of the Interior, United States Geographical and Geological Survey of the Rocky Mountain Region, Part II: 157-241.

1970 Dictionary of the Niskwalli (Nisqually) Indian Language ~ Western Washington. Extract from 1877 Contributions to North American Ethnology 1: 285-361. [Seattle: The Shorey Book Store Facsimile Reproduction.]

Gill, John

1909 <u>Gill's Chinook Dictionary</u>. Portland: JK Gill Company.

Goertz, Jolynn Amrime

2018 <u>Chehalis Stories</u>. Franz Boas Texts. Lincoln: University of Nebraska Press.

Gunther, Erna

1925 <u>Klallam Folk Tales</u>. University of Washington Publications in Anthropology 1 (4): 113-170. August.

1927 <u>Klallam Ethnography</u>. University of Washington Publications in Anthropology 1 (5): 171-314. January.

1928   A Further Analysis of the First Salmon Ceremony. University of Washington Publications in Anthropology 2 (5): 129-173.

1949 The Shaker Religion of the Northwest, <u>Indians of the Urban Northwest</u>: 37-76. Marian Smith, ed. Columbia University Press.

1973 <u>Ethnobotany of Western Washington</u>. The Knowledge and Use of Indigenous Plants by Native Americans. Seattle: University of Washington Press. [1945]

ms. Culture Element Distributions: Puget Sound (Duwamish, Skokomish, Klallam, Makah). Berkeley: Bancroft Library.

Haeberlin, Herman

1916-17 Puget Salish, 42 Notebooks. DC: National Anthropological Archives. # 2965.

1918 SbEtEtda'q: A Shamanic Performance of the Coast Salish. <u>American Anthropologist</u> 20 (3): 249-257.

1924 Mythology of Puget Sound. <u>Journal of American Folklore</u> 37 (143-144): 371-438.

1974 Herman Haeberlin's Distribution of the Salish Substantival (Lexical) Suffixes. M. Terry Thompson, ed. <u>Anthropological Linguistics</u> 16: 219-350.

Haeberlin, Herman, and Erna Gunther

1930 The Indians of Puget Sound. University of Washington Publications in Anthropology 4 (1): 1-84.

Hajda, Yvonne

1990 Southwestern Coast Salish. Handbook of North American Indians, <u>Northwest Coast</u>. Wayne Suttles, ed. Volume 7: 503-517.

Hamp, Eric

1966 Upper Chehalis q'aɬ ~ q'es. <u>International Journal of American Linguistics</u> 32: 84-86.

1967 Another Look at Tillamook Phonology. <u>International Conference on Salish Languages</u>. Seattle, Washington.

1968 Quileute and Salish Lexical Suffixes. <u>International Conference on Salish Languages 3</u>. Victoria, B.C.

1971 Some Phonetic Rules for Mainland Comox Vowels. James Hoard and Thom Hess, eds., <u>Sacramento Anthropological Society</u>, <u>Paper</u> 11: 32-42.

1973 Brief Mention (Minutes of the 7th International Conference on Salish languages, *inter alia*). <u>International Journal of American Linguistics</u> 39: 198-203.

1976 Brief Mention (Conference on Salish Languages). <u>International Journal of American Linguistics</u> 42: 89.

Harmon, Alexandra

1995 Different Kind of Indians. Negotiating the Meanings of "Indian" and "Tribe" in the Puget Sound Region, 1820s-1970s. University of Washington: History Ph.D. Volumes I - 1-365, II - 366-741.

1999 <u>Indians in the Making</u>. <u>Ethnic Relations and Indian Identities around Puget Sound. American Crossroads Series</u>. Berkeley: University of California Press.

Harper, J Russell, ed.

1971 <u>Paul Kane's Frontier</u>. Austin: University of Texas Press.

Harrington, John Peabody

1942a Chehalis Notes. DC: National Anthropological Archives. Microfilm Reels 17, 18.

1942b Quinault, Lower Chehalis, Upper Chehalis, Cowlitz, Chinook, and Chinook Jargon Fieldnotes. Microfilm, reels No. 017-018, remaining data as per Harrington 1910.

1981 The Papers of John Peabody Harrington in the Smithsonian Institution, 1907-1957. Elaine Mills, ed. 30 reels. Millwood, NY: Krause International Publications.

Herbel, Brian, and Randall Schalk

2002 An Archaeological Reconnaissance of the Chehalis River Floodplain for the Centralia Flood Damage Reduction Project. Seattle: Cascadia Archaeology. October.

Hilbert, Vi taqᵂsheblu

1985 Haboo, Native American Stories From Puget Sound. University of Washington Press.

Hilbert, Vi, Jay Miller, and Zalmai Zahir

2001 Puget Sound Geography. sdaʔdaʔ gᵂəɬ dibəɬ ləšucid ʔacaciɬtalbixᵂ. A Draft Study of the Thomas Talbot Waterman Place Name Manuscript and Other Sources, Edited with Additional Material. Seattle: Lushootseed Press.

Hitchman, Robert

1985 Place Names of Washington. Tacoma: Washington State Historical Society.

Hoard, James, and Thom Hess, eds.

1971 Studies in Northwest Indian Languages. Sacramento Anthropological Society, Paper 11 April.

Hodge, Frederick, ed.

1906 Handbook of American Indians North of Mexico. Smithsonian: BAE-B 30, I.

1910 Handbook of American Indians North of Mexico. Smithsonian: BAE-B 30, II.

Holden, Madrona

ms http://holdenma.wordpress.com/culture-and-environment/stay-in-one-place. Accessed 2/28/2011.

Hunn, Eugene

1990 Nch'i-Wana "The Big River": Mid-Columbia Indians and Their Land. Seattle: University of Washington Press.

1994 Place-Names, Population Density, and the Magic Number 500. Current Anthropology 35: 81-85.

1996 Columbia Plateau Indian Place Names: What Can They Teach Us? Journal of Linguistic Anthropology 6 (1): 3-26.

Hymes, Dell

1981 "In Vain I Tried to Tell You:" Essays in Native American Ethnopoetics. Philadelphia: University of Pennsylvania Press.

1987   Anthologies and Narrators: <u>Recovering the Word: Essays on Native American Literature</u>. Brian Swan and Arnold Krupat, eds. Berkeley: University of California Press.

Jackson, Robert

1906 The Story of the Sun. <u>Washington Magazine</u> May.

Jacobs, Melville

1934 Northwest Sahaptin Texts. Columbia University Contributions to Anthropology 19, Part I (English): 168-169.

1959 <u>The Content and Style of an Oral Literature</u>. NY: Viking Fund Publications in Anthropology 26.

1960 <u>The People Are Coming Soon</u>. Analysis of Clackamas Chinook Myths and Texts. Seattle: University of Washington Press.

James, Justine E, Jr., with Leilani Chubby

2002 Quinault. <u>Native Peoples of the Olympic Peninsula</u> - <u>Who We Are</u>: 99-117. Jacilee Wray, ed. Norman: University of Oklahoma Press.

Johnson, Karen

n.d. Claquato Cemetery website. Accessed 28 February 2011.

Jones, Joan Megan

1977 <u>Basketry of the Quinault</u>. Taholah: Quinault Indian Nation.

Jorgensen, Joseph

1969 <u>Salish Language and Culture</u>. A Statistical Analysis of Internal Relationships, History, and Evolution. Bloomington: Indiana University Language Science Monographs 3.

Joyce, Barry

2001 <u>The Shaping of American Ethnography</u>. <u>The Wilkes Exploring Expedition, 1838-1842</u>. Lincoln: University of Nebraska Press.

Judson, Phoebe Goodell

1984 <u>A Pioneer's Search for an Ideal Home</u>. Lincoln: Bison Books, University of Nebraska Press. [1925]

Kane, Paul

1925 <u>Wanderings of an Artist</u> among the Indians of North America, From Canada to Vancouver's Island and Oregon through the Hudson's Bay Company's Territory, and Back again. Toronto: The Radisson Society of Canada. [1858].

Kelly, Klara, and Harris Francis

1994 Navajo Sacred Places. Bloomington: Indiana University Press.

Kinkade, Dale

1963a Phonology and Morphology of Upper Chehalis: I. <u>International Journal of American Linguistics</u> 29 (3): 181-195.

1963b Phonology and Morphology of Upper Chehalis: II. _International Journal of American Linguistics_ 29 (4): 345-356.

1964a Phonology and Morphology of Upper Chehalis: III. _International Journal of American Linguistics_ 30 (1): 32-61.

1964b Phonology and Morphology of Upper Chehalis: IV. _International Journal of American Linguistics_ 30 (3): 251-260.

1966 Vowel Alternation in Upper Chehalis. _International Journal of American Linguistics_ 32 (4): 343-349.

1967 Prefix-Suffix Constructions in Upper Chehalis. _Anthropological Linguistics_ 9 (2): 1-4.

1970 Indian Languages at Haskell Institute. _International Journal of American Linguistics_ 36: 46-52.

1971a Third Person Possessives in Cowlitz. International Conference on Salish Languages 6 Victoria, B.C.

1971b Review of _The Squamish Language, Part II_ (Kuipers 1969). _Lingua_ 26: 433-434.

1971c Roster of Linguists Studying North American Indian Languages. _International Journal of American Linguistics_ 37: 114-121.

1972a The Alveopalatal Shift in Cowlitz Salish. _International Conference on Salish Languages_ 7 Bellingham, Washington.

1972b Roster of Linguists Studying North American Indian Languages [continued]. _International Journal of American Linguistics_ 38: 201-202.

1973 The Alveopalatal Shift in Cowlitz Salish. _International Journal of American Linguistics_ 39: 224–231.

1975a Pluralization in Upper Chehalis. _International Conference on Salish Languages_ 10: 1-55 Ellensburg, Washington.

1975b The Lexical Domain of Anatomy in Columbian Salish. _Linguistics and Anthropology: In Honor of CF Voegelin_: 423-443. Dale Kinkade, Kenneth L. Hale, and Oswald Werner, eds. Lisse, The Netherlands: Peter de Ridder Press.

1976a Areal Features in the Northwest. Paper read at the Northwest Coast Studies Conference, Burnaby, B.C. Published in Laurence Thompson and Kinkade 1990.

1976b The Salishan Languages. Paper read at the Northwest Coast Studies Conference, Burnaby, B.C.

1976c The Copula and Negatives in Inland Olympic Salish. _International Journal of American Linguistics_ 42: 17-23.

1977 Evidence Against the Universality of 'Noun' and 'Verb': Salish. Paper presented at the Annual Meeting of the Canadian Linguistics Association, Fredericton. Published as Kinkade 1983b.

1979 Preliminary Notes on Lower Chehalis (ɬəw'ál'məš) Morphology. _International Conference on Salish Languages_ 14: 108-117 Bellingham, Washington.

1980   The Source of the Upper Chehalis Reflexive.   International Conference on Salish Languages 15: 200–207 Vancouver, B.C. Published as Kinkade 1981d.

1981a Singular vs. Plural Roots in Salish. Anthropological Linguistics 23: 262-270.

1981b The Source of the Upper Chehalis Reflexive. International Journal of American Linguistics 47: 336-339.

1983a Daughters of Fire: Verse Analysis of an Upper Chehalis Folktale. North American Indians: Humanistic Perspectives: 267-278. James Thayer, ed. Norman: University of Oklahoma, Papers in Anthropology 24.

1983b Salish Evidence against the Universality of 'Noun' and 'Verb. Lingua 60: 25-39.

1984a Bear and Bee: Narrative Verse Analysis of an Upper Chehalis Folktale.' David S. Rood, ed. 1983 Mid-America Linguistic Conference Papers. Boulder, University of Colorado, Department of Linguistics 1984: 246-261.

1984b Some Agent Hierarchies in Upper Chehalis. International Conference on Salish and Neighboring Languages 19 (WPLCUV Vol. 4 (2): 236-240. Published as Kinkade 1989c.

1985a The Line in Upper Chehalis Narrative: Wren and Elk. Conference on American Indian Languages 24 (84th Annual Meeting of the AAA, Washington, DC).

1985b More on Nasal Loss on the Northwest Coast. International Journal of American Linguistics 51: 478-480.

1985c   Upper Chehalis Slow Reduplication. International Conference on Salish and Neighboring Languages 20: 189-198 Vancouver, B.C.

1986a Proto-Salishan Colors. Paper presented at the Haas Festival Conference. Santa Cruz, California. Published as Kinkade 1988b.

1986b Passives in Upper Chehalis. Conference on American Indian Languages 25 (85th Annual Meeting of the AAA, Philadelphia, Pennsylvania).

1987a Bluejay and His Sister. Brian Swann and Arnold Krupat. eds. Recovering the Word: Essays on Native American Literature: 255-296. Berkeley: University of California Press.

1987b   Passives and the Mapping of Thematic Roles in Upper Chehalis Sentences. International Conference on Salish and Neighboring Languages 22: 109-124 Victoria, B.C.

1987c   Salmon Names in Tsamosan Salish. International Conference on Salish and Neighboring Languages 22: 181-184 Victoria, B.C.

1987d How to Create a Word in Upper Chehalis, or, Never Trust a Salish Vowel. Conference on American Indian Languages 26. 86th Annual Meeting of the AAA, Chicago. Also Kinkade 1994a.

1988a Felidae ac Hominidae. International Conference on Salish and Neighboring Languages 23: 144-165 Eugene, Oregon. Also Kinkade 1993c.

1988b Proto-Salishan Colors. In Honor of Mary Haas: From the Haas Festival Conference on Native American Linguistics: 443-466. William Shipley, ed. Berlin: Mouton de Gruyter.

1988c Review of Coast Salish Essays (Suttles 1987d). Pacific Northwest Quarterly 79: 158.

1988d Topical Objects and Discourse Tracking in Salish. Conference on American Indian Languages 27 (87th Annual Meeting of the AAA, Phoenix, Arizona).

1989a Prehistory of Salishan Languages. Paper presented at the 88th annual meeting of the AAA, Washington, D.C. Also Kinkade 1990b.

1989b Some Agent Hierarchies in Upper Chehalis. General and Amerindian Ethnolinguistics. In Remembrance of Stanley Newman: 213-218. Mary Key and Henry Hoenigswald, eds. Berlin: Mouton de Gruyter.

1989c When Patients are Topics: Topic Maintenance in North American Indian Languages. International Conference on Salish and Neighboring Languages 24: 1-41, Steilacoom, Washington.

1989d Sorting out Third Persons in Salishan Discourse. Paper presented at the Summer Meeting of the SSILA. Tucson, Arizona. Published as Kinkade 1990d.

1989e Comparative Linguistic Evidence about Salish Prehistory. Paper presented at the 88th Annual Meeting of the AAA, Washington, D.C.

1990a History of Research in Linguistics. Handbook of North American Indians, Northwest Coast. Wayne Suttles, ed. Volume 7: 98-106.

1990b Prehistory of Salishan Languages. International Conference on Salish and Neighboring Languages 25: 197-208 Vancouver, BC.

1990c Salishan Anti-Sonority. Conference on American Indian Languages 29 (89th Annual Meeting of the AAA New Orleans).

1990d Sorting Out Third Persons in Salishan Discourse. International Journal of American Linguistics 56: 341-360.

1990e Speculation on Prehistory of the Southwestern Puget Sound Region. International Conference on Salish and Neighboring Languages 25: 209-212 Vancouver, BC.

1990f Prehistory of the Native Languages of the Northwest Coast. Paper presented at The Great Ocean: International Conference on the North Pacific to 1600, Portland, Oregon. Published as Kinkade 1991b.

1991a Upper Chehalis Dictionary. Missoula: University of Montana Occasional Papers in Linguistics 7.

1991b Proto-Salishan Mammals: The Data. International Conference on Salish and Neighboring Languages 26: 233-240 Vancouver, BC.

1991c Salishan languages. International Encyclopedia of Linguistics. William Bright, ed. New York: Oxford University Press.

1992a Dictionary Appendices: Some Upper Chehalis Solutions. Amerindian Languages and Informatics: The Pacific Northwest. Guy Buchholtzer, ed. Amerindia 7: 31-45.

1992b Kinship Terminology in Upper Chehalis in a Historical Framework. Anthropological Linguistics 34 (1-4): 84-103.

1992c Pseudo-Auxiliaries in Upper Chehalis. International Conference on Salish and Neighboring Languages 27: 22-43 Kamloops, BC.

1992d Translating Pentlatch. Brian Swann, ed. <u>On the Translation of Native American Literatures</u>: 163-175. Washington: Smithsonian Institution Press.

1992e Episode Linking in an Upper Chehalis Myth Cycle. Conference on American Indian Languages 31 (91st Annual Meeting of the AAA, San Francisco, California).

1992f How Much Does a Schwa Weigh? Paper presented in Brisbane, Australia, on February 27, 1992. See also Kinkade 1993e.

1993a The Chimerical Schwas of Salish. Conference on American Indian Languages 32 (92nd Annual Meeting of the AAA, Washington, D.C.).

1993b The Non-Lexical Basis for a Tsamosan Branch of Salish. <u>International Conference on Salish and Neighboring Languages</u> 28: 175-204 Seattle, Washington.

1993c Salishan Words for 'Person, Human, Indian, Man.'' <u>American Indian Linguistics and Ethnography in Honor of Laurence C Thompson</u>. Anthony Mattina and Tim Montler, eds. University of Montana Occasional Papers in Linguistics 10: 163-184.

1993d *S*-Prefixation on Upper Chehalis (Salish) Imperfective Predicates. Paper presented at the SSILA summer meeting, Columbus, Ohio. Published as Kinkade 1994b.

1993e How Much Does a Schwa Weigh? UBC Department of Linguistics Colloquium, February 5. Published as Kinkade 1998a.

1994a Never Trust a Salish Syllable either. Conference on American Indian Languages 33 (93rd Annual Meeting of the AAA, Washington, DC). Continuation of Kinkade 1987d.

1994b S-Prefixation on Upper Chehalis (Salish) Imperfective Predicates. <u>Survey of California and Other Indian Languages</u>. Report 8: 21-30.

1994c Native Oral Literature of the Northwest Coast and the Plateau. <u>Dictionary of Native American Literature</u>. Andrew Wiget, ed. NY: Garland Reference Library in the Humanities, Volume 1815: 33-45.

1994d Lectures on Salish and Northwest Linguistic Areal Features. Sapporo, Japan, January 17 and 21.

1994e Salish Interrogatives. Presentation at Salish Morphosyntax Workshop, University of Victoria, Victoria, BC, March 5. Also Kinkade 1994f.

1994f Salishan Interrogatives from a Diachronic Perspective. Spring Workshop on Theory and Method in Linguistic Reconstruction 5, Pittsburgh, Pennsylvania, April 8-10.

1994g Distinguishing Obsolescing Change from Natural Change in Salishan Languages. <u>48th International Congress of Americanists</u>, Stockholm/Uppsala, July 4-9.

1995a What Aspects Can Be Reconstructed in Salish? Paper presented at the 3rd Annual Salish Morphosyntax Workshop, University of Victoria, Victoria, B.C., January 28.

1995b Speculations on the Origins of an Empty Morpheme in Upper Chehalis. <u>International Conference on Salish and Neighboring Languages</u> 30: 26-27 Victoria, B.C.

1995c Transmontane Contact between the Lushootseed and the Moses-Columbia as Indicated by Vocabulary Borrowing. Paper presented at the 48th Northwest Anthropology Conference, Portland, Oregon, March 23-25. also Kinkade 1995d.

1995c Transmontane Lexical Borrowing in Salish. <u>International Conference on Salish and Neighboring Languages</u> 30, 28-46, Victoria, BC.

1995d A Plethora of Plurals: Inflection for Number in Upper Chehalis. Paper presented at the Summer Meeting of the SSILA, Albuquerque, New Mexico, July 8-9. Published <u>Anthropological Linguistics</u> 37: 347-365.

1995e Is Irrealis a Grammatical Category in Salish? Conference on American Indian Languages 34 (94th Annual Meeting of the AAA, Washington, DC) Published as Kinkade 1998b.

1996a Reconstructing Aspect in Salishan Languages. <u>International Conference on Salish and Neighboring Languages 31</u>: 185-196, Vancouver, B.C. Also at Spring Workshop on Theory and Method in Linguistic Reconstruction 6, Pittsburgh, Pennsylvania, March 22-24.

1996b The Relationship between Lexical Suffixes and Lexical Compounding in Upper Chehalis. Conference on American Indian Languages 35 (95th Annual Meeting of the AAA, Annual Meeting of the SSILA, San Francisco, California, November 20-24).

1997a Cowlitz (Salish) Place Names. <u>International Conference on Salish and Neighboring Languages</u> 32: 249-264 Port Angeles, Washington.

1997b The Emergence of Shared Features in Languages of the Pacific Northwest. Paper presented at the Annual Meeting of the American Association for the Advancement of Science, Seattle, Washington, February 13-18.

1998a Origins of Salishan Lexical Suffixes. <u>International Conference on Salish and Neighboring Languages</u> 33: 266-295 Seattle, Washington, August 5-7.

1998b Native Language vs. English Renditions of Tales and Myths. Carved in the Air Like Spoken Music: Perspectives on Native North American Oral Literature.' Paper presented at the University of British Columbia, Vancouver, March 6-7.

1998c More Thoughts on the Origin of Lexical Suffixes in Salishan Languages: Incorporation Gains Ground. Spring Workshop on Theory and Method in Linguistic Reconstruction 7, Pittsburgh, Pennsylvania, March 27-29.

1998d Salishan Dictionary Making. Conference on American Indian Languages 37 (97th Annual Meeting of the AAA (SSILA Annual Meeting), Philadelphia, Pennsylvania.

2000 An Initial Study of Some Adjectival Modifiers in Upper Chehalis. <u>International Conference on Salish and Neighboring Languages</u> 35: 119-126 (University of British Columbia Working Papers in Linguistics vol. 3, Gessner and Oh, eds), Mount Currie, BC, August 16-18.

2001a Proto-Salish Irrealis. <u>International Conference on Salish and Neighboring Languages 36</u> (University of British Columbia Working Papers in Linguistics, vol. 6), 189-200, Chilliwack, BC, August 8-10. (Bar-el, Watt, and Wilson, eds).

2001b Review of <u>The Salish Language Family: Reconstructing Syntax</u> by Paul Kroeber 1999. <u>Language</u> 77: 573-575.

2001c Review of <u>The Languages of Native North America</u> (Mithun 1999). <u>Journal of Linguistics</u> 10 (2): 297-298.

2001d   The Areal Question: Northwest Coast and California.   Paper presented to the Association for Linguistic Typology, Santa Barbara, California, July 19-22.

2003 Review of <u>Salish Etymological Dictionary</u> (Kuipers 2002). <u>Anthropological Linguistics</u> 45: 245-247.

2004   <u>Cowlitz Dictionary and Grammatical Sketch</u>.   Missoula: University of Montana Occasional Papers in Linguistics 18.

2008 The Kidnapping of Moon: An Upper Chehalis Myth Told by Silas Heck, Dale Kinkade, ed. <u>Salish Myths and Legends ~ One People's Stories</u>. M Terry Thompson and Steven Egesdal, eds. Lincoln: University of Nebraska Press.

MDK Dale Kinkade Papers. Seattle: University of Washington Libraries, Special Collections.

Kinkade, M. Dale, and Jay V Powell

1976 Language and the Prehistory of North America. <u>World Archaeology</u> 8: 83–100.

Kinkade, M. Dale, and William Seaburg

1991 John P. Harrington and Salish. <u>Anthropological Linguistics</u> 33: 392–405.

Kinkade, M Dale, and Wayne Suttles

1987 Linguistic Families. Plate 66, part, New Caledonia and Columbia. <u>Historical Atlas of Canada, Vol. I: From the Beginning to 1800</u>. Harris, R. Cole, ed. Toronto: University of Toronto Press.

Kinkade, M Dale, and Laurence C Thompson

1972   Proto-Salish *r.   International Conference on Salish Languages 7, Bellingham, Washington. Published as Kinkade and Thompson 1974.

1974 Proto-Salish *r. International Journal of American Linguistics 40: 22-28.

Kinkade, M Dale, Kenneth L Hale, and Oswald Werner, eds.

1975 <u>Linguistics and Anthropology: In Honor of C. F. Voegelin</u>. Lisse, The Netherlands: Peter de Ridder Press.

Kiona, Mary

1953 Transcript of Proceedings Before the Indian Claims Commission. 5 August. Simon Plomondon, on Relation of the Cowlitz Tribe of Indians, Docket 218. Seattle.

Kowrach, Edward

1978 Journal of a Catholic Bishop on the Oregon Trail. The Overland Crossing of the Rt. Rev. AMA Blanchet, Bishop of Walla Walla, from Montreal to Oregon Territory, March 23, 1847 to January 23, 1851. Fairfield, WA: Ye Galleon Press.

Krauss, Michael

1990 Kwalhioqua and Clatskanie. Handbook of North American Indians, <u>Northwest Coast</u>. Wayne Suttles, ed. Volume 7: 530-532.

Laird, Carobeth

1975. <u>Encounter with an Angry God</u>. Banning, CA: Malki Museum Press.

Lang, George

2008 <u>Making Wawa</u> ~ <u>The Genesis of Chinook Jargon</u>. Vancouver: UBC Press.

Lane, Barbara

1973 Political and Economic Aspects of Indian-White Culture Contact in Western Washington in the Mid-19th Century. May 10. United States v. Washington.

Lingreen, Minnie, and Priscilla Tiller

1981   Hop cultivation in Lewis County, Washington, 1888 to 1940 ~ a study in land use determinants. Centralia.

Luark, Patterson Fletcher

ms Diary digest at Aberdeen Public Library.

Lutz, John Sutton

2008   <u>Makuk</u> ~ <u>A New History of Aboriginal-White Relations</u>. Vancouver: University of British Columbia Press.

McAtee, WL

1955 folk names of NE birds.

McBride, Delmar

1972   Letter about "squaw chief" mentioned by Wilkes and discussed by Edward Huggins, George Gibbs, William Tolmie, and his own family. State Capitol Museum, 18 July.

McDonald, Lucile

1972a <u>Coast Country</u>. <u>A History of Southwest Washington</u>. Portland: Binfords & Mort.

1972b <u>Swan among the Indians</u>. <u>Life of James G Swan, 1818-1900</u>. Portland: Binfords & Mort.

McHalsie, Albert Sonny Naxaxalhts'i

2007 We Have to Take Care of Everything That Belongs to Us. <u>Be of Good Mind</u>: 82-130. Bruce Miller ed. Vancouver: University of British Columbia Press.

Marr, Carolyn, Donna Hicks, and Kay Francis

1980 <u>The Chehalis People</u>. Oakville: Confederated Tribes of the Chehalis Reservation.

Matson, Emerson

1968 <u>Longhouse Legends</u>. Camden, NJ: Thomas Nelson and Sons.

1972 <u>Legends of the Great Chiefs</u>. Tacoma: Storypole Press.

Matson, RG, and Martin Magne

2007   <u>Athapaskan Migrations</u>. <u>The Archaeology of Eagle Lake, British Columbia</u>. Tucson: University of Arizona Press.

Metcalf, Leon

1951   Tape recording of Upper Chehalis texts from Silas Heck, taken at the Chehalis Indian Reservation, Oakville, Washington.   Ethnology Archives, Thomas F Burke Memorial Washington State Museum, University of Washington, Seattle, Washington.

1952a   Tape recording of an Upper Chehalis text from Murphy Seneca, taken at the Chehalis Indian Reservation, Oakville, Washington. Same bibliographic data as Metcalf 1951.

1952b   Tape recording of Satsop vocabulary from Alice Johns. Same bibliographic data as Metcalf 1951.

1955   Tape recording of Satsop expressions from Alice Johns. Same bibliographic data as Metcalf 1951.

Miles, James

2007   James Swan, Cha-Tic of the Northwest Coast: Drawings and Watercolors from the Franz and Kathryn Stenzel Collection Of Western American Art. New Haven: Yale University Press.

Miller, Jay

1988   Shamanic Odyssey. The Lushootseed Salish Journey to the Land of the Dead. Menlo Park, CA: Ballena Press Anthropological Papers 32.

1989   An Overview of Northwest Coast Mythology. Northwest Anthropological Research Notes 23 (2): 125-141.

1998   Tsimshian Ethno-Ethnohistory: A "real" Indigenous Chronology. Ethnohistory 45 (4): 657-674.

1999a   Chehalis Area Traditions, a Summary of Thelma Adamson's 1927 Ethnographic Notes. Northwest Anthropological Research Notes 33 (1): 1-72.

1999b   Lushootseed Culture and the Shamanic Odyssey. Lincoln: University of Nebraska Press.

2002   Dr. Simon: A Snohomish Slave at Fort Nisqually and Puyallup. Northwest Anthropological Research Notes 36 (2): 145-54 2002.

Miller, Jay, and Vi Hilbert

1993   Caring for Control: A Pivot of Salishan Language and Culture. American Indian Linguistics and Ethnography in Honor of Laurence C. Thompson. University of Montana, Occasional Papers in Linguistics 10: 237-239.

1996   Lushootseed Animal People: Mediation and Transformation from Myth to History. Monsters, Tricksters, and Sacred Cows: Animal Tales and American Identities: 138-156. A. James Arnold, ed. New World Studies. Charlottesville: University of Virginia Press.

2004   That Salish Feeling… Studies in Salish Linguistics in Honor of M. Dale Kinkade. Donna B Gerdts and Lisa Matthewson, eds. University of Montana, Occasional Papers In Linguistics # 17: 197-210. (Vi Hilbert first author)

Morwood, William

1973   Traveler in a Vanished Landscape: The Life and Times of David Douglas, Botanical Explorer. NY: Clarkson N. Potter.

Munger, SH

2003   Common to This Country: Botanical Discoveries of Lewis and Clark. New York: Artisan Books.

National Historic Preservation Act (NHPA)

1966 Section 106, as amended. DC: US Printing Office.

Norton, Helen H

1979 The Association between Anthropogenic Prairies and Important Food Plans in Western Washington. Northwest Anthropological Research Notes (NARN) 13 (20): 434-449.

1980 Evidence for Bracken Fern as a food for Aboriginal Peoples of Western Washington. Economic Botany 33 (4): 384-396.

1985 Women and Resources of the Northwest Coast: Documentation from the 18th and Early 19th Century. University of Washington, Anthropology, PhD Dissertation.

1990   Fort Nisqually: A Little Known Historical Treasure, Index for 1833-1849, Seattle Genealogical Society Bulletin 39 (3, Spring): 103-118.

1990a Fort Nisqually: A Little Known Historical Treasure: Part Two, Seattle Genealogical Society Bulletin 39 (4, Summer): 161-177.

1990b Fort Nisqually Index, Part Two, Index for 1849-1859, Seattle Genealogical Society Bulletin 39 (5, Autumn): 7-14.

1990/1   Fort Nisqually Index, Part Three – Settlers' Accounts of 1841-1879, Seattle Genealogical Society Bulletin 39 (3, Winter): 59-67.

1991 Index IV: Fort Nisqually Servants' Accounts 1836-1867, Seattle Genealogical Society Bulletin 39 (3, Spring): 111-115.

1991 Fort Nisqually Index 5: Women and the Frontier – 1840-1872, Seattle Genealogical Society Bulletin 39 (5, Autumn): 5-10.

ms. Inventory of scrambled pages in Huntington Microfilm.

Norton, Helen

1983 The Klickitat Trail of South-Central Washington: A Reconstruction of Seasonally Used Resource Sites. Prehistoric Places on the Southern Northwest Coast. Robert Greengo, ed. Seattle: Thomas Burke Memorial Washington State Museum, Research Report 4: 121-152.

Olson, Ronald

1925-7   Field Notebooks 1-12. Seattle: University of Washington, Special Collections. Accession 2506.

1936 The Quinault Indians. University of Washington Publications in Anthropology 6 (1): 1-190.

Ott, Jennifer

2008a Centralia February 12 @ *HistoryLink.org* Online Encyclopedia of Washington State History (accessed 28 February 2011).

2008b Chehalis July 1 @ *HistoryLink.org* Online Encyclopedia of Washington State History (accessed 28 February 2011).

Palmer, Katherine Van Winkle.

1918 Paleontology of the Oligocene of the Chehalis Valley, Washington. University of Washington Publications in Geology 1 (2): 69-97.

1925 Honne, Spirit of the Chehalis. The Indian Interpretation of the Origin of the People and Animals. As Narrated by George Saunders. Geneva, NY: Press of WF Humphrey.

Palmer, Katherine Van Winkle, and George Saunders

2012 Honne, Spirit of the Chehalis. The Indian Interpretation of the Origin of the People and Animals. Introduction by Jay Miller. Lincoln: Bison Books.

Parker, Patricia L., and Thomas F. King 1998 Guidelines for Evaluating and Documenting Traditional Cultural Properties. Washington, DC: US Department of the Interior, National Park Service, Interagency Resources Division, National Register Bulletin 38.

Pearson, Flaval

1955 A History of Chehalis. n.p.

Perry, Richard

1991 Western Apache Heritage. People of the Mountain Corridor. Austin: University of Texas Press.

Pettitt, George
1946 Primitive Education in North America. Berkeley: University of California Publications in American Archaeology and Ethnology 43 (1): 1-182. [Submitted 1943]
1950 The Quileute of La Push, 1775-1945. Anthropological Records 14 (1): 1-120.

1970 Prisoners of Culture. NY: Charles Scribner's Sons.

Powell, Jay
1990 Quileute. Northwest Coast. Wayne Suttles, ed. Handbook of North American Indians. Volume 7: 431-437.
Powell, Jay, and Vickie Jensen,

1976 Quileute ~ An Introduction to the Indians of La Push.

1980 Quileute For Kids, Book 6. La Push: Quileute Tribe.

Powell, Jay , and Fred Woodruff,

1976 Quileute Dictionary. Northwest Anthropological Research Notes (NARN), Memoir 3.

Punke, M, A Foutch, AK Blaser, JL Fagan, and J Reese

2009 Archaeological Investigation and Damage Assessment at Site 45LE611 [Opus site], Centralia, Washington. 2 July. Portland: Archaeological Investigations Northwest, Inc.

Raibmon, Paige

2005 <u>Authentic Indians. Episodes of Encounter from the Late-Nineteenth Century Northwest Coast</u>. Durham: Duke University Press.

Ray, Verne

1937 The Historical Position of the Lower Chinook in the Native Culture of the Northwest. <u>Pacific Northwest Quarterly</u> 28 (4): 363-372.

1938 Lower Chinook Ethnographic Notes. <u>University of Washington Publications in Anthropology 7</u>: 29-165.

1966 Handbook of the Cowlitz Indians. Seattle.

1974 Handbook of the Cowlitz Indians. <u>Coast Salish and Western Washington Indians III</u>: 245-315. American Indian Ethnohistory. Indians of the Northwest. David Agee Horr, ed. New York: Garland Publishing.

VRC Verne Frederick Ray Collection, Foley Library, Gonzaga University, Spokane.

Richen, Marilyn C

1974 Legitimacy and the Resolution of Conflict in an Indian Church. University of Oregon: PhD Dissertation in Anthropology.

Robinson, Erik

2009 Tradition of Harvesting Lamprey Lives On. <u>News from Indian Country</u> 20 July 2009, XXIII (14), front page, p4.

Roblin, Charles

1919 Letter to Commissioner of Indian Affairs Summarizing Roll of Landless Indians of Western Washington State. DC: National Archives. 31 January.

Roll, Tom

1974 The Archaeology of Minard: A Case Study of a Late Prehistoric Northwest Coast Procurement System. Pullman: Washington State University, PhD Dissertation, Anthropology.

Rooke, Lara, Jason Cooper, and James Chatters

2011 Centralia-Chehalis Flood Reduction Project. Intensive Archaeological Survey of the Airport, Salzer Creek and Skookumchuck Levees, Lewis County, Washington. Bothell: AMEC Earth & Environmental, Inc. 3 Volumes.

Ross, Alexander

1986 <u>Adventure of the First Settlers on the Oregon or Columbia River, 1810-1813</u>. Lincoln: Bison Books, University of Nebraska Press.

Rubin, Rick

1999 <u>Naked Against the Rain</u> ~ <u>The People of the Lower Columbia River, 1770-1830</u>. Portland: Far Shore Press.

Ruby, Robert, and John Brown

1992 <u>A Guide to the Indian Tribes of the Pacific Northwest</u>. Norman: University of Oklahoma Press.

1996 <u>John Slocum and the Indian Shaker Church</u>. Norman: University of Oklahoma Press.

Rule, Rev William

1945 <u>Riding the Upper Cowlitz Circuit. Fifty Years Ago, 1843-1893</u>. Seattle: University Printing Co.

Schalk, Randall, Matt Breidenthal, Nancy Stenholm, and Mike Wolverton

2005 Archaeological Monitoring and Evaluation for the Centralia Wastewater System Improvements Project. Seattle: Cascadia Archaeology. February.

Seaburg, William

1999 Whatever Happened to Thelma Adamson? A Footnote in the History of Northwest Anthropological Research. <u>Northwest Anthropological Research Notes</u> 33 (1): 73-83.

Sercombe, Laurel

2001 "<u>And Then It Rained: Power and Song in Western Washington Coast Salish Myth Narratives</u>." UW PhD dissertation.

Shepard, Mary Ann Foxwell James

1910 Family Memories. Copy at Aberdeen Public Library.

Shoalwater Bay Tribal Community

1998 <u>Summertime in Georgetown</u>. A Collection of Short Stories by Women and Girls of the Shoalwater Bay Tribal Community.

Sicade, Henry

1940 The Indians' Side of the Story. <u>Building A State, Washington, 1889-1939</u>, XIX: 490-503. Charles Mills and O.B. Sperlin, eds. Tacoma: Washington State Historical Society.

Smith, Allan Hathorn

2006 <u>Takhoma: Ethnography of Mt Rainier National Park</u>. Pullman: WSU Press.

Smith, Herndon

1942 <u>Centralia - The First Fifty Year, 1845-1900</u>. From Materials Written by Students in her English Classes at Centralia High School. 2nd ed 1975, 3rd ed 1995.

Smith, Marian

1940a <u>The Puyallup-Nisqually</u>. Columbia University Contributions to Anthropology 32.

1940b The Puyallup of Washington. Acculturation in Seven American Indian Tribes, Chapter 1: 3-36. Ralph Linton, ed. NY: D. Appleton-Century Co.

1941 The Coast Salish of Puget Sound. <u>American Anthropologist</u> 43: 197-211.

1946 Petroglyph Complexes in the History of the Columbia-Fraser Region. <u>Southwestern Journal of Anthropology</u> 2 (3): 306-322.

Smith, Marian, ed.

 1949 Indians of the Urban Northwest. Columbia University Contributions to Anthropology 36.

Smythe, Charles, and Frederick York, eds.

 2009 Traditional Cultural Properties: Putting Concept into Practice. The George Wright Forum 26 (1).

Sobel, Elizabeth

 2004 Social Complexity and Corporate Household on the Southern Northwest Coast of North America, AD 1450-1855. Ann Arbor: University of Michigan, Anthropology PhD. 2 volumes.

Spier, Leslie

 1936 Tribal Distribution in Washington [State]. General Series in Anthropology 3.

Spier, Leslie, and Edward Sapir

 1930 Wishram Ethnography. University of Washington Publications in Anthropology 3 (3): 151-300.

Stuckley, George, and George Gibbs

 1860 Zoology of the Route. Reports of Explorations and Surveys to Ascertain the Most Practicable and Economical Route for a Railroad from the Mississippi River to the Pacific Ocean in 1853-55. Volume XII, Book II, Part III, Report 2, Chapter III. Washington, DC: Thomas H. Ford Printer.

Suczek, Christopher A, Babcock, R Scott, Engebretson, David C

 1994 Tectonostratigraphy of The Crescent Terrane and Related Rocks, Olympic Peninsula, Washington. Swanson, D.A. & Haugerud, R.A., Editors, Geologic Field Trips in the Pacific Northwest: University Of Washington Department Of Geological Sciences, vol. 1: 1H 1 - 1H 11.

Summers, Camilla

 1978 Go To the Cowlitz Peter Crawford ~ A biography of a northwest pioneer surveyor. Longview: Speedy-Litho.

Suttles, Wayne

 1987 Coast Salish Essays. Vancouver, BC: Talonbooks.

 1989 They Recognize No Superior Chief: The Strait of Juan de Fuca in the 1790s. Culturas de la Costa Noroeste de America. Jose Luis Peset, ed. Madrid: Turner Libros.

 1991 The Shed-Roof House. A Time of Gathering: 212-222. Robin Wright, ed.

Suttles, Wayne, ed.

 1990 Northwest Coast. Handbook of North American Indians. Volume 7. Smithsonian Institution Press.

Suttles, Wayne, and William Elmendorf

1963 Linguistic Evidence for Salish Prehistory: 41-52. <u>Symposium on Language and Culture</u>. Viola Garfield and Wallace Chafe, eds. Proceedings of the 1962 Annual Spring Meeting of the American Ethnological Society. Seattle: University of Washington Press.

Suttles, Wayne, and Aldona Jonaitis

1990 History of Research Handbook of North American Indians, <u>Northwest Coast</u>, Volume 7: 73-87. Wayne Suttles, ed. Smithsonian Institution Press.

Suttles, Wayne, and Barbara Lane

1990 Southern Coast Salish. Handbook of North American Indians, <u>Northwest Coast</u>, Volume 7: 485-502. Wayne Suttles, ed. Smithsonian Institution Press.

Swan, James

20 July 1855 letter from James Swan at Shoalwater to George Gibbs at Steilacoom. NAA

1857 <u>The Northwest Coast, or, Three Years in Washington Territory</u>. NY: Harper and Brothers. [reprinted University of Washington Press, 1972]

1971 <u>Almost Out of the World. Scenes in Washington Territory. The Strait of Juan de Fuca 1859-61</u>. Tacoma: Washington State Historical Society.

Swindell, Edward, Jr.

1942 Report on Source, Nature, and Extent of the Fishing, Hunting, and Miscellaneous Related Rights of Certain Indian Tribes in Washington and Oregon, Together with Affidavits Showing Location of a Number of Usual and Accustomed Fishing Grounds and Stations. Los Angeles: US Department of the Interior, Office of Indian Affairs, Division of Forestry and Grazing. July.

Taylor, Herbert

1974a Anthropological Investigations of the Chehalis Indians. <u>Coast Salish and Western Washington Indians III</u>: 117-157. American Indian Ethnohistory. Indians of the Northwest. David Agee Horr, ed. New York: Garland Publishing.

1974b John Work on the Chehalis Indians. <u>Coast Salish and Western Washington Indians III</u>, as above.

Teit, James

1916 Quinault Vocabulary and Paradigms. Philadelphia: APS Ms 30 (S2a.2), Freeman # 3847.

Terres, John

1980 The Audubon Society Encyclopedia of North American Birds. NY: Alfred Knopf.

Thompson, Laurence, and Dale Kinkade

1990 Languages. <u>Northwest Coast</u>. Wayne Suttles, ed. Smithsonian Institution Press: Handbook of North American Indians 7: 30-51.

Thompson, M Terry, and Steven Egesdal

2008 <u>Salish Myths and Legends. One People's Stories</u>. Lincoln: University of Nebraska Press.

Thomason, Sarah

1981 Chinook Jargon in Areal and Historical Context. Working Papers of the XVI International Conference on Salish Languages. Anthony Mattina and Montler, eds., University of Montana Occasional Papers in Linguistics 2: 295-396.

1983 Chinook Jargon in Areal and Historical Context. <u>Language</u> 59: 820-870.

Thrush, Coll, with Ruth Ludwin

2007 Finding Fault: Indigenous Seismology, Colonial Science, and the Rediscovery of Earthquakes and Tsunamis in Cascadia. <u>American Indian Culture and Research Journal</u> 31 (4): 1-24.

Turner, Nancy

1975 <u>Food Plants of British Columbia Indians</u>. Part 1/ Coastal Peoples. Victoria: British Columbia Provincial Museum, Handbook 34.

1979 <u>Plants in of British Columbia Indian Technology</u>. Victoria: British Columbia Provincial Museum Handbook 38.

USACE

2009 Traditional Cultural Property and Ethnographic Study for the Chehalis-Centralia Flood Damage Reduction Project Study Area. Statement Of Work (SOW). Sole Source Contract to the Confederated Tribes of the Chehalis Reservation, with Participation by the Cowlitz Tribe.

Van Syckle, Edwin

1982 <u>The River Pioneers</u>. <u>Early Days on Gray's Harbor</u>. Pacific Search Press.

1980 <u>They Tried to Cut It All</u>. <u>Grays Harbor – turbulent years of greed and greatness</u>. Friends of the Aberdeen Public Library. [reprinted 1981, Pacific Search Press]

Vancouver, George

1798 A Voyage of Discovery to the North Pacific Ocean and round the World … London: G G and J Robinson and J Edwards.

Walker, Deward

1991 Protection of American Indian Sacred Geography. <u>Handbook of American Indian Religious Freedom</u>: 100-115. Christopher Vecsey, ed. NY: Crossroad.

1996 Durkheim, Eliade, and Sacred Geography In Northwestern North America. <u>Chin Hills to Chiloquin. Papers Honoring the Versatile Career of Theodore Stern</u>. Don Drumond, ed. University of Oregon Anthropological Papers 52: 63-68.

Walls, Robert

1987   Bibliography of Washington State Folklore And Folklife.   Seattle: University of Washington Press.

Waterman, Thomas Talbot, and Geraldine Coffin

1920   Types of Canoes on Puget Sound.   Indian Notes and Monographs, Museum of the American Indian, Heye Foundation, New York.

Waterman, Thomas, and Ruth Greiner

1921   Indian Houses of Puget Sound.   New York: Museum of the American Indian, Heye Foundation, Indian Notes and Monographs, Miscellaneous Series 5.

Waterman, Thomas, and others

1921   Native Houses of Western North America.   New York: Museum of the American Indian, Heye Foundation, Indian Notes and Monographs, Miscellaneous Series 11.

Waterman, Thomas

1920   The Whaling Equipment of the Makah Indians.   University of Washington Publications in Anthropology 1 (2).

1922   The Geographical Names Used by the Indians of the Pacific Coast.   The Geographical Review 12 (2): 175-194.

1924   The Shake Religion of Puget Sound.   Smithsonian Report for 1922: 499-507.

1930   The Paraphernalia of the Duwamish 'Spirit-Canoe' Ceremony.   New York: Museum of the American Indian, Heye Foundation, Indian Notes 7 (2): 129-148, 295-312, 535-561.

1973   Notes on the Ethnology of the Indians of Puget Sound.   NY: Museum of the American Indian, Heye Foundation, Indian Notes and Monographs, Miscellaneous Series 59.

Weinstein, Robert

1978   Grays Harbor, 1885-1913.   NY: Penguin.

Welch, Jeanne

1973   An Archaeological Survey of the Chehalis River Valley in Southwestern Washington.   Olympia: Western Heritage.

1983   The Kwalhioqua in the Boisfort Valley of Southwestern Washington.   Prehistoric Places on the Southern Northwest Coast.   Robert Greengo, ed.   Seattle: Thomas Burke Memorial Washington State Museum, Research Report 4: 153-167.

Welsh, William

1942   A Brief Historical Sketch of Grays Harbor, Washington.   Hoquiam: Rayonier Incorporated.

Wesson, Gary

2000   Archaeological Testing and Evaluation Studies Associated with the Federal Energy Regulatory Commission Relicensing of the Cowlitz River Hydroelectric Project (FERC No 2016).   Lewis County Washington.   January.

Wickersham, James

1898 Nisqually Mythology, Studies of the Washington Indians. <u>Overland Monthly</u> 32: 345-51.

Wilson, Roy

1999 <u>Legends of the Cowlitz Indian Tribe</u>. Lima, OH: Express Press.

2001 <u>Cheholtz and Mary Kiona of the Cowlitz</u>. Lima, OH: Express Press.

Work, John

1912 Journal, November and December 1824. TC Elliott, ed. <u>Washington Historical Quarterly</u> 3: 198-228.

Wray, Jacilee, ed.

2002 <u>Native Peoples of the Olympic Peninsula — Who We Are</u>. Norman: University of Oklahoma Press.

Wyeth, Nathaniel Jarvis

1899 The Correspondence and Journals of Captain Nathaniel Jarvis Wyeth, 1831-36. Eugene: University Press, reprinted by Kessinger Publishing's Legacy Reprints.

firewood, 25, 73f, 91f, 128, 145
fish weirs, 21, 65
flatheads, 62, 79
flowers, 47, 110
Forecasters, 54, 60
Fort Nisqually, 137f
Fort Vancouver, 137, 141
Fox, 7, 108
fungus, 40, 128
fungus target, 84

G

Gate City, 3, 34f, 90, 90f, 145
gender, 23, 33, 124
ghosts, 16, 20f, 27, 30f, 40f, 60, 71, 96, 110
Gibbs, George, 5f, 24*, 123, 135f
Grand Mound, 1f, 30, 40, 46, 67f, 87, 101f,
    110, 115f, 139f, 148
Grandson of Dog, 7
Grey, Stanley, 56f, 60f, 62
Greyback Louse, 72
grouse, 108
grudge disease, 41
guilds, 17, 22f
Gunther, Erna, 89

H

hammers, 82, 96, 112f
heart, 13, 43f, 64f, 74f, 85f, 108, 128
Heck, Bertha, 28f
Heck, Lena, 89
Heck, Lucy, 29, 82*, 124, 147
Heck, Mary, 2f, 28, 34, 43, 67, 78, 87f, 140
Heck, Peter, 2, 7, 25f, 33f, 68f, 82f, 101,
    105, 140
Heck, Silas, 2, 28, 33f, 74, 86, 114, 146
Henness, Captain Benjamin, 141
Heyden, John, 69f, 92, 112f, 134
hide cutout, 42
hoop, 8, 9, 13, 38, 93, 113
hop lice, 145
Hoquiam, 35f, 104, 117f, 130f, 147
horn spoons, 52, 95
Hudson, Bill, 61f, 103
hummingbirds, 38f, 109

I

Iley, Mary, 4f, 32, 37, 72f, 76f*, 94, 104f
Indian Claims Act of 1946, 151
Indian Shaker Church, 37f, 79, 135

J

James Island, 21
James Rock, 32, 117, 130
Jamestown, 82, 147
Jameses, 35, 140f*

K

Kai-kai-sume-lute, *138*
Kamilche, 115
Kanoodle, 49f
Kəmol, 124f; cf Kmol, 127; Kumol, 124
Kinkade, Dale, 6, 28f, 82, 124, 135, 147*
Klaber, 1f, 30, 110, 122, 144
Kwalhioqua, 5
Kwati, 15f, 21f

L

La Push, 21f, 57f
lampreys, 99, 105*, 136
leggings, 94
Leschi, 38, 142
Lighthouse Charley ~ paɬa'ɬc'i), 49
lightning, 19, 38f, 59, 119
Luarks, 134, 138*
Luscier, Emma Millet, 152, 156*
Lummi, 9, 49

M

McLeod, Malcolm Stewart, 153, 156*
macropthalmia, 107
Makahs, 1, 9, 16 #2, 21f, 54f, 125, 132, 139
Marshall, Donald R, 152, 156*
Martin, Adelle, 57
masks, 23, 55f, 64, 74*
McBride, Delmar, 138
menarche, 19
Military Road, 141, 144
Moclips, 118, 129
Moenkopi, 15
Montesano, 29f, 39, 138
Monticello, 2
mo'oɬ ~ hired killer, 79

Please Help Banish Typo Gnomes!!